Ireland's
New
Worlds

HISTORY *of* IRELAND
and the IRISH DIASPORA

James S. Donnelly, Jr., and Thomas Archdeacon, Series Editors

Ireland's New Worlds

*Immigrants, Politics,
and Society in the
United States and
Australia, 1815–1922*

Malcolm Campbell

THE UNIVERSITY
OF WISCONSIN PRESS

This book was published with the support of the Anonymous Fund of the College of Letters and Sciences at the University of Wisconsin–Madison.

The University of Wisconsin Press
1930 Monroe Street, 3rd Floor
Madison, Wisconsin 53711-2059

www.wisc.edu/wisconsinpress/

3 Henrietta Street
London WC2E 8LU, England

Library of Congress Cataloging-in-Publication Data

Campbell, Malcolm, 1963–
   Ireland's New Worlds : immigrants, politics, and society in the United States and Australia, 1815–1922 / Malcolm Campbell.
        p. cm. — (History of Ireland and the Irish diaspora)
   Includes bibliographical references and index.
   ISBN 0-299-22330-2 (cloth : alk. paper) — ISBN 0-299-22334-5 (pbk. : alk. paper)
   1. Irish-Americans—Social conditions—19th century. 2. Irish—Australia—Social conditions—19th century. 3. Irish-Americans—Social conditions—20th century. 4. Irish—Australia—Social conditions—20th century. I. Title. II. Series.
   E184.I6C34   2007
   305.891'62008691209034—dc22   2007011736

Contents

Illustrations

Preface and
Acknowledgments

IN THE PERIOD FROM 1815 TO 1922, approximately 7.5 million men, women, and children emigrated from Ireland to commence new lives abroad. The majority settled permanently in the United States; smaller numbers dispersed elsewhere, to constitute significant minorities in the population of Great Britain and the colonies of the British Empire. By the standards of contemporaneous European migrations, remarkably few Irish emigrants returned home.

For the most part, historians have concerned themselves with the stories of these immigrants in discrete locations across this Irish diaspora. This tendency is unsurprising, given the supremacy of the nation-state as an organizing category in the discipline of history. However, a negative consequence of this approach has been the tendency to reify Irish cultural distinctiveness in accounting for the experiences of the immigrants. In the absence of benchmarks for comparison, the social, political, and economic behaviors of Irish immigrants have often been explained, intentionally or unintentionally, in terms of their *Irishness*, as though this constitutes a homogeneous, coherent, and constant phenomenon.

Oscar Handlin laid the foundation for this scholarly tradition in his celebrated book *Boston's Immigrants*, published in 1941. Handlin recognized that conditions in the new society were influential in shaping immigrants' lives but emphasized that the Irish were "shabbily equipped to meet the multifarious problems imposed upon them by urban life." In both Ireland and America, he believed, the Irish were "victims of incalculable influences beyond their control," a people whose "utter helplessness before the most elemental forces fostered an immense sadness, a deep-rooted pessimism about the world and man's role in it."[1]

Subsequent writers magnified the impact of characteristics assumed to be peculiar to the immigrants to explain both Irish urbanization in the United

States and the nineteenth-century newcomers' subordination in American cities. William Shannon, in his book *The American Irish* (1963), explained that Irish urban concentration was due partly to the newcomers' lack of capital at the time of arrival and partly to the fact that farming in the United States was different from Ireland. However, "beneath these circumstances, there lay a still more profound motivation. The Irish rejected the land for the land had rejected them."[2] Assertions that the Irish, scarred by the experience of the Great Famine, were unable to confront life outside America's cities, continued to permeate the historical literature. The distinguished historian Oliver MacDonagh, in a work that preceded his writing on the Irish in Australia, claimed that the American Irish were unwilling or unable to settle in rural areas because of limited and rudimentary farming experience, lack of capital, and distaste for frontier isolation. More importantly, the Irish "were generally content to drift along where fate had cast them or relatives attracted them until it seemed too late to strike out once again."[3] Similarly, Lawrence McCaffrey argued: "Unequipped to cope with the challenges of large-scale American farming and unwilling to confront the isolation of existence in the vastness of rural America, most Irish immigrants preferred to congregate in cities as the pioneers of the American urban ghetto. Their poverty, loneliness, and psychological insecurity bred alcoholism, crime, violence, and mental disorders."[4]

Kerby Miller's award-winning *Emigrants and Exiles* represents a more recent and influential explanation of Irish adjustment to life in North America in terms of the immigrants' distinctive qualities and prior historical experience. On the basis of an exhaustive reading of Irish and American sources, Miller argued that a deep-seated mentality existed among the Irish that compelled them to view emigration as exile. The consequence of this "exile motif" was that the Irish settled in North America with material and psychological deficiencies that hindered their adjustment to life in a modern, industrial society. According to Miller, "Millions of Irishmen and -women, whatever their objective reasons for emigration, approached their departures and their experiences in North America with an outlook which characterized emigration as exile."[5] Inhibited by this cultural burden, Irish immigrants interpreted experiences and adapted to America in ways that were "often alienating and sometimes dysfunctional."[6]

In contrast to that tradition, the last two decades have seen the emergence of a large body of new scholarship, much of it on Irish immigrants in Australia, Canada, New Zealand, and South Africa, that emphasizes not maladjustment or paralysis in the face of modernization but the abundant adaptability of Irish immigrants in both rural and urban landscapes.[7] In particular, recent scholarship on the Irish in Australia has emphasized the specific conditions encountered in the new society as more critical than antecedent factors in shaping Irish immigrant adjustment. This newer historiography emphasizes considerable diversity of Irish immigrant experience in different regional settings; in many locations at least, a less arduous adjustment to the new society than previous generations of scholars acknowledged; and a propensity for rural life that in many locations differed little from other nativity groups. Much Canadian scholarship has tended to confirm similar patterns. In particular, the iconoclastic work of Donald Harman Akenson has called attention to the rural focus of Irish settlement in Upper Canada. Whatever the conditions of the Irish departure from Ireland or their physical condition upon arrival, he argued, "bodily emaciation should not be equated with cultural impoverishment or with technological ignorance. Typically, [the Irish immigrant] had not been a landless laborer and he did not now become a lumpenprole."[8] Recent scholarship on the Irish in New Zealand has tended similarly to emphasize a fluid and less alienating pattern of adjustment to the new society than traditional accounts allowed.[9]

Concurrent with this proliferation of studies, a series of remarkable regional and community histories has emerged in the United States that does much to sharpen understandings of the range and diversity of the Irish American experience. Books by David Emmons, Timothy Meagher, and David Gleeson and, most recently, Kerby Miller's own exemplary study of the Irish in the colonial and revolutionary periods are to the forefront of works that have revealed the diversity and richness of the Irish engagement within America's borders.[10] Though the local variations exposed in these studies render more difficult the possibility of a national interpretation of the group's experience, their overall result has been to richen immeasurably the historiography of the American Irish.

The comparison of Irish immigrant communities in this study provides an opportunity to break out from the constraints of national historiographies and explore in greater depth the impact of different New World settings on the lives and experiences of Irish immigrants.[11] More than a century ago James Francis Hogan commenced his book *The Irish in Australia* by observing that "for more than thirty years two great streams of emigration have been flowing from Ireland, the larger shaping its course across the Atlantic and discharging its human freight on the shores of the Great Republic of the West, the smaller in volume turning to the south, and, after traversing half the circumference of the globe, striking against the sunny shores of Australia."[12] Hogan's stirring reference to two great streams of emigration was undoubtedly guilty of exaggerating the relative scale of Irish departure to the Australian colonies (though not so its local importance). However, it did demonstrate appropriate recognition that, as well as bearing national importance and national implications, these two distinct migratory movements were at the same time subordinate components of a larger pattern of emigration from Ireland. As such, the experience of the Irish in each of these New World societies provided a benchmark against which the life of the other might be assessed.

Comparative history offers a valuable strategy to explore current controversies within the historical literature and to test the methods and explanations of scholars working in this field. Lord Acton once declared that "the process of civilization depends on transcending nationality. Everything is tried by more courts, before a larger audience. Comparative methods are applied. Influences which are accidental yield to those which are rational."[13] That need to move beyond nation and nationality has been reiterated many times since, though it remains the case that few historians in general, and fewer in this specific area of immigration history, have seen fit to embrace such an approach and to apply it.[14] There are many reasons why comparative history has had limited appeal for historians, including the national orientation of the history profession in most universities and some historians' skepticism toward the value of the genre.[15] Another is uncertainty about the meaning and method of comparison. Skocpol and Somers identified three specific types of comparative history: comparison as a parallel demonstration of theory, comparison as a contrast of contexts, and comparison as macrocausal analysis. In the first of these typologies, comparison is used to demonstrate the application of a theory to a range of cases to show the general validity of that theory. In contrast, the second utilizes the process of comparison to draw out the unique features and distinctive patterns from each example. In the third case, the focus of comparison is rather different. Here the principal purpose of comparison is to scrutinize existing explanatory models and hypotheses through testing on approximate case studies. However, these three methods are not mutually exclusive, and this present study draws heavily on the second and third of these modes of comparison to explore the lives of nineteenth-century Irish immigrants in both societies.[16]

To undertake cross-national comparison and explore the importance of a variety of structural differences is not to deny the agency of the immigrants themselves, nor should it be construed as denying the importance of the immigrants' homeland, regional backgrounds, language, or prior experiences.[17] In fact, one cannot examine the lives of nineteenth-century Irish immigrants without being forcibly struck by their determination to fashion their individual and communal lives, by their adaptability and responsiveness to life's vicissitudes, and by their desire to attain secure futures for themselves and their descendants. However, notwithstanding these features, comparison of the experiences of Irish immigrants in the United States and Australia, both at a national and subnational level, reveals key differences in setting that contributed to significantly different experiences in each location.

Two particular points of distinction stand out in comparing the experiences of Irish immigrants in the United States and Australia in the period 1815–1922. First, the different stages of economic development in each location did much to condition the broader experiences of Irish newcomers. The United States' earlier experiences of industrial development and urbanization shaped specific patterns of settlement and employment for the Irish-born, producing residential and occupational profiles that differed fundamentally from those of their compatriots who settled in the Australian colonies. Whereas America's Irish-born in the second half of the nineteenth century were concentrated in urban centers and were overrepresented in unskilled or lowly skilled employment compared to the total United States population, Australia's Irish showed a greater propensity for rural settlement and farm work, which was at least the equal of the colonial population at large. In both locations, the structural conditions encountered in the New World ultimately proved more important than factors specific to the immigrants themselves in shaping the broad outlines of their engagement with the new societies. Consequently, explanations of Irish distribution in America that emphasize their urban proclivity as the product of various psychological barriers to rural settlement, or as the product of particular cultural traits, rather than primarily the result of the specific economic context they encountered must in the end be regarded as erroneous. The microhistorical studies of Irish adaptation in America and the Australian colonies contained in this book confirm the greater importance of specific conditions in shaping the richly hued tapestries of nineteenth-century Irish immigrant life.

Second, throughout the nineteenth century the United States and the Australian colonies constituted widely different political and ideological entities, and these influenced in telling ways Irish immigrants' engagement with their new societies. Throughout the period from 1815 to the Irish Civil War, republican America prescribed ideals of thought and behavior and sanctioned actions by immigrants that were not regarded as appropriate in British colonies. Most specifically, the United States environment stimulated a level of Irish national consciousness and enabled immigrant activism in support of Irish demands for independence from Great Britain in ways that went beyond what was possible in the more inhibited colonial context. Conversely, a good deal of evidence supports the contention that for much of the nineteenth century the Australian colonial context fostered an environment of greater religious tolerance than was enjoyed by Irish immigrants in the United States. In both cases, specific milieus proved tremendously influential in shaping the nature and tone of Irish immigrants' engagement with their New World neighbors.

Neither in the United States nor the Australian colonies did the parameters of immigrants' lives remain static across the course of the century after 1815. In the United States the market revolution, the Second Great Awakening, urbanization, civil war, and the expansion of manufacturing in the latter decades of the nineteenth century were but some of the factors producing shifts that materially and psychologically affected Irish immigrants and their descendants. In Australia, convictism and the end of the convict system, the discovery of gold, and late-nineteenth-century industrial growth and urbanization did the same. Likewise, the global zenith of nationalism near the end of the nineteenth century did much to affect Irish immigrants' positions in their new societies and the terms of their engagement with Ireland. The advent of the Irish Civil War then caused many in Ireland's New Worlds to distance themselves permanently from affairs in the old homeland.

*

This book has taken a long time to complete and I have incurred many debts along the way. A Fulbright Postdoctoral Award from the Australian-American Educational Foundation first enabled me to visit the United States, where I was fortunate to spend the best part of the year working with Kerby Miller at the University of Missouri–Columbia. Like so many other scholars I have benefited enormously from Kerby's generosity ever since. I was also lucky to have the opportunity to meet and work with David Doyle at Missouri, who gave generously of his time and ideas. Beth R. McIntyre and Stephen McIntyre provided kind friendship and guidance during that year. I am also pleased to acknowledge the Humanities Research Centre at the Australian National University and its director at the time, Iain McCalman, for the award of a Visiting Scholarship that provided a period of research and writing time without which this book would not have been completed.

I owe substantial debts for support and encouragement to numerous historians in Ireland, the United States, Australia, and New Zealand including Don Akenson, Jean Allman, Andy Bielenberg, Philip Bull, Enda Delaney, David Emmons, David Fitzpatrick, Lyndon Fraser, Keith Jeffery, Joe Lee, Brad Patterson, Benjamin Penny, Bob Reece, Eric Richards, and David Roediger. The late Patrick O'Farrell influenced my understandings of Irish and Irish Australian history from my time as an undergraduate until his death. I would also like to acknowledge help received from librarians and archivists in all these countries and to the National Library of Australia and the State Library of New South Wales for permission to reproduce images in the book.

I am fortunate to have the day-to-day friendship and support of wonderful colleagues in the Department of History at the University of Auckland, and especially Barry Reay, my near-neighbor for many years. My work has been supported generously by grants from the Auckland University Research Committee, for which I am very grateful. Tim Nolan produced the maps and Charlotte Hughes assisted with the production of images used in the text.

A version of chapter 3 first appeared in *New Hibernia Review* and was subsequently included in Andy Bielenberg's collection, *The Irish Diaspora*; chapter 4 first appeared in *Pacific Historical Review*, published by the Pacific Coast Branch of the American Historical Association and the University of California Press; an account of the Redmond visit to Australia in chapter 6 was published in more extended form in *History*; and a version of the final chapter appeared in *Irish Historical Studies*. I am grateful to the editors of all these publications and anonymous referees for their comments.

I would like to thank the editors of the series in which this book appears, Tom Archdeacon and Jim Donnelly, and the staff of the University of Wisconsin Press for their support of this book.

Finally, deepest thanks are due to my wife, Leanne Comer, and our sons Tobias, Finn, and Eamon for so much that is good and enjoyable in life.

Ireland's
New
Worlds

Map 1. Nineteenth-Century Ireland: Provinces and Counties

1 Contrasting Fortunes
*Irish Lives from
1815 to the Famine*

IN THEIR BROAD DESIGNS, IMMI-
grants' lives are molded by the prevailing economic conditions and social
patterns of their new host society. For this reason, Irish emigrants embarking in 1815 upon the transoceanic journey to the United States had strong
grounds to feel optimistic about their futures. Notwithstanding doubts and
emotional anxieties elicited by their abandonment of the Old World, and
the fears and uncertainties aroused by the prospect of life in the New World,
emigrants in 1815 were making conscious choices to better their lives. Their
decisions, based upon hopes for greater material prosperity or desires for
superior political and religious liberties, were considered, calculated, and
deliberate. They invested their hopes in a new nation, where Irish men and
women had already made their mark, where opportunity was believed to
be abundant, where economic liberalism and republican idealism were secular creeds, and where the battle against the oppressions of the old order
seemed to have been resolved.

In contrast, the Irish dispatched to the Australian penal colonies in the
decade after 1815 had no such grounds for optimism. Their lives were des-
olate prospects. The antipodes, at the time remote and little known, prof-
fered no dream but servitude, no reward except continued life itself. Australia held out no grand visions of abundant wealth or political or religious
liberty, for to its English architects, its colonies were merely bureaucratic
blueprints, the most expedient solutions to criminal overcrowding. And perhaps worst of all, transportation to Australia involved no expression of liberty or desire, no exercise of choice or initiative, and held out only the
remotest prospect of ever returning to Ireland's shores again.

In the course of the next three decades, these positions were nearly reversed. By the onset of the Great Famine, the prospects for Irish immigrants' futures in the two societies had altered beyond expectation, almost beyond reason. By the 1840s convict transportation to New South Wales had been abandoned and the major Australian colonies were on the path to responsible government and the introduction of universal male suffrage. The Irish-born constituted nearly one-fifth of the colonial population and were spread across all strata of society, if unevenly so. Religious liberty had been secured, at least as far as most people considered necessary in what was a not-very-religious society. The Irish constituted a visible minority but were in tone and demeanor a mainly contented group, even a complacent one. In contrast, in the United States, by the eve of the famine the optimism that had prevailed in 1815 was nowhere near as strong as it had been. The immigrants' prior mood of confidence had been supplanted by defensiveness, the bright future vision of economic abundance and political liberty now overshadowed by a much harsher reality. The Irish stakes in American society, previously secure and well positioned for the future, seemed by the mid-1840s to be less bold, more marginalized.

This chapter examines the major currents in Irish American and Irish Australian life in the period from 1815 to the famine and seeks to account for the remarkable reversal in the fortunes of the Irish in both societies. In doing so, it charts the decline of America's Irish from a position of fair strength and assurance in their new society to a much more tenuous one, a movement well under way even before the arrival of the first famine immigrants in the late 1840s. In contrast, in the period from 1815 to the famine's eve, Australia's Irish moved from margin to mainstream, from poverty to promise. In fact, from this prefamine period emerged much of the tone and character that would shape the immigrants' experience in each of the settler societies for the remainder of the century: attitudes toward Ireland, responses to the host society, and their place in each nation's future. These three decades were therefore of profound importance; indeed, they constituted arguably the pivotal phase in the casting of Irish America and Irish Australia. Yet this prefamine period remains frequently overlooked in favor of the postfamine years in analyses of the Irish immigrant experience.

*

Though the peoples of Ireland had for centuries been on the move in Europe and the Atlantic world, Ireland's "new worlds" were ultimately born of the century of mass migration that commenced with the economic and social crises of 1815. A sharp decline in prices for agricultural exports after the Napoleonic wars triggered a severe downturn across the Irish country-side. In Drimoleague, County Cork, for example, the parish priest observed a decline in laborers' wages and the lesser availability of constant work. Potato plots previously worked by women and children "were now attended by themselves, for the want of general employment."[1] The hardship was felt most sharply in Munster, where the price rises before Waterloo had been among the strongest of any region. Falling prices also contributed to a financial crisis that occurred in the province, where half of the banks were forced to close. However, the signs of less favorable economic conditions were clearly visible elsewhere, especially in the midlands.[2]

It was not only the agricultural sector that was troubled. Manufacturing, too, was affected, though with significant regional variations. Particularly hard hit was Cork, the second-largest urban center. The termination of lucrative army contracts was a heavy blow to the local woolen industry, where levels of employment fell to a third of those two decades before. Domestic demand was unable to compensate for the loss of wartime orders: declining commodity prices ensured farmers had no spare income with which to boost the demand for manufactures.[3] There were other hardships too. Repatriations of discharged soldiers, a run of poor harvests, and a typhus epidemic all exacerbated the severity of the postwar crisis and con-tributed to the distress among the rural population. Moreover, the rate of population growth, now close to its peak, ensured no respite from the dis-turbing signs of rural impoverishment. Across large parts of Ireland protests mounted against the worsening state of affairs, violence escalating to an intensity not seen since the 1790s.[4]

In the face of this crisis Irish emigration assumed a scale and momentum that differed markedly from the outflows of the previous century. Shipping agents specializing in the passenger trade now emerged as some thirty-five thousand emigrants departed for North America in the years 1815–18.[5] How-ever, despite the intensification in their rate of departure, these emigrants shared many of the characteristics of the eighteenth-century waves of Irish migration to North America. Drawn predominantly from Ulster, the major-ity who ventured across the Atlantic were Protestants of mixed denomina-tions. Well-to-do farmers, traders, and artisans were to the forefront, while over half the emigrants traveled to North America in family groups.[6]

Emigration leveled off after this initial upsurge, the slowdown attribut-able not so much to any dramatic improvement in conditions in Ireland but to the temporarily troubled state of the United States economy. The depressed level of economic activity in America in the years 1818–21 greatly reduced the demand for immigrant labor, and as this news was communicated across the Atlantic, the rate of departures from Ireland slowed. However, the post-1815 outflow had by then been of profound importance in eroding resistance to emigration in parts of the Irish countryside, widening the provincial base of the movement. Now, William Forbes Adams asserted, there were "in many districts discontented groups who looked to America for the ultimate solution of their difficulties." Consequently, when in the mid-1820s Ireland suffered under the effects of a severe British financial crisis, inhibitions toward emigration had diminished considerably, and the Irish were primed to resume their movement abroad.[7]

From its resumption in the mid-1820s, emigration from Ireland to North America maintained its upward momentum until the mid-1830s when a severe economic downturn in the northeastern United States caused a short-term decline.[8] Ulster continued to be at the forefront as Irish men and women chose to forsake their homeland and risk their chances abroad. As a result of the operation of the Passenger Acts, most emigrants in these years sailed first to Canada, though many subsequently traversed the border to the United States. William Bowman Felton, a legislative councilor in Lower Canada, was of the opinion that 80 percent of emigrants arriving in Quebec who were not part of organized migration schemes moved on to the United States: "The wages of labor being higher in the adjoining states of the Union, in consequence of public works being carried out there, there is a greater demand for the services of those people." This pattern of on-migration was not confined to the Catholic Irish. The emigration agent Alexander Buchanan reported, "Many of the emigrants I am acquainted with go from the north of Ireland; their feelings would induce them to settle under the British government but, hearing so much of the prosperity of the United States, and great demand for labor, they are never satisfied until they have taken a general range."[9]

Overall, in excess of one million emigrants departed from Ireland for North America in the three decades after 1815, the majority settling finally in the United States. Details on the Irish origins of these prefamine North American immigrants are patchy, with the best general guide being David Fitzpatrick's calculation of cohort depletion in the four Irish provinces during the years from 1821 to 1841. This confirms Ulster's position as the leading source of emigrants, with Leinster and Connacht ranked together some distance behind. Munster experienced the lowest rate of emigration in this period. During these decades families constituted a greater proportion of the emigrants than would be the case later on, and greater numbers of men traveled abroad than women. Emigrants were drawn from all classes and occupations, but with artisans and farmers especially prominent among the earlier departures to the United States.[10]

The outflow was dynamic, though, and reflective of regional transitions occurring in prefamine Irish society. Consequently, from the 1830s the origins of the emigrants became gradually more diverse, and the occupational profile of those departing Ireland broadened to include increasing numbers of agricultural laborers and lowly skilled workers. Hence, in the mid-1830s the numbers of Roman Catholics leaving Ireland first exceeded Protestants, and from 1837/38 more Irish men and women were sailing from Cork than from Belfast. A fundamental shift was at work at this time: emigration was more and more coming to permeate all regions and sectors of Irish life. As one historian observed, "Many contemporaries believed that the desire to leave home was so widespread that only a lack of means prevented a tidal wave of eager emigrants from deluging American shores."[11]

Figure 1. Irish emigrants leaving home—the priest's blessing (London: *Illustrated London News,* 1851). S2844, National Library of Australia.

*

Men and women in Ireland were well aware of the attractions of the United States even before the surge in emigration commenced in 1815. In Ulster, the eighteenth-century waves of emigration to North America had served to establish strong familial connections through which information was conveyed back to Ireland's then most emigration-prone province. In Belfast and Dublin books on the United States, including the works of Dickinson and Crèvecoeur, were published to enthusiastic audiences. Their capstone message, one historian observed, "was the commonplace that human betterment and political improvement, preferably republican, were interdependent; and the more obvious lesson that the Americans, who had broken the connection with England, were the exemplars of that commonplace."[12] Even among Ireland's less literate people, messages of the liberty and opportunity present in postrevolutionary America were understood, even if the finer details of New World settlement remained as yet vague.

Irish emigrants who sought to build new lives upon American shores in the last decades of the eighteenth century or in the first two decades of the

Figure 2. Emigrants arrival at Cork—a scene on the quay [1850?]. S2838, National Library of Australia.

nineteenth century were mostly well informed about their new host society and found much to their liking upon arrival there. They were uplifted, in the first instance, by goodwill borne of the Irish contribution to the establishment of the nation. Wider horizons for Roman Catholics and the demise of indentured labor further contributed to America's appeal for the Irish audience: "Community, livelihood and religious freedom, all were waiting in one society."[13] This is not to suggest that the United States was a panacea for the ills and wants of Irish immigrants or that material progress was easily attained. Conditions were not always benign. Even immigrants of notable stature confronted obstacles: for example, Thomas Addis Emmet, lawyer and United Irishman, arrived in New York in 1804 and had to campaign for the right to practice at the bar while awaiting naturalization.[14] But despite its tribulations, the tone of life in America was rather conducive to Irish achievement. Nudged along by the successful Irish mercantile communities of the mid-Atlantic states, many immigrants on the eastern seaboard established firm and, for the time being, secure niches. No lesser building than the White House itself, the work of Dublin-trained mason James Hoban, stood as a metaphor for the centrality, confidence, and vibrancy of the republic's Irish-born population.[15]

Irish immigrants who arrived in the decade after 1815 were inheritors of this pluralistic and confident milieu. In 1826 a Limerick-born Quaker arrived in New York, "one of the first commercial cities in the world, inferior in its commerce to London & Liverpool alone." Impressed by the lively mercantile culture of the city, he recognized its beneficence to shrewd and attentive newcomers: "Here are no religious distinctions, all men of good character are eligible to every public office without exception, the laws are mild but rigorously executed, thefts not so frequent as in Ireland, perhaps because the people are not so poor."[16] Similar confidence existed in Philadelphia, which in the years after the revolution hosted a vibrant Irish population. Baltimore presented a similar picture as to the influence of the Irish in civic affairs.[17]

Further north in New England the situation was more volatile than in the mid-Atlantic states. The Puritan inheritance augured less well for Irish immigrants, although across the region local contacts between the new arrivals and the host society varied widely, from readily negotiated compromises to hostility and outright rebuke. For example, in Worcester, Massachusetts, where in 1718 a group of Ulster Irish immigrants had been harried for their attempt to establish a separate meeting house, a community of Irish now decamped after the construction of the Blackstone Canal. Worcester's Irish

9

workingmen of the 1820s were more commonly enterprising contractors or master artisans than navvies, married men with families who held secure and responsible employment. Many had spent transitional time residing in Britain; most commonly their children were American-born. In Worcester they anticipated prosperous futures in a town that seemed immune from more virulent nativist sentiment. But within the space of decades, as the numbers of lowly skilled immigrants from Ireland continued to rise and the proportion of Roman Catholics within the immigrant stream increased, that early optimism would prove to be misplaced.[18]

Along the eastern seaboard in the late 1810s and 1820s, therefore, grounds existed for at least moderate optimism, even among the lesser skilled. Economic expansion fuelled a steady demand for labor, a resource the Irish were well able to provide. The proof of this was everywhere in northeastern America in the years after 1815. Certainly, unskilled laboring was arduous, dangerous, and poorly rewarded, but for many Irish immigrants in the prefamine years employment opportunities promised in time to extend beyond the most mundane and hazardous forms of work.

The immigrants' confidence in the years after 1815, a certain Irish American ebullience, flowered in the democracy of the New World to a degree that disconcerted their critics. It especially raised the ire of Englishmen uneasy at their own alienation in America after the War of 1812 and antagonized at the conspicuous influence of the Irish in American affairs. One man so affected was the English diplomat Augustus John Foster. In America, Foster complained, "good people are often to be found represented by men who are not even natives of the soil—noisy blustering Germans or Irishmen who live by agitation, and [who] from their European knowledge and tactics, possession of the press and so forth, have an immense influence over all the wild unruly young adventurers of the western woods." Such a people, Foster believed, were "like tinder ever ready for blazing up." Who were the agitators Foster identified? In Philadelphia, John Binns, Irish-born editor of the *Democratic Press,* and William Duane, born in New York State of Irish parents and deported from Calcutta having edited the *Indian World.* Both were Irish men of American influence but, in Foster's resentful eyes, no more than inspirers of hatred, "who live upon doling out abuse of the country they had been obliged to abandon, and of whom there [are] no small number scattered thro' the states."[19]

The antipathy toward England present in early-nineteenth-century America was, in fact, one factor that helped consolidate the position of the immigrant Irish. Put simply, suspicion of England translated into a general, if thinly veiled, sympathy for Ireland as a victim of English misrule.[20] The question of Catholic emancipation provided a further telling point of demarcation between English policy and American idealism. Pro-Jackson newspapers editorialized in favor of the removal of civil distinctions based on religion, identifying English laws that restricted the civil and political rights of Irish Catholics as anathema to the spirit of American republicanism. Public sympathy for the cause of emancipation provided the backdrop for Irish Catholics' arguments in favor of reform of the offending laws: support for repeal, they declared, was their right and their responsibility as American citizens, an enunciation of principles fundamental to their new society. Irish immigrants were encouraged in their mobilization on the emancipation question by the intervention of George Washington Parke Custis, stepson of the founding president, who reminded Americans, "Irish hearts, and Irish sinews were with you in your arduous struggle for independence." The Republic, Custis declared, would not forget the plight of those who had striven on its behalf. This link to the nation's foundation was given symbolic acknowledgment in Philadelphia in 1829, when the Liberty Bell in Independence Hall was rung to signal the final achievement of emancipation.[21]

In 1827 Thomas Addis Emmet reflected on his two decades of life in the United States in a letter to a longtime friend, Archibald Hamilton Rowan. During this time, Emmet wrote, he had seen civil restriction become less onerous and party antipathy diminish:

> America is not what you saw it, nor even what your sanguine mind could anticipate. It has shot up in strength and prosperity beyond the most visionary calculation. It has great destinies, and I have no doubt will ameliorate the condition of man throughout the world. When you were here party raged with a fiend-like violence, which may lead you to misjudge of what you may occasionally see within an American newspaper, should you ever look in one. Whether the demon be absolutely and for ever laid, I cannot undertake to say; but there is at present no more party controversy than ought to be expected, and perhaps ought to exist in so free a country; and sure I am it does not interfere with general welfare and happiness; indeed I think it never can—their roots are stuck so deep.[22]

However, Emmet's optimistic evaluation of the prospects of his new homeland overlooked fundamental changes taking place in the organization of capital and labor, transformations recently initiated and for which the full implications were then scarcely visible. Within two decades, rapid economic reconfiguration would dramatically undermine the position of Irish immigrants in America and erode severely the ties that bound the Irish to their new nation.

*

As in North America, the Irish presence in Australia also predated 1815, although the circumstances of the island continent's colonial conquest ensured a very different reception for those who arrived there. The European occupation of Australia commenced in 1788, with the arrival in Sydney of the first fleet under the command of a royal navy captain, Arthur Phillip. For several decades historians have debated the motives of the Westminster authorities in establishing the penal colony of New South Wales, revisionist scholars emphasizing the importance of trade and strategic concerns in imperial reckoning.[23] Notwithstanding those arguments, it is clear that the new settlement was seen as providing at least a partial solution to problems posed by the increasing number of prisoners incarcerated in Britain, a situation exacerbated by the recent termination of convict transportation to the American colonies.[24] It was within this peculiar penal society that the Irish first laid roots in Australia.

Irish-born convicts were present from the time the first ships landed in Australia, though the earliest to arrive were in fact prisoners convicted in English courts. Indeed, it has been estimated that 4 percent of the convicts tried in Britain were Irish-born, nearly eight thousand in all. The first prisoners transported directly from Ireland to New South Wales followed soon after the colony's establishment, dispatched from Cobh aboard the *Queen* in 1791. On that ship were some 133 male convicts, 22 females and 4 children of convict women; the felons ranged in age from eleven to sixty-four. This was the first contingent of nearly forty thousand convicts who were sent direct from Ireland to eastern Australia in the period until 1853. Together, these two strands, plus small numbers of Fenian prisoners transported to Western Australia in 1867, saw the Irish-born comprise about one-quarter of all convicts transported to the Australian colonies.[25]

Though the convicts accounted for only 12 percent of the Irish to settle in nineteenth-century Australia, their influence in shaping subsequent patterns of migration from Ireland to Australia far exceeded their numbers. Freed to prosper on Australian soil, several became the linchpins that held together hubs of Irish settlement that endured for several generations.[26] Comprehensive data on the convicts' place of birth is elusive, but several studies have collated information on the place of trial of Irish convicts. Leinster appears to have been the site of the greatest number of convictions, accounting for approximately 40 percent of those transported. Its position as the leading source of convicts was most pronounced in the period prior to 1816, influenced to a considerable degree by the number of prisoners transported to Australia in the wake of the failed 1798 rising. Next in importance was Munster, where nearly one-third of the convicts sent directly from Ireland to Australia were tried. The Munster counties, especially Cork, Tipperary, and Limerick, contributed especially strongly in the wake of the post-Napoleonic downturn. The upsurge of agrarian violence that so alarmed Dublin Castle at this time saw significant numbers of rural protesters transported to New South Wales. Ulster and Connacht ranked third and fourth as provinces where the Irish convicts transported to Australia were tried, accounting for approximately 17 percent and 10 percent of the total respectively.[27]

Until the 1970s, Australian historians were greatly concerned to ascertain the true culpability of the convicts, the criminal foundations of the nation having been a long-standing source of shame and embarrassment. This interest was even more pronounced among a group of historians and antiquarians to whom it seemed the demonstration of overt political motives might distinguish and enhance the reputation of Irish convicts compared to common criminals transported from England. In a carefully documented study published in 1954, T. J. Kiernan estimated that in the period from 1791 to 1803, 61 percent of Irish convicts were political rebels who did not belong to the "ordinary criminal class." Over the quarter century to 1816, he believed, 49 percent of those transported had been either participants in the 1798 rebellion or active rural protesters, the remainder convicted "mainly from city trials, of the common offences against the normal kind of laws."[28] Despite the difficulties involved in classifying crimes of social protest, it now seems Kiernan's limited study significantly overestimated the proportion of political offenders among the Irish transported to Australia. A more detailed analysis published in the 1960s dramatically lowered his estimates and placed the number of Irish convicted of broadly defined political offences at less than 10 percent over the entire convict period. A subsequent study suggested the need for even further downward revision.[29]

Since the 1980s, however, Australian historical writing has moved away from concern with this question. Quantitative studies, concerned to refute the chapter in Australian historiography that casts the convicts as habitual criminals and "n'er do wells," have recently been to the fore. These works have focused more on the skills and economic potential of the women and men forcibly removed to the Australian colonies and cast the convicts more in the role of economic migrants than transported criminals. Though not without conceptual limitations, these studies have served to draw a well-rounded and less mythologized picture of the Irish in early Australia.[30] A major study of convicts arriving between 1817 and 1840 indicated that four out of five Irish sent to Australia were males, the mean age of both men and women being between twenty-one and twenty-five years of age. Two-thirds of the Irish were drawn from rural backgrounds compared to half the English convicts and less than one-third of those from Scotland, with little difference apparent in the origins of Irish men and women. Protestants comprised 15.7 percent of convicts tried in Ireland: not surprisingly, they were more likely to be from urban backgrounds than Catholic convicts, though only by a slight margin. Fewer Irish convicts were able to read and write than their English or Scottish counterparts, with the proportion of Irish women unable to perform these tasks three times greater than among English women and seven times greater than among Scottish women.[31] But despite this educational disadvantage, the profile that emerges of Irish convicts in Australia is of a group of considerable regional and social diversity, comprised not of the very poorest or least able in Irish society but rather of individuals with either urban experience or a degree of rural savvy.

In addition to the convict population, the Irish-born were present in Australia after 1788 within the military establishment and colonial administration and as clergymen. A small number of other Irish immigrants, perhaps five hundred by 1828, chose to migrate freely to the colony to try their luck as merchants or landholders. These early settlers, whose number included a liberal sprinkling of Protestants, hailed from a wide range of counties across Ireland, including those of Ulster.[32] However, the long voyage and greater costs of emigration to Australia—and perhaps most importantly at this time, the odious reputation of the convict colonies—served to deter departure for Australia on any larger scale.

Despite the hindrances of immense distance and ill repute, there were some individuals who from an early stage sought to promote the immigration of free men and women to Australia on a larger scale. In 1827 Hanbury Clement, a retired naval officer, proposed taking five hundred Irish families to Australia and providing all with provisions and employment on arrival in return for a grant of two hundred thousand acres of Crown land. Questioned by a House of Commons committee, Clement stated his desire to recruit Protestant artisans from Longford, Cavan, Leitrim, and Fermanagh. When challenged by committee members over his preference for

Protestant immigrants, Clement disclaimed any sectarian bias, testifying that he desired to avoid the "inconvenience" of conveying a group of mixed denomination settlers. Though Clement's scheme found only limited support among members of the committee, it foreshadowed both the vital role assistance schemes would play in subsequent Irish emigration to Australia and the sensitivity to the motives and religious predilections of those involved in the selection process.[33]

Eventually, in August 1838, a select committee of the House of Commons, chaired by Sir William Molesworth, signaled the imminent termination of convict transportation to eastern Australia. The Molesworth committee, which was philosophically committed to ending the scheme, sounded the death knell with its assertion that convict transportation was a form of slavery with no effectiveness as a deterrent. "Transportation, though chiefly dreaded as exile undoubtedly is much more than exile; it is slavery as well. . . . It is the restraint on freedom of action, the degradation of slavery, and the other moral evils, which chiefly constitute the pains of transportation, and of which no description can convey an adequate idea to that class in whom transportation ought to inspire terror."[34] In its report, the committee estimated that nearly seventy-five thousand convicts had been transported to New South Wales; almost thirty thousand more had been sent to Van Diemen's Land (Tasmania). Given its decision to recommend the ending of the convict system, the most critical question confronting the committee was an economic one: how would the Australian colonies continue to develop without the labor supply previously procured by transportation? James Macarthur, a representative of the colonial pastoral interest, supported the replacement of convicts by free laborers but warned of the dire consequences that would flow if arrangements were not made for an alternative labor source.[35] In the colonies, consideration was given to the introduction of indentured laborers from India or China, and several small-scale ventures to procure such workers were initiated before opponents forced their abandonment. This avenue closed, the only answer to the labor shortage lay in Europe, but it was obvious to all that urgent measures would be required both to rehabilitate the reputation of the Australian colonies as a destination for emigrants and make financially viable the movement of an alternative work force to the antipodes.[36]

Transforming the identity of the "colony of thieves" was a gradual but ultimately successful process.[37] Emigrant guides, pamphlets, and testimonials were used extensively to persuade the laboring populations of Britain and Ireland that migration to Australia would result in an improved diet, better health, and a more independent existence for all those willing to toil.

Typical was a collection of statements published in 1847 by the English advocate of emigration, Caroline Chisholm. *Comfort for the Poor! Meat Three Time a Day!* encouraged readers in the United Kingdom to make their own decisions about emigration but portrayed Australian colonial society in an extremely positive light. Testimonials by Irish settlers emphasized the bounty of the new land and the optimistic future it promised for the young immigrants. John K——of Dublin informed readers that Australia "was twice the country at home. . . . I can kill my own cattle here, and have a store of 150 bushels of wheat. I am better off than ever my father was at home— he could not feed me as I can feed my children."[38] Such descriptions, repeated in numerous other publications of the period, were undoubtedly appealing to the increasingly impoverished Irish population for whom the consumption of meat was a rarity and secure access to land was becoming more difficult.

However, success in revising the colonial reputation depended not just upon promotion of the material benefits of life in Australia but also demonstration of the improving moral tone. Molesworth's committee had noted with grave concern the overwhelmingly male population in Australia, especially in remote rural areas, where the imbalance was as great as seventeen males to each female. In the opinion of the committee members, this produced a society unique in its degradation, "a peasantry unlike any other in the world; a peasantry without domestic feelings or affections, without parents or relations, without wives, children, or homes; one more strange and less attached to the soil they till, than the negro slaves of a planter."[39] Such pronouncements were in fact nothing new, and colonial reformers had long decried the condition of laborers in the inland and demanded action by government to attract free, single women to New South Wales. In 1831 Edward Smith Hall had pleaded for the introduction to the colony of "a thousand or two sober, industrious women," who would prove themselves good wives and mothers to a new Australian-born population. Definitely not wanted were more convict women, "very bad characters," who would perpetuate the immoral demeanor of society. And indeed, it was in this pursuit of moral reform that the colonial governments first began to provide substantial assistance to emigrants from the United Kingdom.[40]

The recruitment of labor for the Australian colonies was hindered not only by reputation but by the much greater cost of a passage there than to America's East Coast. In the mid-nineteenth century the fare to Australia (up to fifteen pounds) was approximately five times the price of a passage to the United States.[41] Commencing in the 1830s, assistance schemes were introduced aiming to help allay this disadvantage. As a first measure, in 1831 ninety-nine girls from Cork's Foundling Hospital were shipped to New South Wales at the expense of the British government. In the wake of that very limited exercise, a broader scheme of female assisted immigration was initiated. But influenced by the theories of Edward Gibbon Wakefield, and concerned at the burden assistance schemes placed on the imperial treasury, the colonial office determined that future emigration should be funded from the proceeds of the sale of Crown lands in Australia. Consequently, nearly three thousand women were shipped from the United Kingdom to Australia in the period 1832–36, many of them Irish. That scheme was terminated in the face of mounting criticism over the moral character of the women selected, and colonial governments looked to alternative methods of recruiting emigrants.[42]

In the period from 1836 to 1850 several other systems were initiated whereby colonial governments, either directly or through the payment of a bounty to intermediaries, acted to select emigrants and subsidize the cost of their passages to Australia. The Irish responded with enthusiasm to the opportunities made available by these schemes. Some thirty-two thousand Irish adults received assistance to undertake the journey to New South Wales and Port Phillip (later Victoria) between 1837 and 1850, so that the Irish comprised 52 percent of all United Kingdom emigrants receiving assistance at this time. Though little more than a trickle in the great torrent of Irish departures for North America, the scale of Irish assisted emigration to the colonies in the years before midcentury was of great importance in its Australian context. By 1846 one-quarter of the New South Wales population was Irish-born.[43]

*

If the position of the Irish in the United States before 1830 was a mildly sanguine one, the Australia colonies offered their early-nineteenth-century compatriots much less reason for comfort. Within a decade of the establishment of the penal settlement at Sydney the Irish were stigmatized by the colonial administration, identified as a grave threat to the future of the remote penal outpost. In January 1798 the governor, John Hunter, wrote to the Duke of Portland warning "that if so large a proportion of these lawless and turbulent people, the Irish convicts, are sent to this country, it will scarcely be able to maintain that order so highly essential to our well-being." Not without reason were the Irish convicts Hunter referred to restless and irritated. Not only were they ostracized, cast either as dangerous villains, or as simpletons and fools, offensive to the sensibilities of the English middle-class establishment, but critical records pertaining to their convictions and sentences were not forwarded to the colony. As Hunter wrote impatiently to Portland, it was essential "as a matter of common justice" (not to mention as a sensible palliative to their repeated attempts at escape) that such information be forthcoming.[44]

The standing of the Irish convicts in eastern Australia worsened further in the subsequent decade, due to political developments in Europe. War with France and rebellion in Ireland served to heighten the anxieties of colonial officials stationed at the very periphery of the British Empire, the settlement's naval administrators being acutely conscious of its vulnerability to internal uprisings and external interdiction. Convict escapes and small-scale disturbances fueled this trepidation, so that by 1801 a near hysterical tone entered viceregal dispatches to London. Governor Philip Gidley King, writing after the arrival of the convict transport *Ann,* described the Irish prisoners as "137 of the most desperate and diabolical characters that could be sentenced throughout that Kingdom." The United Irishmen in the colony, now numbering nearly six hundred, were "only awaiting an opportunity to put their diabolical plans into execution."[45] King's worst fears seemed to be realized in March 1804 when four hundred to six hundred convicts assembled west of Sydney proclaimed their intention of taking control of the colony, their battle cry "Death or Liberty" a stark reminder of the United Irish presence in the penal settlement. When the uprising was ruthlessly put down, scrutiny passed immediately to the most prominent United Irishmen in the colony. "General" Joseph Holt, one of the most high profile of the Irish exiles, denied any involvement in the affair and in his memoir maintained, "I endeavored to persuade them from any such thing, but they, being foolhardy, they made up their minds and I always seen a weakness in men."[46] But if not Holt and his United Irish cadres, who? And why?

The most persuasive analyses of the 1804 convict uprising point to the middle rank of Irish convicts as primary instigators of the rebellion, those involved drawn from neither the upper echelons of the prisoners nor the most downtrodden. Prominent among those punished were married men in their thirties, who might be expected to feel most poignantly their separation from homeland and loved ones. However, English convicts joined the Irish prisoners, too, their united front signaling that the uprising was no simple or uniform expression of Irish identity or national sentiment.[47] Though the rebellion included many Irish convicts and carried the unambiguous imagery of Irish protest, the colony's fearful English rulers played a part in consigning its Irish identity upon it.

The manner in which the Castle Hill rebellion was deemed an Irish affair focuses attention directly upon the complexities of Irish identity in early colonial Australia. On 29 May 1801, the king's birthday, celebrations were held in Sydney to mark the Union of Great Britain and Ireland. The royal proclamation was duly read and the new union flag raised to salutes from gun batteries on sea and shore, accompanied, in the governor's words, by "other demonstrations of joy." The responses of the Irish women and men present on this occasion, whether convict or jailer, can only be a matter of speculation. For some, the event most likely represented abject failure and humiliation, a loss of Irish autonomy and prestige. Others, perhaps, welcomed the new constitutional arrangement. For a small minority, the moment was one of newfound liberty, as several Irish prisoners were released in celebration of the new constitutional relationship. And for others still, the celebratory issue of a ration of one pound of fresh beef to all prisoners victualled from the government store was probably of paramount importance.[48] But for certain, the event affirmed very visibly the penal settlement's colonial status and emphasized that Britain's antipodean colonies would prove no free and fertile ground for the cultivation and maintenance of Irish nationalist sentiment. Official records suggest the presence in subsequent years of a simmering level of unease and resistance among the Irish-born, a friction that found expression in sporadic acts of defiance.[49] But even if such acts constituted a form of protonationalism, their ambition was repeatedly suppressed and mocked in the suspicious and constrained world of the convict colony.

From the very beginning of the nineteenth century, then, the colonial relationship between Britain and the Australian settlements distinguished the experience of Australia's Irish from that of their compatriots in the United States. The Irish population in America included forceful and articulate advocates of the old country, immigrants whose conceptualization of, and aspirations for, Ireland as a nation were well developed. Robert Emmet and William Macneven in New York, and Mathew Carey and John Binns in Philadelphia were but some of those for whom the milieu of republican America provided fruitful ground for the growth and development of nationalist sentiment.[50] Their legacy was a tradition of Irish American nationalism, unmatched in its stridence and popularity by the national sentiment for Ireland present among their Australian sisters or brothers.

At the same time, there is a danger in ascribing too widely to the Irish in either society in the early decades of the nineteenth century any clear sense of nationality that was sufficient to transcend or displace entirely older local and familial identifications, save those molded in their new immigrant worlds. In the Australian context, the ship's surgeon Peter Cunningham observed early in the century the tendency of Irish convicts to split into distinct groups along complex lines, partly religious and partly provincial: "the 'Cork *boys*,' the 'Dublin *boys*,' and the 'North *boys*'; and these are so zealous in upholding their respective tribes, that when two individuals of different classes quarrel, there is no possibility of arriving at the truth—since a dozen of each class will run forward, and bawl out at once, in favor of their respective comrades, evidence of the most conflicting, contradictory nature."[51] So, too, in 1816 Irish prisoners involved in a suspected mutiny on the convict transport *Surrey* were identified by their shipmates as the "Tipperary men," a label that in its context implied not only a regional basis but also the subterranean complexities of Irish factional identities. Even at midcentury, the strength of regionalism remained evident. The Roman Catholic lawyer Roger Therry observed that onboard the ships conveying workhouse inmates to Australia, the women "formed themselves into detachments, taking their names from counties from which they respectively came. . . . There was much rivalry amongst these ladies on the passage, in their speculations as to their future destiny, the ground of jealousy being whether the Kilkennys or the Limericks would get the best in the colony."[52]

These patterns have resonance and meaning in the American context, too, where evidence points to the persistence of subnational identities among many of the immigrants. In the 1820s and 1830s Irish canal workers engaged in internecine skirmishes, the Fardowns versus the Corkonians, the division in part sectarian but also a reflection of a highly persistent localism that was eroded only slightly by a nascent sense of nation.[53] Even well after midcentury, ambiguity over Ireland as the primary focus of identification remained evident among some Irish communities, such as in Pittsburgh's "Point" district, where immigrants drawn mainly from western Connacht preserved what they could of a closed, provincial world in their new homeland.[54] But gradually, inevitably, the lived experience of immigration and the newcomers' standing as a minority community in their new societies operated to diminish old localisms and forge an Irish national identity. In doing so, this process forced a myriad number of individual accommodations to the demands that Irish national identity imposed in each destination.

*

As the numbers of Irish immigrants entering the United States increased after 1815, a fundamental economic transition in American life was in progress that drastically undermined their prospects. The gradual demise of the artisan system and its replacement with the market relations of bourgeois capitalism, evident in New England and the mid-Atlantic states from the beginning of the nineteenth century, heralded gradual economic and ideological shifts that adversely affected the Republic's immigrant populations and the Irish in particular. As Joyce Appleby wrote recently of "this profound economic transformation," "the flood of immigrants, starting with the Irish in the 1840s, provided the factory fodder that enabled native-born Americans to ignore the cruelest forms of exploitation that industrialization brought."[55]

Between 1820 and 1860 the United States population increased from ten million to thirty million. Though at the end of this period the majority of the United States population still resided outside urban centers, these decades were marked by substantial growth in the populations of America's major cities and in the proportion of the nation's population who were urban dwellers. New York City's population rose by a remarkable 750 percent between 1820 and 1850, while numerous other towns in New England and the mid-Atlantic states grew rapidly in size and complexity, if on a smaller scale. The movement of people to these expanding cities was initially the drift of the native-born—only after 1846–47 did immigrants assume a dominant position in the continued expansion of urban America. The influx of newcomers of different classes, backgrounds, and religions to the close living of the city was a new, exciting, and confusing experience, but in a time of economic change and dislocation, a sure source of uncertainty and anxiety too.[56]

As the nation was transformed, new Irish arrivals possessed of trades or other marketable skills entered America's East Coast cities under a dual disadvantage. First, they encountered a labor market determined to increase production and minimize costs rather than to preserve the pride and traditions of the old, established crafts. As one study of nativism pointed out, the "immigrants clustered in trades that were among the first to make the transition from traditional craftsmanship to contracting and putting-out, where cheap unskilled labor was in demand."[57] Second, the Irish arrived in urban labor markets attracting large volumes of native-born labor from the countryside. While the prevalence of "No Irish Need Apply" signs has been hotly disputed of late, what is beyond doubt is that labor market competition often saw Irish immigrants treated less favorably, consigned to compete with free black labor for the least skilled and most poorly remunerated work.[58] As midcentury loomed, and as the numbers of new arrivals from Ireland year upon year increased, this tendency became ever more pronounced. Ample contemporary evidence confirms this trend. For example, in 1855 the Massachusetts Commission on Lunacy observed that few of the state's Irish possessed much capital: "Most are struggling with poverty [and] many find great difficulty in supplying their wants." The result of the confluence of the market revolution and mounting competition between native-born and foreign labor was not only continued downward pressure on workers' standards of living but also a labor market in which new Irish arrivals were cast as outsiders, pressed to the more tenuous margins of the workers' world. Their marginality was reflected in high rates of mental illness, according to the commission: "Their lives are filled with doubt, and harrowing anxiety troubles them, and they are involved in frequent mental, and probably physical, suffering."[59]

These tendencies were amply demonstrated in Sean Wilentz's study of antebellum New York. "As work was divided and put out a large share of underpaid work [fell] to the least-skilled, destitute immigrants (particularly the Irish) who would work for whatever price they could get."[60] However, contrary to commonplace assumptions, the invidious position of Irish workers was only partly attributable to their alleged lack of skills. Analysis of the occupations of Irish immigrants entering the United States in the years 1819–20, and New York specifically during the period 1820–46, compels reconsideration of the emphasis placed upon the lack of skills of the newcomers in analyses of their labor market performance. Figures compiled by Cormac Ó Gráda indicate that in the years 1819 and 1820 no more than one-third of unaccompanied Irish emigrants, and less than one-fifth of workers within family groups, were laborers or servants—that is, among family groups, 80 percent of Irish workers were skilled farmers, artisans, textile workers, or white-collar workers. Through the longer period of emigration to New York, the figures for skilled workers are considerably lower: 61 percent of unaccompanied workers were laborers and servants, and 52 percent of those in families similarly lacked skills.[61] However, Irish sources emphasize the southward shift of the emigrant stream through the 1830s, as well as the broadened socioeconomic base of emigration as the famine decade approached. Inevitably, then, skill levels declined among the later arrivals. Put simply, attempts to explain the prefamine Irish position in the American labor market on the basis of the immigrants' lack of aptitude risks ignoring the levels of skill that the post-1815 immigrants did in fact possess. As the New York Association for Improving the Condition of the Poor recognized in 1852, "In this city, where there is so large a redundance of labor, even the possession of industrial skill affords no guaranty either for employment or good wages."[62] In addition to overlooking the immigrants' skill base, analyses also frequently understate the extent of the Protestant Irish component within the immigrant stream. Wilentz suggested "New York's early national journeymen . . . were [virtually all] white, and most had been born either in this country or in Protestant Britain; Irish Catholics and blacks, as yet a small fraction of the city's population, were consigned largely to manual labor and casual work in and around the port." That during this period the majority of Irish immigrants were from Ulster, and very likely Protestant, poses questions yet to be satisfactorily answered in the literature of the American Irish about the fate of these newcomers, and whether in antebellum America ethnicity was as influential a determinant as religion in patterns of Irish employment.[63]

To reiterate the point, despite a scarcity of hard quantitative data it is not in dispute that Irish immigrants fared poorly in the eastern United States in the antebellum period, though there were of course a considerable number of immigrants who enjoyed solid success in their new society. However, before the mid-1840s, Irish subordination within the reconfigured economy should be understood as less the product of their lack of skills than of the increasingly hostile nature of the urban communities they came to inhabit. In contrast to the position of the Irish-born in the first quarter of the nineteenth century, the ideological shifts that accompanied the market revolution produced a social context that tended to marginalize the Irish and push them to the fringes of American life. New World conditions were more influential than the baggage of the immigrants themselves in determining their adverse engagement with the host society.

American society was not intrinsically hostile to the Irish after 1815. Continuing acknowledgment of Irish involvement in the revolution, recognition of the legitimacy of Ireland's aspiration to greater independence, an environment moderately tolerant of religious diversity, and the plaudits won by Irish workers' involvement in such high-profile projects of nation building as the Erie Canal, all augured well for the newcomers. But with the market revolution came further fragmentation and contestation of the meanings of republicanism and, eventually, a new hegemony much more hostile to the Irish presence in the United States. The rise of Protestant evangelicalism; the dilemmas posed by reformist campaigns for abolition and temperance; widespread fears over undue Irish political power and partisanship, especially in cities; and staunch antipathy to the unskilled and undeserving poor—all these were factors that created especial discomforts for the immigrant Irish and rendered the adjustment of new arrivals to American life difficult in the extreme. These factors, in combination with the more tenuous Irish position in the labor market, produced a sharp diminution in the prospects of many Irish Americans in the second quarter of the nineteenth century.

The market revolution produced considerable disorientation and apprehension among America's native-born population. Old certainties crumbled in the face of change, and as anxiety increased thousands of Americans turned toward evangelical Protestantism in the search for stability and security. Indeed, the evangelical movement attracted such huge numbers of followers and exerted such wide influence over American life that one historian recently judged it "the principal subculture in [antebellum] American society."[64] This movement, the "Second Great Awakening," profoundly touched the lives of the immigrant Irish; it also contributed to the creation of lasting divisions between Protestant and Roman Catholic Irish in the United States.

It is difficult to overstate the importance of worsening sectarian relations in accounting for the deteriorating standing of America's prefamine Irish Catholic immigrants. Unlike Protestant Irish newcomers, they received an implacably hostile reception as they settled in the new land. To American evangelicals, the Roman Catholic Church was repugnant not only for its doctrines but also for the manner in which its organization infringed on the "true" meaning of republicanism. The increasing numbers of Roman Catholic immigrants from Ireland were unwelcome, not just for the threat they posed as agents of "popedom" but also because their values were judged to be incompatible with the future of a Protestant American society. "Poor, often disorderly, unsympathetic to the teetotal, Sabbatarian code of Puritanism, unversed in democratic politics, Catholic immigrants seemed a pestilential threat to the evolution of a healthy, virtuous, and Christian republic"—so one historian summed up evangelicals' objections to the ever-increasing numbers of Roman Catholic immigrants.[65] Opposition to the newcomers crystallized over the issue of education. In Massachusetts, Protestant reformers had from 1830 advocated a public school system to inculcate the values of republican citizenship upon new arrivals. By the end of that decade, the commonwealth's education system was controlled by a state department, and the school curriculum it endorsed was far from disinterested in its teaching on the relative merits of Roman Catholic and

Protestant doctrines.[66] Along the East Coast, the Roman Catholic Church staunchly opposed Protestant challenges. For example, in 1839, under the leadership of Bishop John Hughes, the Church strenuously resisted the American Bible Society's attempts to have the King James Bible read in New York's public schools. Controversy over Bible reading also spread to Philadelphia, the bitter dispute hardening sectarian divisions in American society and imbuing Irish America with an increasingly defensive tone.[67] By the early 1840s accommodation was under threat as politics labored under the weight of religious divisions. On 13 April 1842 New Yorkers witnessed conflict on the streets over the issue. "We had some hard fighting yesterday in the Bloody Sixth, and a grand no-popery riot last night, including a vigorous attack on the Roman Catholic Cathedral with brick bats and howls, and a hostile demonstration on Hughes's episcopal palace, terminating in broken windows and damaged furniture," recorded George Templeton Strong. "Well, this is the beginning of the end, the first fruits of that very abominable tree—the School Bill."[68]

The rise in sectarian fervor was worst on the northeastern seaboard, where the market revolution was more advanced. Further away, in cities such as New Orleans and Saint Louis, which had strong Roman Catholic foundations, the situation for Irish Catholics was generally a little better. In those places, long-standing Roman Catholic populations made for greater community accommodation and more strenuous neighborhood resistance to the intrusion of sectarian disputes. But in those regions where the Irish were most strongly concentrated, in New England and the mid-Atlantic states, the mood of the host society was ever more hostile. The rising level of nativist antipathy provided Protestant Irish immigrants with every reason to distance themselves from their embattled Roman Catholic countrymen, and this many appear to have done.

The Second Great Awakening also profoundly influenced the major reform movements of the antebellum period: the struggle against slavery and the fight against intemperance.[69] For the Irish in mid-nineteenth-century America, no issue posed more immediate discomfort nor did more long term damage than abolition. The ranks of Irish America had for many years included prominent opponents of slavery. In January 1805, soon after his arrival in the United States, Thomas Addis Emmet rejected the pleas of his longtime friend Joseph McCormick to settle in the South, writing "you know the insuperable objection I have always had to settling, where I could not dispense with the use of slaves, and that the more they abound, the stronger are my objections."[70] However, there was no uniform Irish response to slavery, and many among the numbers of Irish who entered the United States after 1815 harbored support for the maintenance of black servitude. Already in competition with free black labor for the most lowly paid employment along the Atlantic seaboard, the expanding Irish population had no wish to see that contest made more acute by the termination of slavery.

The dilemmas posed by the question of abolition were pressed to the foreground of Irish American life by the vocal and articulate public stance of Daniel O'Connell, Ireland's foremost political leader of the prefamine period. From the early 1820s O'Connell was a strident and unrelenting critic of the institution of slavery and of America's persistence with it. He corresponded with leading American abolitionists and in 1833 met William Lloyd Garrison in London.[71] "The Liberator" vehemently rejected invitations to visit the United States while slavery remained in force and declared he would refuse to shake hands with any defender of slavery, telling one meeting, "I should be sorry to be contaminated by the touch of a man from those states where slavery is continued."[72]

O'Connell's opposition to slavery caused embarrassment for many Irish Americans. In 1838 reports of his speeches, especially the comment that "the people of the United States instead of being the highest in the scale of humanity are the basest of the base and the vilest of the vile," prompted a public rebuke from leading Irish citizens in Philadelphia. Stressing their affection for Ireland and high regard for O'Connell, his critics explained, "You will instantly perceive how jealously and suspiciously we may be looked upon by our native American fellow citizens if the man, whom we have delighted to honor, shall by them be believed to have *en masse* deemed them the basest of the base and the vilest of the vile." They requested from O'Connell explanation and exoneration, "to remove from the natives of Ireland American citizens the odium which in the eye of their Native American fellow citizens had been cast upon them from their devotion and disposition to love and laud the man who had libelled them."[73] Their pleas went unanswered. Indeed, the American Anti-Slavery Society in New York was at the same time urging on O'Connell a different course of action, beseeching that he not back down to the demands of his critics but speak directly and unwaveringly to the American Irish. "They will listen to *you*," wrote Elizur Wright Junior to O'Connell in October 1838.[74]

O'Connell did not retreat. And despite his steadfast rejection of slavery, Irish American support for his leadership remained strong in the early 1840s as the campaign for the repeal of the union with Great Britain gained strength. Enthusiastic repeal associations formed throughout the United

States, and large sums of money—"repeal rent"—were raised to sustain O'Connell's political campaign in Ireland.[75] However, the foundations of American Irish support were gravely shaken when, in January 1842, abolitionists unveiled at a public meeting in Boston an "Address of the People of Ireland to their Countrymen and Countrywomen in America." The document, signed by sixty thousand Irish supporters of abolition including Daniel O'Connell and the renowned temperance campaigner, Father Theobald Mathew, called on Irish Americans to "unite with the abolitionists, and never to cease your efforts until perfect liberty be granted to every one of her inhabitants, the black man as well as the white man."[76] Taken by surprise, the Irish American press swiftly dismissed the address as a hoax, while Bishop John Hughes of New York declared that O'Connell's signature was almost certainly a forgery. However, when the address was authenticated, its significance and ramifications were only too apparent to Irish Americans. Put simply, they were compelled to publicly declare whether their loyalties were dictated by leaders of the old nation or whether they were an independent and freethinking people whose primary loyalty lay with their new society. The answer was given unambiguously and without hesitation. In New York, Hughes denounced outside interference in American affairs, while in Pottsville, Pennsylvania, Irish miners gave a similarly unequivocal response— "We do not form a distinct class of the community, but consider ourselves in every respect as *citizens* of this great and glorious republic—that we look upon every attempt to address us, otherwise than as *citizens,* upon the subject of the abolition of slavery, or any subject whatsoever, as base and iniquitous, no matter from what quarter it may proceed."[77]

Irish American opposition to abolition has been explained on numerous grounds: that immigrants struggling in their period of adjustment had not the time or energy to devote to the antislavery cause; that the Irish were fearful of the consequences of emancipation for their own tenuous position within the labor market; that confronted with charges of disloyalty, they were anxious to distance themselves from the charge of being susceptible to external influence; and that many were fundamentally racist. There is, in most, an element of truth. But if the Irish hoped their rejection of O'Connell's pleas might confirm their republican credentials and cement their standing in American life, they were sadly mistaken. As nativism surged during the 1840s, the immigrants' rejection of abolitionists' appeals brought forth the charge from William Lloyd Garrison that America's Irish were incapable of making a decision other than one "effectually controlled by a crafty priesthood and unprincipled political demagogues."[78]

In addition to abolition, the other great reform movement of the antebellum period was temperance. On this issue, as on slavery, the Irish-born found themselves increasingly out of step with the sentiment of their American-born neighbors. In colonial and early republican America, the consumption of alcohol was part of the routine of everyday life. In their love of drink and participation in the congenial world of the tavern, Irish immigrants then differed little from the host society. But this pattern changed in the post-Jacksonian period when, fanned by the winds of evangelical religion, drink became identified as a root cause of the nation's social ills.[79]

Reformers' campaigns to end intemperance were not then understood as movements of reaction but as measures affirming the belief in the possibilities of human improvement. As one historian explained, "Reformers sanctioned the acquisitive and individualistic economic order developing in America, and they optimistically predicted the improvement of the moral state of society on a firm basis of material progress."[80] As temperance movements assumed huge followings, those who stood in opposition to reform were cast as intransigents, ill informed, and in conflict with the true values of the nation. This burdensome judgment fell heavily on European immigrants generally, but most susceptible to the shadow it cast were the Irish, who in the decades before midcentury were seen as the least adaptable and least provident of all new arrivals on American shores. "Molloy missing [from the office] this morning. . . . I met him in the street smoking a cigar and he said he was sick, but it struck me he was cocked," wrote George Templeton Strong in his diary on 26 October 1840. To Strong, Irish men and women appeared to possess a predisposition to drink: "It's as natural for a Hibernian to tipple as for a pig to grunt," he declared.[81] However, American circumstance, particularly on the eastern seaboard, made the world of drink central to many immigrants' lives. Mired increasingly in poorly paid and irregular unskilled work, the tavern was for the Irish a crucial space of consolation, information, and restoration. It was a place, a space, and a moment that could not and would not be easily surrendered.

To vocal reformers, as well as to an increasing proportion of the population at large, it was essential that the Irish embrace the temperance crusade for their own—and, indeed, for Ireland's own—benefit. Strong believed this: "Separation from England and national independence are brought far nearer to probability when the people have thrown off the chains of *one* tyrant and become thereby sober and capable of resolute, steady, prudent and united action."[82] So, too, Charles Dickens viewed the American Irish most favorably when he came upon a temperance convention in Cincinnati in 1842. "I was particularly pleased to see the Irishmen, who formed a distinct society among themselves, and mustered very strong with their green scarves; carrying their national Harps, and their Portrait of Father Mathew, high above the people's heads," he wrote. "They looked as jolly and good-humored as ever, and working the hardest for their living, and doing any kind of sturdy labor that came in their way, were the most independent fellows there I thought."[83] Steady, prudent, independent—these were the qualities that distinguished the good citizen of the republic in the mid-nineteenth century. These were the values, supporters of temperance maintained, the war against liquor produced.

The further Irish immigrants moved in time from the optimistic post-Napoleonic years, the less possible the adoption of the values deemed most desirable by American society actually became. Less possible, not just because worsened economic circumstances and the rising tide of immigration precluded many Irish immigrants from fulfilling the ideals of social mobility and self-improvement the new nation held dear, but also because of the increasingly rigid stereotypes within which Irish immigrants were typecast. As one historian observed recently, "There was a discernible change in the nature of the Irish stereotype in American verbal culture. The change that took place was not merely a matter of words but captured public gropings for a different formulation of American nationality itself."[84] More and more, Irish adherence to the Catholic Church, supposed intemperance, and the newcomers' perceived lack of receptivity to the modernizing and reforming tendencies of American life were viewed as fixed, immutable, culturally specific characteristics.

The Irish defied the hopes and expectations of their nativist critics in other ways too. In a nation that celebrated enterprise, thrift, and self-reliance, the immigrants—especially the poor, unskilled, and desperate new arrivals of the 1840s—were cast as outsiders, their dependence one further reason for them to be despised.[85] In politics, too, the Irish were identified as an out-group, inflexible supporters of the Democratic Party and self-interested opponents of municipal reform. In 1835 Philip Hone wrote with acrimony on the situation in his city: "These Irishmen, strangers among us, without a feeling of patriotism or affection in common with American citizens, decide the elections in the city of New York."[86] Unsurprisingly, given the strength of such sentiments, demands were made for electoral reform to restrict the voting rights of newcomers in order to protect the sanctity of the ballot box.

*

In contrast to the frenetic changes associated with the market revolution in the United States, Australia's remoteness bred a sedate ambience. In the first half of the nineteenth century the colonies experienced none of the dislocations of industrialization that so traumatized antebellum America. Despite its tenuous beginnings, the economy in eastern Australia expanded rapidly, stimulated by generous government land grants to military officers, ambitious free immigrants, and convicts whose period of servitude had expired. The provision of land was supplemented by the assignment of convict workers, and not surprisingly, the demand for labor far outstripped the available supply. This combination of immense amounts of land and state-provided labor proved a boon for landholders, but the rapid expansion of European settlement posed difficulties for the colonial administration. By October 1829 the New South Wales government established a boundary to constrain the uncontrolled spread of the settlement, though this proved to be wholly ineffective in containing the expansion of the pastoral industry. One historian accurately captured the mood of the expansion, the insatiable hunger of the settlers for land, when he wrote that "soldiers could not have stopped them, and certainly not the feeble proclamations of a Sydney government."[87] Though there were fewer large landholders of Irish birth than English, many Irish ex-convicts managed to secure a comfortable stake on the land; others found employment as rural laborers in a generally favorable labor market.

In the first half of the nineteenth century, pastoralism dominated the Australian economy, while urban development lagged far behind. In 1828, forty years after the arrival of the first Europeans, the population of the Sydney district numbered just over ten thousand and the colony of New South Wales' entire population was only thirty-three thousand. The major town had a coterie of merchants, some with connections to companies in Britain; sealing and shipbuilding also developed, though still on a minor scale. The first colonial bank had opened its doors in 1817, but the development of industry remained slow. Only gradually did mills, breweries, and other small-scale manufacturing enterprises develop in the colony. The scale of production was usually small: workshops often comprised only a tradesman assisted by several journeymen. Such economic growth as did occur in the towns was then adversely affected by depression in the 1840s, so that in its wake Sydney could claim few successful capitalists and less than a dozen substantial companies.[88]

The economic context of Australian settlement therefore ensured a society devoid of major class realignment along the lines then occurring in the major American cities, but the colonies nevertheless had their own divisions to confront. Principal among these was the split between the exclusives—the faction of European settlers devoid of the criminal taint—and the emancipists, who as ex-convicts claimed the "colony of thieves" as their rightful inheritance. What was at stake then was not so much a question of proprietorship (though economic privilege rested more heavily with the exclusives) but one of rights and access to political power: would those with a criminal past eventually be entitled to the same civil status as those who arrived free? The seeds of the dispute were sown early and bloomed during the reign of Governor Lachlan Macquarie (1810–21), when to the outrage of the conservative elite a few select ex-convicts received invitations to dine at Government House.[89] The crucial struggle came later, however, and centered on questions of the right of the ex-convicts to sit on juries and local councils and whether questions related to civil status (convict background) would be included in the 1841 census. The Irish-born were to be found on both sides of this caste divide, though in greater numbers on the side of the emancipists. And it was the ex-convicts who eventually prevailed, with the Irish-born among their most effective leaders. Especially prominent in the campaign was the Anglo-Irish radical Henry MacDermott, a native of County Roscommon, who arrived in New South Wales as a sergeant in the 39th Regiment. After his discharge he settled in Sydney as a wine and spirit merchant, but also developed interests in pastoralism. MacDermott was strongly committed to the defeat of those measures that sought to restrict the civil rights of emancipists and in 1840 campaigned to enable emancipists to sit on the newly formed district councils and to defeat the inclusion of civil distinctions in the census. W. A. Duncan, the Scottish-born editor of the Roman Catholic newspaper the *Australasian Chronicle,* claimed in his autobiography that it was to himself "and to Mr. Henry MacDermott, a merchant who usually acted with me on those occasions they [the emancipists] were altogether indebted for their triumphs of this year."[90] However, MacDermott was closely associated with leading Catholic campaigners, too, highlighting a strong spirit of bipartisanship that characterized most dealings between Protestants and the Catholic Irish across eastern Australia before 1850.

The other major line of fracture in colonial life was religious. Suspicion of the Irish during the early years of the penal settlement resulted in restrictions on the practice of Roman Catholicism and savage attacks upon the faith from Church of England clergymen. The Reverend Samuel Marsden, the most vituperative opponent of Catholicism in the colonies, warned in

1807 that New South Wales would be lost to Great Britain within twelve months were the practice of the Roman Catholic religion permitted. "Was the Catholic religion tolerated they would assemble loyally from every master not so much from a desire of celebrating mass as to recite the miseries and injustice of their punishment and to inflame one another's minds with some wild scheme of revenge."[91] Opposition to the Roman Catholic Church was maintained in a more subdued way through the episcopacy of William Grant Broughton, Bishop of the Church of England in Australia from 1836 until 1852. However, the English church's hopes for exclusivity and the entrenchment of its privileged position were thwarted in the Australian colonies. Following the removal of civil restrictions on Roman Catholics in the United Kingdom, two Irish Catholics were appointed to significant positions in New South Wales: Roger Therry, in 1829, as commissioner of the court of requests and John Hubert Plunkett, in 1832, as attorney general. Both had strong connections to Daniel O'Connell—Therry a kinsman and Plunkett a well-known political supporter. At this time, too, a new governor was appointed to the colony, Richard Bourke, born in Dublin in 1777 to a Protestant family with landholdings in Limerick and Tipperary. Daniel O'Connell is reported to have "rejoiced" in the House of Commons upon hearing the news of Bourke's appointment. Within the space of just a few years, three important posts in the principal Australian colony fell into Irish hands, and within a short time the religious climate of colonial society underwent far-reaching change.[92]

The position of the Irish Catholic population was irreversibly transformed by the most significant reform of Richard Bourke's governorship, the Church Act of July 1836. The new act, which remained in force until 1862, legislated for the provision of state assistance to all major religious denominations relative to their number of adherents. In doing so, it effectively stripped the Church of England of any claim to special status. The new law, which was attacked by its critics as the work of an O'Connellite clique, was an important liberal measure, instituted by men experienced in the sectarian calumnies of Irish life and anxious that Old World divisions not be replicated in new Australia. The Church Act set the tone for a general state disinterest in doctrinal matters that was to prove resilient in nineteenth-century Australia. It gave a remarkable stimulus to the underresourced churches in the colony too: in the five years after the passage of the act the number of ministers of religion in the colony rose threefold.[93]

Significant, too, in the Australian context was the absence during the early decades of European occupation of an evangelical movement of comparable character and strength to that which exerted such power on the American scene. This is not to say evangelicalism was unimportant in the colonies, only that its relative influence was less profound. Here once again the convict heritage proved crucial. As a leading historian of evangelical Christianity in Australia has noted, the penal foundation "helps explain the conspicuous and often-observed difference between the religious scene in Australia and that in America."[94] Gradually, however, religion's importance in the lives of Australians did escalate, prompting Manning Clark's observation that by the end of the 1840s there was "a visible increase of religious consciousness and the growth of a sentiment of fidelity towards the church."[95]

New South Wales did have prominent clergymen of an evangelical bent, including John Dunmore Lang, a Presbyterian whose upbringing and education in towns along the River Clyde in Scotland instilled a deep-seated antagonism to Irish immigration and the Roman Catholic Church. Lang was keenly interested in the United States, toured America in 1840, and was impressed by the religious fervor and the strength of republican democracy he observed.[96] However, Australia was not the United States, and the colonial status of the antipodean settlements, the ethnic composition of the population, and the temper of its peoples all operated to circumscribe Lang's attitudes and actions. A case in point was the controversy that erupted over the appointment of the English Benedictine, John Bede Polding, to the position of Roman Catholic archbishop of Sydney. When Polding returned to Australia from Rome in 1843 the Anglican bishop of Australia, William Broughton, protested vigorously that only one head within the colony could wear the miter and that his own should be the one. Lang, no close ally of Broughton, declared he could not see "why Dr. Polding, as a British subject, has not as good a right to set up the machinery of his anti-scriptural church in this territory as Dr. Broughton has to set up a whole machinery of his." This stance represented no softening of Lang's opposition to the Roman Catholic religion, and he reiterated his disdain for its "monstrous system of priestcraft and superstition." But to Lang there was an overriding principle involved: "[Roman Catholics'] civil and religious liberties as British subjects . . . we shall always esteem it our bounded duty to advocate and contend for, precisely as if they were our own."[97] Yet this duty evidently extended only to those already settled on Australian shores, and Lang agitated stridently against further Irish immigration to the Australian colonies.

If Governor Richard Bourke's initiative in funding all denominations did much to tone down the potential for sectarian controversy, his attempts to introduce the Irish national education system to New South Wales had the reverse effect. Bourke envisaged a secular, state-controlled education system, with daily readings of scriptures acceptable to both Protestant and Roman Catholic churches and catechism taught weekly by visiting clergymen to the children of their own denomination. The proposal foundered, much to the governor's dismay. The Church of England insisted its catechism only should be used in schools; the Presbyterian Lang objected that "New South Wales was a British colony and should not be treated like an Irish one"; and Roman Catholic support for the Irish scheme only served to heighten the antagonism of all Protestant denominations. The education controversy showed that, despite Bourke's initiatives, religious bigotry remained well and truly alive in colonial Australia, though much less virulent than in antebellum America.[98]

Bigotry also underpinned debates about the future peopling of the colonies after the report of the 1838 Select Committee of the House of Commons sounded the death knell for convict transportation. Pastoralists' attempts to recruit cheap labor from India or China were extinguished by the fledgling mercantile bourgeoisie, anxious to ensure that the privileged position of the landholders was not further entrenched. They found staunch allies in their campaign among the colony's mechanics and laborers, fearful of the consequences for wage levels of cheap colored labor.[99] All eyes turned then to the British Isles—and some, to Ireland in particular—transfixed with the question posed by John Dunmore Lang: "Is this colony to be transformed into a Province of Popedom?"[100]

In the 1840s, the numbers of Irish immigrants arriving in the Australian colonies proved highly contentious. The *Sydney Morning Herald* warned in August 1840, "We have repeatedly called the attention of our readers to the unfair manner in which this colony is flooded with ignorant and unskilled Irish Roman Catholics, contrary to the wishes of those who are the chief contributors to the Land Fund, namely, landholders of the colony, nine-tenths of whom are Protestants of various denominations." Its fear rested not only on the boost for Roman Catholicism that would come through increased immigration from the southern Irish provinces but also on disturbances to the public order it feared would arise from the Irish presence. As early as 1840, Australian newspapers and commentators invoked the example of the United States, which, they claimed, demonstrated the disadvantages of uncontrolled Irish migration. "Hordes of Irish Roman Catholics have been periodically poured forth on the shores of Canada and the United States till their numbers have become a political nuisance," the

Herald explained. But the threat to Australia was, it argued, a greater one than confronted America: "There they are soon lost in a crowded native Protestant population; but here twenty or thirty thousand such importations would in a contested election give them as mischievous and pernicious a weight and influence as they have exerted in Ireland itself."[101] Proposals to regulate assisted immigration in proportion to the relative sizes of the British Isles populations were discussed, a measure too lenient for most irascible opponents of the Irish, but a palliative nonetheless. However, quotas proved impossible to implement if colonial demands for labor were to be met. For, as the *Herald* also acknowledged in late 1840, "the consequences of the want of labor are fearfully ominous at this time. . . . We dread to think of them."[102]

*

On Saint Patrick's Day 1840, the Catholic newspaper, the *Australasian Chronicle,* editorialized on the spirit of veneration in which Ireland's saint was held at home and abroad. "We regret however to say this praiseworthy spirit has yet to manifest itself in Australia! For, although it may fairly be said that more than one half of the white inhabitants of New South Wales are Irishmen, either by birth or descent, and although many of these are much more wealthy than their ancestors—where shall we look for a standing memorial of their national faith and patriotism. Where are we to look in this colony for a school or hospital under the patronage of great Saint Patrick? Where shall we look on this 17th day of March for a proof that Irishmen have not forgot their country, save in the tavern and the tap room?"[103] Though not recognized at the time as such, the *Chronicle's* disillusionment was testimony to the remarkable transformation in Irish fortunes in Australia in the half century after European occupation. The longevity and size of the Irish component in the Australian population, the religious liberalism introduced initially during Richard Bourke's governorship, the continuing requirement for labor, and the exertions of the Irish-born themselves all contributed to an environment where the immigrants were no longer inevitably marked as outsiders but were for much of the time nearly invisible in the colonial mainstream. Their Australian environment was tolerably beneficent, and few decisive political issues existed to set them apart from their fellow colonists.

Just as importantly, there was as yet no well-developed sense of Australian nation or national identity with which to try the performance of the Irish.

Whereas in antebellum America republican idealism saw harsh judgments cast on Irish behavior, the colonies' possessed no directly comparable ideological or cultural prescriptions. Instead, Australia struggled with the inferiority of the colonial subject. In the wake of the damning criticisms contained in the 1838 Molesworth Inquiry and other adverse comments, the *Sydney Morning Herald* complained that Australia "has utterly lost caste among civilized nations, and is now, it is to be feared, in the general estimation, little better than 'a desolation, an astonishment, a hissing and a curse.'" The answer to this libel, the *Herald* argued, was for party differences to be subsumed to the greater interest of all the people. "Protestant and Catholic, Christian and Jew, are equally implicated in the foul slander and are equally called upon to come forward and vindicate their fame."[104] Only by the 1840s, liberated from transportation and forced to confront the future through a different prism, did a proto-nationalist movement really begin to emerge in Australia; it was a movement in which Irish participation was expected and in which the Irish would demand and eventually find a satisfactory niche.

If in this way the Australian scene was propitious for the Irish, the reverse was true in the United States. In May 1844 the Philadelphia suburb of Kensington erupted in violent sectarian riots. Native-born workingmen, influenced by the tide of evangelical Protestantism, turned on Irish immigrant weavers and identified them as outsiders and intransigents, opponents of reform, and bitter rivals across a range of issues including education, liquor control, and politics. To Philadelphia's protesting workers, the Irish were implacable antagonists.[105] The eruptions on Kensington's streets signaled just how remarkably the position of the American Irish had shifted in the thirty years after 1815. Once proud legatees of the revolution and acknowledged citizens of the republic, the Irish-born were now ostracized and pushed further to the margins of American life, subject to increasingly virulent and violent attack. Images and stereotypes of the Irish hardened at this time: increasingly the immigrants were seen in racial terms, their faults and deficiencies general to the Irish character and fixed in biology.[106] As America turned inward, the Irish were cast in the most unenviable of positions, and the new American immigrants of the famine years entered what was by far the more hostile and antagonistic of Ireland's new worlds.

2 Crisis and Despair
The Famine and Its Aftermath

BY THE EVE OF THE IRISH FAMINE, THE crucial outlines of the Irish immigrant experience in the United States and Australia were set in place. In America, the profound economic and ideological transformations that accompanied the market revolution struck the post-1815 Irish arrivals with peculiar severity, so that by the time of the "Great Hunger" their economic standing and social reputation were inferior to those of any other major European immigrant group. The Irish were concentrated most heavily in poorly remunerated laboring work, and the increasing proportion of Roman Catholics within the Irish immigrant stream were subject to virulent religious bigotry. Admittedly, within the vast and dynamic landscapes of nineteenth-century America, there were diverse local experiences. In cities such as New Orleans and Saint Louis, where a Roman Catholic presence had long been significant, middle-class Irish communities enjoyed the benefits of more tolerant host communities and more open economic structures than those found along the northeast coast. In the towns and farmlands of the Upper Mississippi Valley, too, conditions were more benign. California, following the discovery of gold, would provide the Irish with another, more liberating, American experience. But in the areas of greatest concentration—New England and the mid-Atlantic states—the realities of mid-nineteenth-century life were grim and disheartening. Imposed upon this foundation, the mass emigration of the famine years proved a heavy burden for Irish America. The arrival of more than one million immigrants from Ireland in the period 1847–54 aggravated the position of the Irish in the labor market in America's major East Coast cities and exacerbated nativist fears of the consequences of unrestrained immigration.

In contrast, the Irish position in Australia half a century after European occupation was a curiously strong and influential one. In the decades after the Napoleonic wars, Irish ex-convicts and free settlers had carved a satisfying niche in colonial life, beneficiaries of the liberal political and religious policies of successive colonial administrations and the colonies' insatiable demand for labor. Though economic hardship in the early 1840s dealt a blow to antipodean confidence, the longer-term prospects for the Irish in Australia remained positive. Furthermore, Australia remained relatively untouched by Irish emigration during the worst of the famine years. It was simply too distant, too expensive, and too complex a destination for emigrants to reach during the headlong flight of the late 1840s. Fast relief was then necessary, and Australia's colonies provided no analgesic to the famine's distress. The most traveled route to salvation was to go quickly to Liverpool, in all its chaos and complexity, then onward across the Atlantic.[1] There were exceptions to the rule. Between 1848 and 1850 some 4,175 "orphan girls," women selected from workhouses and charitable institutions across Ireland, were provided with clothing and provisions and a passage to the Australian colonies. There they met a mixed response, welcomed by employers eager for servants and more so by single men desperate for wives, but disdained by Protestant clergymen and politicians whose voices of fearful outrage drowned out the cool headed. Amidst this din, and an accompanying level of opposition within Ireland, the scheme was terminated.[2] Emigrants were also assisted under an old scheme, temporarily revived—that of reuniting convicts with their families. Between 1849 and 1852 the imperial government funded the migration of over six hundred Irish women and children to Sydney under such auspices. Small numbers of other Irish men and women came, too, their emigration sponsored by landlords concerned with their tenants' welfare and eager to clear the land.[3] Yet, as important as these various schemes were in their intimate, human terms, they stood minute and insignificant against the Atlantic emigrant tide. Only with the discovery of gold in 1851 would Australia achieve greater prominence as a destination for the Irish.

Just as the vast torrent of emigration during the famine years impacted upon Ireland's new worlds in different ways, so the political turbulence in Ireland in the late 1840s affected its emigrant communities with different force and different consequences. The rise of Young Ireland, set within the broader context of the dramatic rise of European nationalism, aroused great excitement among the Irish in the United States, their reaction intensified by America's own revolutionary heritage. Ireland's plight and America's example constituted a potent mix of idealism and emotion, one into which more than one million new Irish men and women were directly cast by the hunger and dislocation of the famine years. From this wellspring of Ireland's past, the powerful evocation of America's republican heritage, and the fearsome brutalities of midcentury urban life, a new and powerful form of identification arose. Irish American nationalism, born in this crucible of deprivation, resentment, and bold aspiration, emerged as a form of identity and belonging that would until the 1920s pursue its own remarkable life course on American soil.

Australia, too, was touched by Young Ireland, but in very different ways. Its leaders were sent into exile in Australia, to a distant colonial setting where at midcentury the Irish-born constituted nearly one-fifth of the total population. However, despite the presence of this substantial component within the Australian population and the enduring legacy of convict transportation and forced labor, no Irish nationalist movement took root in Australia to rival the intense nationalism present among Irish immigrants in the United States. Though in the two decades after the Great Famine Irish Australia experienced significant changes in setting, leadership, and tone, the immigrants' experiences remained for the most part widely different from those of their compatriots in the United States. Distance, background, economic conditions, and colonial setting all served to delineate Ireland's two new worlds abroad. Only later, in the 1860s, with the spread of Fenianism and gradual transformations in Australian life, would significant convergence commence.

This chapter evaluates the major currents in Irish life in the United States and Australia in the decades from the famine to the Fenian upsurge of the late 1860s. It demonstrates that the principal differences in national experiences already evident in the decades after 1815 were maintained across the middle of the nineteenth century and that the widely differing socioeconomic and ideological contexts of the two societies provide the principal explanation for the different patterns of immigrant adjustment in this period.

*

In July 1846 the Repeal movement in Ireland split, the division precipitated finally by disagreement over the use of physical force. "Abhor the sword? Stigmatize the sword?" the Young Irelander Thomas Meagher taunted the Repealers, before delivering his memorable rejoinder—"No, for at its blow, and in the quivering of its crimson light a giant nation sprang up from the waters of the Atlantic, and by its redeeming magic the fettered colony became a daring, free Republic."[4] Attempts to achieve rapprochement between Young Ireland and Daniel O'Connell's supporters failed, though the Irish Confederation was soon wrought with its own internecine strife. John Mitchel, estranged from Charles Gavan Duffy, split from the *Nation* at the beginning of 1848 to publish his own newspaper, the *United Irishman.* It soon gained notoriety for the Derry-born Mitchel, with its remarkable, acerbic attacks on Dublin Castle. However, as news of uprisings on the continent inflamed Irish nationalist imaginations, the cracks within Young Ireland were hastily plastered over. Inspired by news from Europe, Duffy all too optimistically prophesied that "Ireland will be free before the coming summer fades into winter. All over the world—from the frozen swamps of Canada, to the rich corn fields of Sicily—in Italy, in Denmark, in Prussia, and in glorious France, men are up for their rights."[5] The confederate factions assembled together for a meeting in Dublin on 21 March, when Mitchel and Duffy addressed a crowd of between ten and twenty thousand. However, in spite of this show of unanimity, fundamental differences remained in the ranks of Young Ireland, and the course of events in Ireland took on the mantle of illusion. Amidst confusion, disorganization, and acrimony, Mitchel was convicted under the newly proclaimed Treason Felony Act and sent to Bermuda, then onward to the grim reality of penal exile in the Australian colony of Van Diemen's Land.[6]

Later in the year other Young Irelanders followed the same path as Mitchel, convicted in the trials that followed July's showdown in the Widow McCormack's cabbage patch. William Smith O'Brien, Thomas Meagher, Patrick O'Donoghue, John Martin, Kevin Izod O'Doherty, and Terence Bellew MacManus were, like Mitchel, exiled to Australia. Thomas Darcy McGee and Richard O'Gorman gained respite only through their hasty escape to America. Charles Gavan Duffy, acquitted at trial through the advocacy of Isaac Butt, later joined the ranks of those who departed from Ireland, sailing to commence a new life in Australia. Left behind was a cadre of followers who would eventually embrace the Fenian cause.[7]

In the volatile atmosphere of 1848, Ireland and Irish America proved sparks to each other's tinder. The Irish in the United States watched, first with trepidation, then with rising hope, the political maneuverings in Ireland after Daniel O'Connell's death. In February 1848 Irish men in Cincinnati formed the Emmet Club and responded enthusiastically to the powerful rhetoric of the Irish Confederation. "It is the duty of every Irishman in this country to hold himself prepared, for the purpose of assisting the Irish people to attain their independence, whether their efforts be by peaceable agitation or the sword," they resolved.[8] Clubs formed in other American cities, too, linked by a national directorate, to help bring revolution to Ireland. However, not all Irish Americans were so strongly committed to the use of force. In New Orleans, anxious attempts were made to heal the rift between immigrants still loyal to O'Connell and the supporters of Young Ireland, while in New York the large Irish population was fragmented in its support for the different nationalist groups at home. All, however, believed earnestly that America's Irish had an important role to play in the drama unfolding at home. The *New York Tribune* was anxious that the American Irish not be seen to incite disorder in Ireland but maintained that just "in case [the Irish] *should* be driven into forcible resistance to the tyranny that grinds and crushes them, we *are* anxious that they should be sustained by the 'sympathy' of our countrymen not only, but of those who in all countries love Freedom and Justice and hope to see wrong righted."[9]

The reactions of America's Irish were not shaped exclusively by developments in the old country. American stimulus was also critical. In March 1848 George Washington Parke Custis, stepson of the founding president and long-standing advocate of Ireland's political liberation, addressed a mass meeting of Irish immigrants in Washington, D.C. Two decades earlier, Custis had been a supporter of the campaign for Catholic emancipation in Ireland. His name had provided a visible link between America's revolutionary heritage and Irish Catholic demands for religious equality. Now, in 1848, Custis's reappearance on stage in the name of Irish freedom reaffirmed that association between America's past and the Irish present. It fashioned for thousands of newly arrived Irish men and women a vitalizing nexus between the revolutionary heritage and republican idealism of their new society and the, as yet, unfulfilled national aspirations of the old. Amidst the gloom and the poisoned atmosphere that enveloped Irish America in the wake of the 1844 Kensington riots, the prospect of Ireland's liberation seemed to hold out promise for both famine-ravaged Ireland and Irish America, providing a desperately needed tonic to an immigrant population ostracized from the currents of popular republicanism. For Irish America, the turbulence of 1848 hinted at an opportunity to demonstrate its republican credentials, regain pride, and restore the standing that had been so significantly eroded in the difficult years of the 1830s and 1840s. When at this time the Boston *Pilot* imagined pikes raised and rifles leveled against the British and pleaded desperately "God grant it," it prayed as much for the futures of its immigrant readers as for their compatriots still at home.[10]

While events in Europe nourished the aspirations of the Irish in the United States, so, in a pattern that would be maintained for decades to come, nationalists in Ireland were directly affected by the actions and reactions of their compatriots in America. In 1848 the fervor of the Irish American reaction to events in Europe did much to shape the contours of nationalist Ireland's own response. Mitchel's *United Irishman* published extensive coverage of American reaction to events in Europe and developments in Ireland in particular. Its reports highlighted Irish American fund-raising and broached the possibility of armed American intervention in Irish affairs. Yet while such news did much to raise the hopes and ambitions of the nationalist cause in Ireland, it simultaneously imposed constraints and dependency upon Irish actions. So when the American League of the Friends of Ireland announced plans for a national convention in July to coordinate the response to events at home, its timetable frustrated the plans of nationalists in Ireland. Thomas Darcy McGee wrote to the conveners of the congress with scarcely concealed frustration: "Events in Ireland will not allow us to wait for your aid until late in August, as wait we must till then, if you do not meet before the end of July. . . . Summon, therefore, your convention; summon it quickly; organize the contribution you propose to levy for Ireland."[11]

In the final analysis, 1848 proved a time of disillusionment and distress for both Ireland and the Irish in America. The year of revolution drew to a close with the nationalist movement in Ireland grossly depleted; many of its most talented leaders exiled; and no coherent strategy in place to pursue the objective of Irish independence. Moreover, with the Great Famine wreaking destruction and emigration rising to previously unimaginable levels, the very future of Irish society lay shrouded in uncertainty and despair. For the Irish in the United States, too, the unfulfilled hopes of 1848 proved painful. Just as the United States was a golden exemplar for Ireland's national aspirations, so the failure of Young Ireland, measured against that American example, was all too easily open to interpretation as an abject failure for Irish Americans. And just as the rapidly rising tide of famine emigration posed its own tragedy for the homeland, the seemingly endless flight of men and women to the United States compounded the difficulties of the Irish already settled in America. Poorly positioned, and soon to be confronted by a vituperative outpouring of nativist bile, America's Irish had few havens to which they could escape.

*

Australia's Irish-born population was not nearly so affected by the tremors of 1848 as their compatriots in the United States. The distance from Dublin to Sydney was an insurmountable obstacle to meaningful involvement in the affairs of the homeland, and this remoteness from the Irish scene bred detachment and apathy. Such news of Irish affairs as did intermittently reach the major Australian newspapers invariably passed through the imperial center, London, and arrived in the colonies filtered and sanitized, containing little to excite the passions of the local Irish population. On 19 July 1848 the *Sydney Morning Herald* carried Irish news—details of a meeting of the Irish Confederation. Its source was London's *Daily Mail,* and the report was nearly four months out of date. Along with the redundant information of the meeting's speeches came unrevised editorial comment from the English newspaper, its opinions on Irish affairs inadequately informed and wholly unsympathetic. The message conveyed to the *Herald*'s Australian readers from the heart of the empire was that "the Irish government continues to receive, day by day, uncontestable proofs that the great mass of the population is still favorable to the present order of things, and that the revolutionary principle has only for its disciples 'the men of no property,' crackbrained theorists, and the turbulent agitators."[12]

The arrival of Young Ireland's leaders on Australian shores failed appreciably to change this situation. On 27 October 1849 William Smith O'Brien and several of his Young Ireland colleagues landed in Van Diemen's Land (Tasmania) aboard the *Swift.* The prisoners were offered release into the society at large, subject to giving assurances that they would make no endeavor to escape from the island, that each would reside in separate locations, and that all would report regularly to the authorities. O'Brien courageously refused this offer of probation and, subject to strict and lonely confinement on Maria Island, devoted his time to writing a two-volume treatise, *Principles of Government, or, Meditations in Exile.* In time, solitude bore down on O'Brien's health. Thomas Meagher, concerned for his friend, wrote to the colonial governor, William Denison, that O'Brien's "strength has been greatly weakened, and his health in general very seriously impaired."[13]

The other Young Irelanders were dispersed across Tasmania. Despite the strict terms imposed upon the prisoners, Governor Denison remained deeply suspicious of their activities. Not surprisingly, Patrick O'Donoghue's outlandish proposal to found a new newspaper, the *Irish Exile,* aroused particular anxiety. However, the governor's fears proved exaggerated, for the conditions of life in Tasmania provided little nourishment either for Young Ireland's political activism or any local manifestation of fervent Irish nationalism. Certainly, some among the colony's population exhibited a degree of sympathy for the Irishmen. But this warmth was in the main a reflection of the curiosity aroused by the infamous new arrivals and an expression of broader local anxiety over the persistence of convict transportation rather than an endorsement of their earlier nationalist activities in Ireland.[14] In fact, few on the island colony embraced Young Ireland; and there were fewer people still in Tasmania that the high-profile Irishmen would really have wished to have as supporters.

Despite the stringent restrictions imposed on the Young Irelanders by the colonial administration, the exiles managed to maintain contact with the outside world. Most kept up a steady correspondence with colleagues, friends, or family, while O'Doherty, Martin, and Meagher succeeded in arranging regular, semiclandestine meetings, inviting local sympathizers to join them for picnic lunches. But despite these fleeting encounters, all the exiles were affected by a gnawing sense of restlessness in their new and distant setting. Dissatisfied, daily watching their lives pass by, MacManus, Meagher, Mitchel, and O'Donoghue planned and executed escapes from Tasmania. Eventually, all four traveled to the United States, a setting infinitely more receptive to their unfulfilled nationalist ambitions. By the middle of 1854 the remaining Young Irelanders received news that they would be permitted to leave the island legally, having been granted pardons by the Crown.[15]

The Young Irelanders' detention in Australia did little to boost the stocks of Irish nationalism in Australia or to incite in Australia the fervor of either Irish or continental European reform. Most of the exiles remained at the margins of Australian life, aloof from the population as a whole, disparaging of convict-tainted society into which they had been removed. John Mitchel wrote in his *Jail Journal*, "It is hateful to me to come down from our remote pastoral district of Bothwell, to mingle in the unclean stream of travelers by this public road. . . . Every sight or sound that strikes eye or ear on this mail road, reminds me that I am in a small misshapen, transported, bastard England; and the legitimate England itself is not so dear to me that I can love the convict copy."[16] To be sure, the Irish nationalists did from time to time take a minor interest in Australian issues. During his confinement on Maria Island, William Smith O'Brien drafted a new constitution for Tasmania and submitted it to the *Launceston Examiner* newspaper for public discussion. Even John Mitchel's remarkable writing is at times suggestive of a bond of affection toward the landscape of the island to which he had been exiled. Following the arrival of his family he was moved to write: "methinks I shall have something like a fireside again. . . . Here we have pure air, glorious forests, lovely rivers, a thinly peopled pastoral country, and kind friends."[17] John Martin, too, would look back on his exile with a measure of fondness, if only for the personal contacts made during his time there. In August 1851 he wrote to an admirer of the exiles, "I shall never forget the true Irish heartiness of the hospitality with which you, Mr. Connell, your daughter and your son received my 'rebel' comrades and myself. . . . It was both very sad and very delightful for me to find in a forest in the Antipodes the warm Irish feelings and the grace and intelligent nature of the Irish character, and to think that all that is fast being extirpated at home."[18] But such glimpses of comfort or solace are fleeting ones, and there is everywhere in the writings of the Young Irelanders an underlying tension and a sense of unease and discontent at their contact with colonial Australia.

Just as was true of the Australian Irish in general, the great distance between the colonies and Ireland sapped the energy and enthusiasm of these fiercely committed men. The Australian scene was simply too remote to remain focused and engaged. John Mitchel, the man who had aroused such trepidation in Dublin Castle, now awaited news of Irish nationalists in the United States in letters from his mother. Writing on the heated discussions among Irish nationalists, Mitchel could but confess his estrangement: "I know not the merits or demerits of the questions at issue. . . . It is easy for me, here at the antipodes, cut off from the whole scene of bustling life as by the shearing scythe of death—with the whole mass of the planet lying between me and my former work and life." Australia was so far away, so far behind activities on either side of the Atlantic, that it induced lethargy. "Surely it is not good for us to be here. I wish at times to be awake; long for a rattling, sky-rending, forest-crashing, earth-shaking thunder-storm, and fancy that the lightning of heaven would shoot a sharper life into blood and brain. Lazily and sleepily we even look into the papers that bring us periodical news from the northern hemisphere—news perhaps four months old; and how is it possible for us to feel that keen human interest in transactions whose effects may all have been reversed, and their movers and actors all dead long before the sound of them has reached our ears?"[19] Mitchel's listlessness does much to explain how, for those of lesser commitment than the Young Irelanders, distance was a near insurmountable obstacle to support for the Irish nationalist cause. Always the last to know and the most hazily informed about Irish affairs, Irish nationalists in Australia required a faith that few were able or eager to sustain.[20]

*

As the tide of unrest washed over Europe in 1848, the *Sydney Morning Herald* pointedly emphasized the liberties enjoyed by the Australian population and the distance of the road down which the penal settlement had traveled. "There are, it is true, some few restrictions upon our local rights of which we have reason to complain," it acknowledged, but "when we remember the infancy of our settlement, and the recency of our deliverance from penal thralldom, we should rather rejoice that our advancement has been so considerable. All the solid benefits pertaining to a free people are already ours."[21] Though the *Herald* wrote as the voice of conservatism in the colony, it accurately enough captured the temper of a society that would in 1848 see no local enactment of the tide of reformism that swept across Europe.

There were, certainly, issues of local importance that aroused strong feelings in Australia. Liberals and workers were determined that convict transportation would not be resumed, no matter how doggedly it was sought by conservative pastoralists. Colonists also united to demand that the British government yield them self-government, to enable local control of land and revenue matters. In the outlying regions of the foundation colony, New South Wales, local populations advanced their own separatist demands. Through the late 1840s and early 1850s all these claims were pursued vigorously, and in the course of campaigns on these issues the emergent colonial bourgeoisie were often to be found mobilized with the colonies' artisans and working men against the old landed elite. The demands of the liberal reformers were effectively put and in time their position became ascendant, so that by the mid-1850s the Australian colonies were on the verge of parliamentary government and, by the end of that decade, had achieved universal male suffrage.

The tide of reform in the early 1850s was advanced, too, by the remarkable demographic transformations that occurred in eastern Australia in the wake of gold discoveries in New South Wales and Victoria in 1851. The rapid influx of immigrants—in Victoria alone, the settler population rose by 450 percent from 97,489 in December 1851 to over 540,000 one decade later—posed a major challenge to colonial conservatives, destabilizing established power relationships in society and exciting fears of the excesses of democracy.[22] In that peculiar world, the *Dublin University Magazine* informed its readers, were "brief-less barristers and Cornish miners, *ci-devant* doctors, and 'old hands,' broken down swells and wild Tipperary boys." It was, the Irish magazine declared, "a heterogeneous mass of people, in a state of admirable fusion, or confusion."[23] Such disorder, with all its risks and opportunities, contrasted markedly with the more regimented and ordered convict society of a half century before, and its dynamism proved attractive to numbers of adventurous new arrivals.

Prominent among the vast immigrant stream that arrived to seek fortunes on the gold fields were Irish men and women, some of whom arrived in Australia politicized by their experiences of the Repeal movement or the invective of Young Ireland. Other Europeans, too, came touched by the currents of Chartism or the turbulence of the 1848 revolutions on the continent. These diverse, radicalizing influences surfaced in Australia in 1854, when a number of gold diggers on the Eureka field near Ballarat rose in protest against the excesses of state authority and demanded concessions from the Victorian government. A variety of issues were at stake: diggers' license fees, the administration of the goldfields, the widening of the franchise, even demands for land reform. But the administration of Governor Charles Hotham was oblivious to the extent of discontent, or so it seemed

Figure 3. Frederick Grosse, Emigrants landing at the Queen's Wharf, Melbourne [ca. 1860]. S2853, National Library of Australia.

to contemporaries. As Melbourne's *Argus* commented with prescience, "It is very plain the government [understand nothing] but Irish hints."[24] Following a clash with troops, on 30 November 1854 diggers enclosed themselves in a stockade to resist the authorities. Two days later, in the early hours of a Sunday morning when few remained in camp, troops fired on the stockade and took control. Approximately thirty protestors were killed and about half that number of troops killed or wounded. The victory proved a fleeting one: the affair destroyed the governor's reputation and in their own gesture of defiance Melbourne's juries refused to convict prisoners brought to trial on charges of treason.[25]

The Eureka rebellion, as the protest became known, acquired a privileged place in Australian nationalist and labor mythology. The distinguished politician and jurist H. V. Evatt was later to christen Eureka "the birthplace of Australian democracy." This was an exaggeration, as the great constitutional reforms of the 1850s were in fact already well in train by the time of the rebellion. But the power of the Eureka myth was then, and remains today, a strong one, and allied to it is a legend of the crucial roles played by the Irish in the achievement of Australia's democratic reforms. Much evidence does indeed point to Irish immigrants' prominence in the disturbance at Eureka. Peter Lalor, son of an Irish member of Parliament from Queen's county and brother of the more renowned nationalist James Finton Lalor, was the diggers' most prominent leader; half the casualties of the fracas were Irish; pikes were produced in the Irish style (by a German blacksmith) for the impending showdown with authority; and the password for entry to the rebels' stockade, "Vinegar Hill," was an unmistakable throwback to Ireland's own 1798 rebellion.[26] However, the extent to which the affair should be described as distinctively Irish is a vexed one, much debated by historians. Most insightful and measured was Patrick O'Farrell's assessment that the event "points to the centrality of Irish initiatives in that [national] myth-making process, not so much in their having any necessary monopoly of bellicose oratory, or aggressive posturing, but in their lending to these things a distinctive flavor and emphasis."[27]

This period of reform in the late 1840s and the early 1850s also witnessed the emergence of a first wave of Australian republicanism. Principal advocates of republicanism in the colonies were the Presbyterian clergyman John Dunmore Lang, who during a visit to the United States in 1840 had been strongly influenced by America's republican idealism, the Australian-born poet Charles Harpur, and an Australian son of Irish convict parents, Daniel Henry Deniehy. However, their early republican aspirations then weighed only lightly upon the consciousness of Australian society and were in no way comparable to the strength or influence of republican ideology in the United States. Moreover, in contrast to the American scene, republicanism in the colonies seems to have exerted only the most minimal pressure either on Irish Australian attitudes toward Ireland or upon attitudes to Irish immigrants themselves. Certainly, Dan Deniehy had visited Ireland and returned to Australia impressed with the spirit of the Young Ireland movement, and Charles Harpur was an acknowledged sympathizer with Ireland's struggle for independence. But empathy with Ireland was not a universal or consistent feature of early Australian republicanism: the Scots-born Lang was, in fact, one of the most vituperative opponents of Irish immigration and Irish influence in Australian colonial life. With its leaders divided over Ireland, and insufficiently powerful to displace the strength of the colonies' imperial attachments, the first wave of Australian republicanism failed to provide a significant stimulus to the cause of Irish nationalism.[28] If the United States was at this time a model for a future republican Ireland, the Australian colonies provided only a model for a better, more enlightened colonial relationship. But in Australia this was not viewed with opprobrium, and mid-nineteenth-century Australia's Irish population seem on the whole to have been well satisfied with their stake in the colonial enterprise.

In August 1856 Charles Gavan Duffy arrived in Victoria, where the substantial sum of £5,000 had been subscribed to a public appeal to obtain a qualification so that he might sit in the colony's legislative council. Residents of Sydney had also sought to entice Duffy to enter public life there, but to their disappointment he opted to settle in Melbourne, then a "thriving village" but soon to become the beacon of Australian prosperity and the symbol of nineteenth-century Australasian progress.[29] At a meeting in his new home city, Duffy graciously accepted the endowment as "a noble retaining fee to serve the interests of Australia, according to my best abilities." The vision he espoused to his supporters was of a peaceful, ecumenical Australia: "I cannot see what any man, high or low, wise or foolish, can hope to gain in the long run by setting Protestant against Catholic, and Catholic against Protestant. We may destroy the peace and prosperity of the country, but we cannot possibly destroy one another."[30] In the 1850s and early 1860s, Duffy and most of his compatriots who occupied positions of political and social influence in Australia imparted a tone of tolerance, openness, and "Europeanness" that would otherwise have been absent from the Australian scene. Their presence imbued the wider landscape of Australian public life with an appreciation of the Irish, and of Irish civility and public virtue, to a degree that was not paralleled in the United States.

Most of the leading Irish figures in Australian public life at this time retained an interest in Irish affairs, but more importantly, they felt a predominant concern with the Australian scene and the Irish position within it. They were far from Ireland; they were making colonial lives. Few, if any, could be called radical; fewer still, radical in any Irish nationalist sense. One in this mould was John O'Shanassy, born in Ballinahow, County Tipperary, in 1818, who immigrated to Australia in 1839 and became premier of Victoria in 1857. One contemporary recalled that O'Shanassy was "in strong sympathy with the mass of his countrymen" but "decidedly conservative in a general socio-political sense of the word."[31] Likewise Peter Lalor, the diggers' hero at Eureka, was of a decidedly conservative bent. His disposition matched his privileged background and defied simplistic English stereotypes of Irish lawlessness and disorder. While a member of the Victorian parliament (during a career that lasted more than three decades and that included a term as speaker of the legislative assembly) Lalor exhibited no leveling tendencies but displayed behavior consistent with his Irish upbringing and Trinity College education.[32]

*

As the famine spread devastation across Ireland in the late 1840s and early 1850s, Irish men, women, and children took flight to America in unprecedented numbers, encouraged by the ready availability of cheap passages and news and promises from relatives already there. Not surprisingly, few who left at the height of the distress carried with them large sums of capital, and most initially resided in those cities and states where they disembarked. In 1850 by far the greatest concentration of Irish immigrants, some 343,111, were found in the state of New York, where they comprised 11.1 percent of the population. The other great concentrations were in Pennsylvania, where the 151,723 Irish-born made up 6.6 percent of the total population, and Massachusetts, where 115,917 Irish constituted 11.7 percent of the state's population. Smaller numbers of the Irish-born moved westward, venturing along transport routes to states including Illinois and Wisconsin, while few Irish (as indeed, few immigrants of any nationality in the mid-nineteenth century) sought new lives in the southern states.[33]

First reports of the Irish distress were greeted with sympathy in America, and strenuous fund-raising took place to provide relief for victims of the hunger. However, compassion soon hardened as America's East Coast cities threatened to burst at the seams under the weight of this unprecedented influx of newcomers. The great tide of European immigration, its haste, and its immediate and inescapable visual impact on urban America raised to new levels the fears of a society already unnerved by the pace and extent of economic restructuring. Gradually, the antagonism and bigotry that had been held in abeyance since the Philadelphia riots in 1844 returned to boiling point.

As the sectarian feuding deteriorated, strident attacks were made on the Roman Catholic Church. Nativists also expressed deep disdain at what they branded the immigrants' domination and corruption of the political process.[34] These charges were most frequently laid, and weighed most heavily, on the Irish. In 1852 the Order of the Star Spangled Banner, a nativist organization, began to mobilize in New York City, prompting the newspaperman Horace Greeley to warn of the expanding influence of the "Know-Nothing" movement. The appeal of the Know-Nothings spread rapidly, and by 1854 their influence was felt across the northeast. In Massachusetts, the Know-Nothing candidate, Henry J. Gardner, was elected governor by a large majority and the party dominated the state legislature, while in New York, Know-Nothing candidates won one-third of the positions in the state assembly and more than half of the state's congressional seats. The party also polled strongly in Pennsylvania.[35] Even before the strength of the nativists' electoral appeal was fully known, George Templeton Strong noted the ominous signs afoot. "[A]nother Catholic *vs.* Protestant row at Newark—Irish church gutted; those infatuated, pig-headed Celts seemingly the aggressors, as usual. We may well have a memorable row here before the fall elections are over, and perhaps a religious war within the next decade, if this awful vague, mysterious, new element of Know-Nothingism is as potent as its friends and political wooers seem to think it."[36] Strong was no Know-Nothing and plainly declared their religious intolerance to be unacceptable, but neither was he unsympathetic to the cascading political campaign. By late 1855 he noted, "Antipathy to the Pope and to Paddy is a pretty deep-seated feeling. Were I about to enter political life, and selecting an available set of principles, I should be very apt to cast in my lot with the Natives. I could very honestly pronounce in favor of material changes in our Naturalization laws."[37]

For the most part, Know-Nothings fared less well away from the eastern seaboard, and the differences in political climate and economic prospects between the most densely populated East Coast cities and inland regions were well recognized at the time.[38] Irish emigrant organizations and community leaders sought actively to encourage new arrivals to move west, away from the most poverty stricken and hostile conurbations. To Thomas Darcy McGee, one of its most prominent advocates, internal migration of Irish settlers was absolutely essential "to win respect for a fallen race— to straighten the way of the stranger, and prepare a favorable public opinion to receive him—to watch over the growing passions of a young state [and] to direct wisely less experienced emigrants who follow."[39] Judgments such as McGee's were dismissed by opponents, including New York's Archbishop John Hughes, who was reluctant to support the large-scale movement of Irish immigrants away from the secure and regimented world of priest and parish. However, notwithstanding Hughes's objections, McGee's exhortations paved the way for the Irish Catholic Convention for the Promotion of Agricultural Settlements in America, convened in Buffalo, New York, in February 1856. The convention aimed to develop strategies to settle the Irish on the land, but well-meaning advice was one thing—many immigrants eager to follow such guidance were constrained from fulfilling their goal by the lack of means.[40] Margaret McCarthy, newly arrived in New York, wrote to her family in Kingwilliamstown, County Cork, in September 1850: "There is one thing that Ruinin this place Especially the Frontiers towns and Cities where the Flow of Emmigration is most [of] the Emmigrants has not money Enough to take them into the Interior of the Country which obliges them to remain here in York and the like places for which Reason Causes the less demand for Labour and also the great Reduction in Wages."[41] Organized settlement schemes were subsequently instigated to overcome immigrants' shortage of capital, though these initiatives mostly failed to fulfill the expectations of their sponsors.

By the mid-1850s, under the weight of the nativist attack, the position of Irish immigrants in the most populous states of the United States had deteriorated markedly from that which prevailed even a decade before. Increasingly, the Irish were cast in rigid, racial terms, viewed as fixed in temperament, unchanging in nature, and ultimately unable to assimilate to American life. That deleterious shift was evident in comments such as George Templeton Strong's, that "our Celtic fellow citizens are almost as remote from us in temperament and constitution as the Chinese."[42] Such sentiments were repeated widely in the popular press of the time, and religious bigotry as well as the impecunious circumstances of so many of the immigrants' lives served to reinforce the power of damaging stereotypes.

Ample evidence demonstrates the material disadvantage of the American Irish at this time. Econometric studies indicate consistently that the Roman Catholic Irish who came to America as a result of the famine were the least prosperous of all the midcentury's major immigrant groups and that they experienced the greatest difficulty making the transition from unskilled to skilled or semi-skilled work. This was particularly the case in the major East Coast cities. In 1850 the real wealth of Irish newcomers in New York was 28 percent that of British immigrants, 38 percent that of Germans, and a mere 10 percent of the real wealth of the native-born. In 1860 the Irish position in Boston was worse, the mean wealth of the Irish a paltry 4 percent that of the native-born. Even in Chicago, a site of rapid economic growth after 1850 and where by 1860 the mean wealth of males exceeded the national average, the Irish had the lowest proportion of any major nativity group employed in white-collar jobs, and their mean wealth was less than one-fifth that of the native-born. While several studies identify the immigrants' occupation and age profiles as the principal determinants of a nativity group's levels of wealth accumulation, Steven Herscovici goes further in his study of Boston and identifies Irish nativity itself as a critical factor in accounting for the group's relative disadvantage.[43]

The Irish position was not a static one, however, and the extent of the wealth difference between the Irish and other immigrants seems to have diminished slightly between 1850 and 1860.[44] Yet the relative disadvantage of the Irish was not lost on their hosts, who placed them lowest in their ranking of desirable newcomers, targeting them as objects of scorn and derision. In New Orleans, Frederick Law Olmstead observed Irish laborers working alongside slaves, where "no man who had any regard for his position among his fellow-craftsmen would ever let himself be seen." Black workers, he noted, joked about the lowly status of the Irish laborer: "Hallo! You is turned Irishman, is you," they taunted each other when forced to carry mortar on a building job.[45]

Less well acknowledged in the historical record are the experiences of earlier Irish immigrants and their descendants who had garnered positions of prosperity before the famine and who maintained their station through the troubled years, whether in business or the professions. Numerous examples of immigrant success stand out: Eugene Kelly, founder of the Catholic University of America, in banking and insurance, and John McDonald in New York's building and construction industry are but two.[46] But below this elite level, and across all regions of the nation, Irish immigrants were found in positions of solid standing. Restaurants, saloons, tailor shops, grocery stores, and bookshops were but some of the avenues utilized by Irish immigrants to fashion their working lives and provide employment to friends or relatives.

*

When a severe financial crisis struck the northeastern United States in 1857 the opportunities available to new arrivals deteriorated further still. Building projects in many major eastern cities ground to a halt. Thousands of Irish men, women, and children struggled against destitution. Lacking work, mired in shanties adjacent to the cities and towns, they desperately awaited signs of an economic recovery. In these conditions disease and malnutrition took hold—responsibility for a cholera epidemic in Philadelphia was laid at the feet of impoverished Irish immigrants.[47] However, many others strove to move on, across town, to the hinterland, to adjacent counties or states, or further across the American expanse, desperately hoping to improve their fortunes. Though risky, transience often proved beneficial. Recent evidence suggests lowly skilled immigrants who did venture elsewhere in search of better opportunities between 1850 and 1860—and especially to the cities and towns of the new urban frontier—were rewarded for their endeavors. Within a decade, those who risked relocation were likely to enjoy levels of personal wealth and social advancement in excess of those who had remained stationary.[48]

Partly in reaction to the harsh vicissitudes of life in industrializing America, and partly to help facilitate their own adjustment and that of the friends and relatives who would follow in their footsteps, the Irish in cities and towns of New England and the mid-Atlantic states turned inward. Strong, cohesive, self-reliant communities not only provided essential support and sustenance for the newly arrived, they also facilitated a more forceful and effective Irish response to nativist opposition.[49] In Worcester, Massachusetts, for example, the adverse climate engendered by the anti-immigrant upsurge reunited an Irish population that had previously fractured upon generation and class lines and instilled a new camaraderie and sense of common purpose to their ranks. However, though this development was in some senses advantageous, it also encouraged a tone of remoteness and defensiveness that exaggerated the distance between the Irish and the host society. That gap, most identifiable in areas where the Irish gathered in the greatest absolute numbers, contrasted starkly with their earlier, more agreeable engagement with American life.[50]

Three main institutional pillars underpinned the emergence of more insular and self-reliant Irish communities in the decade prior to the Civil War.[51] The first was the Roman Catholic Church, which throughout the antebellum period took on an increasingly Irish tone. Indeed, by the time of the famine, Irish-born bishops controlled important dioceses including New York and Philadelphia, and the church was set on course to fulfill a central role in immigrant life.[52] American Catholicism, like versions of Roman Catholicism elsewhere through the Irish diaspora, was subsequently affected by the reinvigoration that followed the 1850 Synod of Thurles. The heightened emphasis on institutional structures, parish life, church attendance, and devotions that followed the Cullenite revolution ultimately transplanted well to Irish America and provided a range of familiar rituals and experiences that unified, comforted, and strengthened the immigrant community.[53] However, like the nativist threat, developments within American Catholicism were far from uniform. From midcentury, internal tensions simmered between those bishops committed to accommodation with mainstream American life and those bent on preserving more rigid interdenominational boundaries. Geographical differences were significant too. A number of historians contend that in the Midwest and on the West Coast Roman Catholicism exhibited a less defensive and less strident tone in its public dealings than was the case in cities such as New York and Boston. But on the Atlantic coast, the assertiveness of the Roman Catholic hierarchy alarmed Protestant leaders and was interpreted by nativists as confirmation of the danger of unrestrained Catholic immigration.[54]

The second pillar upholding inward-looking Irish communities was the Democratic Party. Democratic politics offered the immigrants an opportunity to exercise power when few other avenues of influence appeared open to them. Courted as white workingmen, and on the premise that they, unlike the native-born, invariably acted in concert, the Irish utilized their strength to achieve considerable influence in national politics and at the level of the urban machine. There was, in this movement, some assimilatory impulse: as one historian observed, "Democratic politics speeded the naturalization of Irish newcomers and provided them with jobs in exchange for their votes."[55] But there was a more deleterious side, too, for the Irish adherence to the Democratic Party sharpened the lines of division between themselves and their most vocal native-born opponents. It also extended the gap between the immigrants and the major reform movements of the antebellum period and ensured that antipathy to the Irish political style was preserved for decades to come.[56]

The third and final pillar upholding and unifying the Irish in America was their intense nationalist yearning. In his influential study of Irish nationalism in the United States, Thomas Brown emphasized the primary importance of conditions in America in accounting for the strength of nationalist sentiment among the immigrant population. The immigrants, lacking possessions and skills but bearing an intense commitment to Roman Catholicism and a deep hatred for England, felt anger and despair at both their own and their old nation's plight, their humiliation all the greater "living among Americans—the people of get-up-and-go to whom poverty was sinful." Brown maintained that it was possible to identify the impulse toward Irish American nationalism here in "the realities of loneliness and alienation, and of poverty and prejudice."[57] Irish nationalism, rooted in failure and despair, was embraced most strongly by the ambitious and socially mobile, by those who yearned for but were denied prestige and opportunities for leadership in American society. The commitment to Irish nationalism—to the removal of Ireland's colonial status—was seen by middle-class Irish in the United States as a strategy through which they might assert their own independence and renounce their exclusion from mainstream American life. Nationalism was, for the Irish, a path toward securing a niche in middle-class Anglo-America.[58]

Together, the institutional structures of the Roman Catholic Church, the powerful pull of Democratic politics, and the unifying force of immigrant nationalism, nourished the large numbers of predominantly Catholic Irish who arrived in flight from the famine. But much less well understood is the institutional life of Protestant Irish immigrants in the famine and postfamine periods. This is partly due to the weakness of extant census data, but it also reflects a resilient (though receding) current in Irish American historiography that plaintively declined to acknowledge the dimensions of nineteenth-century Irish Protestant immigration to the United States. The most important of the specifically Irish organizations was the Loyal Orange Institution of the United States of America, present from the 1820s and which by 1850 enjoyed a presence across five states. However, Irish Protestants were also to the forefront in numerous Protestant associations that formed in the antebellum period to oppose the spread of Roman Catholicism, their influence strongly in evidence among the more militant organs of the Protestant press.[59]

*

The debilitating condition of Irish American life in the aftermath of the Great Famine has proved critical in fashioning historians' wider interpretations of the Irish experience in the United States. Particular controversy attended the attempt by the American historian Kerby Miller in the mid-1980s to explain the Irish predicament. Drawing especially on sentiments expressed in immigrants' letters, Miller argued that Irish emigrants traveling to the New World were burdened by an "exile motif," an outlook rooted in Gaelic language and historical experience that inhibited their adjustment to a new, modernizing society.[60] That interpretation was quickly challenged by scholars including David Fitzpatrick, not only on the ground that the particular forms and conventions present in immigrant letters had not been adequately interrogated, but also because of the absence of any firm quantitative analysis of the letters' contents.[61] More recently, such attempts at overarching explanations of the Irish experience in America have become less fashionable, and later works by historians, including Miller himself, have tended more toward dissecting individualized and localized experiences of migration and settlement. The case of the Australian Irish has also served as a counterpoint to globalizing interpretation of the legacy of the Irish past. In particular, Fitzpatrick utilized Australian Irish correspondence luminously to challenge Miller's interpretation and reading of evidence, writing that the antipodean letters "give scarcely a hint of banishment, whether constructed in terms of political, economic, social, or familial pressures."[62]

This study lends weight to Fitzpatrick's position in that dispute. If from the time of the famine Irish America was affected by a mounting aura of unease and besiegement, the same bearing was not evident among their compatriots in Australia. In its inaugural issue the Sydney *Freeman's Journal,* founded by the Tipperary-born, Maynooth-educated priest John McEncroe, declared, "The Australian colonists are at present comparatively a 'free people,' and are on the eve of obtaining a considerable accession to that freedom."[63] Irish convicts and their descendants as well as Irish free settlers and their families had been among the foremost beneficiaries of the liberalizing tendencies evident in colonial life through the 1840s. By and large this trend continued through the 1850s. Sectarian predilections among immigrants to Australia at this time were greatly diminished by the raw conditions of Australian life—there was no repeat in the colonies of the religious invective then so prevalent across the more heavily populated American states. In fact, the midcentury experience of the Australian Irish echoed much more closely that of their compatriots in the United States who ventured westward to the prairie states or to distant California. Established in a more encouraging environment than most of America's Irish, Australia's immigrants focused their attentions principally on matters of local importance: the attainment of satisfactory colonial constitutions, the introduction of responsible government, and the achievement of an extended franchise.[64]

It would be misleading to deny that the Australian colonies lacked national and sectarian tensions—accurate only to say that, until the mid-1860s, they were for the most part sporadic and then well contained. The ebbs and flows of the colonial scene were particularly well demonstrated in the controversy that surrounded the immigration of the so-called orphan girls, women shipped from Irish workhouses to the Australian colonies in the period 1848–1850. Australia received few immigrants direct from Ireland during the famine, though some 4,175 Irish women, selected from workhouses and other charitable institutions, were provided with clothing and provisions and a passage to the Australian colonies. The response to their arrival was a mixed one. The staunchest opponent of Irish immigration to Australia, the Reverend John Dunmore Lang, objected: the Irish women, he asserted, were "selected as free emigrants for Australia, expressly with a view to their becoming the wives of the English and Scottish Protestant shepherds and stockmen of New South Wales, and thereby silently subverting and extending the Romanism of the colony." Others joined him in opposing the settlement of these Irish women: even in the labor-starved inland areas, with chronic shortages of female settlers, strenuous complaints against the scheme were laid. The *Goulburn Herald* newspaper declared, "The specimens we have already had have suffered to show that the class is utterly useless to the colony, and in fact mischievous. The papers are full of the misdoings of these girls, and where they are not absolutely depraved they are so stupid they are fit for nothing."[65] Eventually, in the face of a considerable local opposition as well as trenchant disapproval from nationalists in Ireland, the scheme was terminated.

At the height of the controversy, the Sydney *Freeman's Journal* reacted to the anti-immigrant agitation and declared, "For our own part, we would prefer to leave many of these girls exposed to the dangers of starvation at *home,* than to have them exposed to the taunts and bad treatment which some of them have received *here.*" This was an overreaction to the agitation, and perhaps a slightly disingenuous one too. Though public debate was heated, on the ground much cooler heads prevailed. Community reaction to the women's arrival proved to be much more muted and tolerant. In the New South Wales rural township of Yass, for example, the women were welcomed and praised in the local press for their "orderly, cleanly, and healthy appearance." Three weeks after their arrival, the positive impression of the

Irish women remained undiminished, and a large number had secured satisfactory employment. The *Goulburn Herald*'s correspondent in Yass now expressed regrets at the reflections that had been cast upon the girls elsewhere, "for in this township they are highly appreciated and respected." This was the opinion, too, of forty-eight leading residents of Yass, who signed a forceful public address expressing complete satisfaction at the conduct of the women and welcoming their presence in the rural region.[66] The positive reaction to the women was reiterated in evidence collected by a select committee of the New South Wales parliament appointed to inquire into the scheme. Daniel Egan, a Roman Catholic member of parliament, reported the comments of one influential landholder that "they turned out the best servants they had there."[67]

This case of Irish women's immigration demonstrates a measure of the complexity of the colonial Australian response to the Irish. In a society where the Irish-born constituted nearly one-fifth of the total population (and even more when the descendants of the Irish-born are taken into account), and where the development of a distinctive national identity was much less advanced than in the United States, there was simply less scope for the Protestant British majority to inflame tensions and encourage rancor. The predominantly rural scene in Australia also bred interdependence across the lines of class and ethnicity to a considerable degree, though that tendency was much less in evidence in the interactions of white settlers and indigenous Australians. In other words, unlike the situation then present in much of Great Britain and the United States, the combination of predominantly rural settlement, the absence of rapid and tremulous urbanization, and a sizeable Irish-born population mitigated against any repeat of the intense antagonism that greeted the Irish in those other destinations. Only later would the Australian colonies experience the ramifications of industrial transformation and its attendant experiences of urbanization and displacement to any marked degree, with the result that in the mid-nineteenth century they were devoid of much of the dislocation and despair then pervading the lives of the Irish in many American cities and towns.

In the dissimilar economic and political context of mid-nineteenth-century Australia, the pillars of Irish American institutional life—church, party politics, and immigrant nationalism—took on very different forms and complexions. The English Benedictine foundation of Australian Catholicism fostered moderation and integration in colonial life and provided little encouragement to Irish separatism. Archbishop Polding's church, while cognizant that the laity was predominantly Irish, and sympathetic to their spiritual and material needs, was emphatically not an Irish church. Only gradually did this situation change, as Irish-born clergy sought to wrest control from the Benedictines. This occurred as a succession of Irish bishops were appointed to the colonies' dioceses: James Quinn to Brisbane in 1859, his brother Matthew to Bathurst in 1866, Daniel Murphy to Hobart in 1866, William Lanigan to Goulburn in 1867, and the Quinns' cousin, Timothy O'Mahony, to Armidale in 1869. The arrival of these men, students of the Irish College in Rome, ardent admirers of Paul Cardinal Cullen, and deeply influenced by the Synod of Thurles, ensured impressive programs of church construction and parish formation.[68] However, the Australian Irish and their descendants observed the Irish clerical takeover with guarded circumspection, still ready to determine and be guided by their own pragmatic assessments of their material and spiritual interests. In nineteenth-century Australia the clergy had to earn respect through words and deeds, not just through titles and dress, and not all sent from Ireland passed the inspection of their Australian flocks.

Just as the church in Australia lacked the degree of organization and discipline found throughout most of the American church, so, too, the immigrants in the colonies were more fragmented politically than their compatriots in the United States. In the colonies' systems of factional politics the Australian Irish enjoyed their share of political power, but there was no party system or voting bloc to rival Irish America's commitment to the Democratic Party. In the towns and the countryside colonial politics were more fluid, with personalities and local issues to the fore in elections for the various parliaments. This sometimes produced examples of one-sided Irish support for a candidate—most famously in the strongly Irish Catholic village of Grabben Gullen, New South Wales, where in the 1880s successive elections returned votes of 162 to 5, 148 to 10, and 100 to 6. Similar results were occasionally produced in other Irish enclaves, too, prompting opponents of the Irish to complain ruefully of the adverse influence of the Irish on American politics and to warn of its impending recurrence in Australia. Yet this was mostly just alarmist talk, fear, and prejudice not supported by the practice of colonial politics. Indeed, the absence of Irish political unity was visible early and proved resilient, much to the chagrin of the more politicized Irish clergy of the 1860s when they attempted to assert control over their people. As early as 1858 a priest stationed in a strongly Irish community in rural New South Wales bemoaned "the utter confusion between the lay and clerical element. . . . We have done great things of late in this diocese but yet things are rotten. Brother hates brother—no fraternity."[69]

In the mid-nineteenth century Irish nationalism, too, was largely an impotent force in Australia, a pale imitation of its vigorous American manifestation. For whereas America's republican tradition encouraged active support for Ireland's emancipation, Australia's colonial status imposed restraint and promoted only the most moderate expressions of sentiment or contemplation of Ireland's relationship with the British Empire. The Australian Irish were, to be fair, keenly interested in Ireland and its welfare. When news of distress in western Ireland reached the colonies in 1858, the Reverend McEncroe initiated a Donegal Relief Fund, and this received enthusiastic public subscriptions.[70] But more overt expressions of nationalist sentiment were mostly deemed out of place, the friction generated by them interpreted as a barrier to Irish involvement in colonial life rather than as an avenue of acceptance or a path to higher status.

Newcomers, including members of the clergy, were sometimes insensitive to, or disregarding of, the cautious mood and low-key disposition of Australia's Irish. Archbishop Polding, well versed in the colonial context and cognizant of the temper of the immigrant Irish, had cause to regret speeches made in 1867 at a celebratory dinner for the newly consecrated bishop of Goulburn, William Lanigan. "Just as I forewarned them in Rome," Polding wrote frankly to his friend Abbot Henry Gregory, "this 'importation of Irish bishops' . . . has been the unfortunate cause of, or pretext for, raising a no-popery cry, and has been used to influence the votes for the passing of the most obnoxious Education Bill. At the consecration of Dr. Lanigan at Goulburn there was a dinner, and, of course, speeches after, which I am sorry to say contained much to inflame. It might have suited the atmosphere of Dublin but here was sadly out of place."[71] However, just as the Irish clergy assumed control of the Australian church, significant changes were also beginning to affect the lay Irish population in Australia. The early 1860s saw a new group of Irish immigrants, termed by one historian as the "forties generation," take a more prominent place in Irish and Irish Australian affairs. These were men—all too little is known of the nationalist proclivities of Irish women in Australia at this time—who arrived in Australia in the 1840s, often as children accompanying parents or as rather young men themselves, now in their mid-thirties or forties. "Nostalgic for Ireland and, having recently discovered an identity as Irishmen over and against Englishmen, [they] persisted in retaining that identity in the colony."[72] This new, proto–Irish nationalism would assume importance in Australia as intergroup relations soured in the late 1860s and 1870s.

*

The American Civil War touched the lives of millions of men and women in the United States and in Ireland. The war coincided with a series of serious crop failures in Ireland, and the decline in the flow of remittances home during the troubled years of the conflict resulted in grave hardship for families heavily dependent on contributions from sons or daughters abroad.[73] But the interest of Irish men and women ran deeper than the pecuniary one. Many in Ireland waited anxiously for news of relatives or friends serving in the field or followed with pride reports of the martial qualities of Irish regiments in the service of both the Union and the Confederate armies. Others debated the political dimensions of the conflict, most pertinently reflecting upon the attempt of the Confederate states to secede from their own unsatisfactory Union. On the merits of the war, no unanimous Irish position emerged. Some nationalists, probably a minority, argued that a Union victory would enhance the prospect of American intervention in Ireland's affairs. But a greater number were in sympathy with the Confederacy and drew upon the obvious parallel of the South's aspiration to independence to justify their stand. Other supporters of the Confederacy reasoned less convincingly that the instability produced by the breakdown of the American Republic would hasten Ireland's liberation from the tyranny of empire.[74]

For the Irish resident in the United States the war was a personal, divisive, and bitter affair. About one hundred and fifty thousand Irish-born soldiers served in the Union army; a quarter of that number fought for the South. Prominent Irish advocates were to be found for both sides of the conflict. Among the Young Irelanders who had fled Australia for new lives in America, John Mitchel and John Martin spoke for the Confederacy. Mitchel, in fact, lost two sons in the war. To them, consistency demanded support for the South. John Mitchel wrote that he was unable to "understand the process of reasoning" that persuaded northern Irishmen to the view that "the repeal of one union in Europe depends on the enforcement of another union in America."[75] William Smith O'Brien was another Southern sympathizer and argued that the Irish should arbitrate to facilitate peace, not war. Yet this was the position of a detached and rather naive outsider—of an Irishman and not an Irish American—who enjoyed a luxury of choices and coolness of reasoning not available to those forging new lives abroad. In contrast, their former colleague Thomas Meagher now took up the sword for the Union army and attained the rank of brigadier general.[76] For him, and most other Irish immigrants in the north, the matter was a much more straightforward one: it was essential to demonstrate loyalty to their adopted land. Other Irish joined for less idealistic reasons (those faced with unemployment or paid a bounty) or, later, because they were drafted. But few Irish, most accounts concur, sought the liberation of slaves: one soldier wrote, "ninety-nine soldiers out of one hundred say that if the abolitionists are going to have to carry on this war, they will have to get a new army."[77]

At the commencement of the war, especially in the Northern states, uncertainty reigned about the loyalty of the Irish and their willingness and ability to fight. These anxieties were allayed, in part, by the success of Irish regiments in recruiting immigrants to enlist. Pennsylvania's 116th Regiment, Massachusetts' Ninth Irish Brigade, and New York's 69th and 88th regiments garnered prominence and public acclaim. Performance in the field confirmed these initial impressions. After the battle at Fredericksburg, where Meagher's regiment was decimated, no doubt remained about their bravery or commitment to the Union cause.[78] High-profile individuals such as Philip Sheridan and James Shields, who served as general officers in the Union army, ensured the Irish a share of public attention. At the same time, the smaller number of Irish in service in the Confederate army also achieved acclaim. The presence of units including General Patrick Cleburne's Fifth Confederate Regiment; Richmond, Virginia's Emmet Guards; and the Emerald Guards from Alabama testifies to the geographic diversity and widely varied dispositions of America's huge Irish-born population in the years after the famine.[79]

The war years, though, were not without moments of deep distress. In July 1863 New York City was disturbed by violent rioting, a period of disorder in which the Irish were prominent participants. The causes of the draft riots have been fully explored elsewhere: changing economic relationships, anger at the inequities of the proposed draft system, the underlying frustration and fears of the group that identified itself as most at threat by emancipation, and the recklessness of powerless and resentful young men—all played a part in the complex rituals of violence that swept the metropolis during the days of the riot.[80] For some Americans, the demonstrations reignited all the old prejudices that had been temporarily submerged to the Union cause. George Templeton Strong wrote colorfully on 19 July: "No wonder St. Patrick drove all the venomous vermin out of Ireland. Its biped mammalia supply that island its full average share of creatures that crawl and eat dirt and poison every community they infest." "For myself personally," he wrote the following day, "I would like to see war made on Irish scum as in 1688."[81] But the riots were a New York phenomenon, not repeated elsewhere. The confinement of the violence salvaged much for Irish America. In the wake of the Civil War, and in the course of Reconstruction, it would be the strength of the Irish contribution rather than the memory of the draft riots that stood more visibly to the fore.

3

Irish Rural Life
Minnesota and New South Wales Compared

WHILE THE VAST MAJORITY OF MID-nineteenth-century Irish immigrants settled adjacent to the United States eastern seaboard, a minority moved away from the nation's emerging urban centers to pursue lives in the agricultural lands of the West. However, the history of these rural Irish, unlike that of their countrymen and women who took to farming in Australia, remains at present very much underdeveloped. The extensive attention in American historical writing given to Irish urban settlement, mobility, and nationalism as well as the Irish position at the intersection of ethnicity and race has seen the experience of the rural Irish largely bypassed.

The absence of significant recent work on America's rural Irish is puzzling for two reasons. First, a group of scholars writing in the 1950s, including Grace McDonald, James Shannon, and Merle Curti, laid a foundation for studies of the rural Irish that is unparalleled elsewhere in the Irish diaspora.[1] Given the refreshing changes in approach to rural history in the last four decades, it is surprising that few attempts have been made to build upon these writers' pioneering endeavors or revisit issues raised in their works. Secondly, given the high profile of rural studies in recent overseas scholarship on the Irish diaspora and the significant controversy they have provoked, it is curious that the implications of these works for the American Irish have seldom been pursued.

This chapter contributes to redressing the omission by comparing Irish rural settlement in the American state of Minnesota and the southwest region of the Australian state of New South Wales. While cross-national comparison of the experiences of immigrant groups remains rare, comparison undertaken at a local or regional level is rarer still.[2] Yet such intensely focused comparison provides an opportunity to compare the experiences of an emigrant group in different destinations in much finer detail than is usually possible in a transnational study. It also lends itself to a more precise assessment of the relative influences of cultural heritage and local conditions in shaping immigrant experiences, and to assessing the validity of the commonplace assertions that the Irish were unsuited to, alienated from, or incapable of, rural life in the New World.[3]

Minnesota and southwest New South Wales share a number of features that suggest their potential for comparison. In the mid-nineteenth century, both experienced rapid increases in their European populations as the frontier gave way to more established settlement. In both regions, the Irish-born were prominent among the early arrivals who sought to take advantage of the opportunities available in the still unrefined settings. In 1850, 68 percent of the British Isles–born population in the Minnesota Territory was of Irish birth, while in southwest New South Wales between one-third and a quarter of the settler population was Irish-born, others the children of Irish immigrants.[4] Parallels continued in the second half of the nineteenth century too: settlement extended and became more intense, towns developed to service farming communities, and as the population in each location increased, a significant Irish presence remained a feature of both regions.

However, during the last quarter of the century significant differences emerged between the two. In southwest New South Wales the large Irish-born population gradually diminished in significance, though the presence of second- and third-generation Irish ensured the region maintained its reputation as a location of intensive Irish—and by that time, Roman Catholic—settlement. In Minnesota, while the proportion of Irish-born in the population declined, the organization of Irish settlement underwent significant changes. Colonization schemes, especially those organized by Bishop John Ireland and the Irish-American Colonization Company, achieved prominence, and increasingly these ventures departed from the processes that had underpinned the successful establishment of Irish settlers in the state. These colonization schemes undermined old configurations and, for the most part, proved unsuccessful in promoting viable Irish rural communities. Yet as this chapter shows, in the historical literature it is the less auspicious second phase of Minnesota's experience that has achieved the most prominence, with the result that stereotypical assertions about the Irish incapacity for rural life have been reinforced.

*

In 1850 the Irish-born, though few in number, constituted 4.5 percent of the total population of the infant Minnesota Territory and 13.2 percent of the total foreign-born. A decade later their presence was more pronounced, Irish immigrants then comprising 7.2 percent of the state's total population and nearly 22 percent of the foreign-born. Indeed, as previous studies have indicated, the Irish were therefore overrepresented in Minnesota compared to their share of the total United States population throughout the period from 1850 until 1870.[5] However, although these figures are indicative of a strong Irish presence, they are of little use in identifying Minnesota's broader, multigenerational Irish ethnic group. For example, the largest foreign group in Minnesota in the 1850 census were those born in (then) British North America, some 23 percent of the territory's total population, a significant proportion of which were likely to be Irish-born or the children of Irish immigrants. Obscured, too, in the available census data are those second-generation Irish born elsewhere in the United States who chose Minnesota.

Information on the regional origins of the Irish who settled in mid-nineteenth-century Minnesota is also sparse. One study of Irish settlers in Scott County during the period 1853–70 found Counties Cork and Kerry each contributing one-fifth of the total Irish-born, with significant contributions from Clare, Galway, Sligo, and Mayo. There were also concentrations of Scotch-Irish settlers at Eden Prairie in Hennepin County and Long Prairie in Todd County—in the former the immigrants were drawn mainly from counties Tyrone, Monaghan, and Cavan.[6] Overall, the patchy evidence available points to considerable diversity in Minnesota's Irish immigrant base, though in the absence of further research, firm conclusions are difficult to draw. David Fitzpatrick argued that variations existed in the social composition of the different Irish emigrant streams—the United States drawing from the surplus subsistence rural population, whereas Australia drew more heavily upon semiskilled farm workers. This is partially born out here: Sligo and Mayo, though noteworthy contributors to Minnesota's Irish population, were the least significant counties to contribute to Irish-assisted immigration to Australia. On the other hand, the presence of a strong Clare contingent in this American rural sample mirrors that county's importance as a major contributor to those entering Australia. In sum, comparison of these rural regions supports the view that variable streams did exist in the Irish migration to these New World destinations; however, it is difficult to see this as an adequate explanation of the widely differing interpretations of Irish life

Map 2. Minnesota

experiences in the new lands. As Fitzpatrick himself observed, "The structure of the host societies was a far more important factor."[7]

Initially, the open land and infant economy of Minnesota held considerable attraction for Irish settlers. Michael Callaghan, a native of County Cork, arrived in America in 1845 and initially worked in a salt mine in Syracuse, New York. However, in 1849 he moved westward in search of a better climate for his ailing wife's health. Three years later he wrote to his brother in the East advising him to follow in his footsteps, and alerting him to the favorable conditions he would encounter. "This country is not tried much farming yet but what I see is the finest I ever see in America so far as potatoes and vegetables. . . . If you do come this fall you are better buy your flour, sugar and coffee and such things in Galena and a cow and a sow pig—they are very dear here and if you have money enough get a yoke of cattle they will cost you about eighty dollars here. . . . I think the best route for you is to Chicago and Galena . . . I think you will like this country well enough. . . . People say it will be a good place for there is a good many railroads started there. It is a good place for James Coughlan for there is plenty of whiskey."[8] For some settlers, the declining availability and increasing cost of land elsewhere made Minnesota an attractive destination. Mary Jane Anderson was born in 1827 into an Anglican family in Baileborough, County Cavan, and immigrated to the United States with her husband Robert in 1850. After short periods in New Orleans and Saint Louis, the couple moved on to Galena, Illinois, where Robert had two sisters and a brother. Mary Jane recalled, "By this time all the homesteads in Illinois had been taken up, and it was expensive to buy." However, in 1853 Robert's uncle, already settled in Minnesota, came south to purchase stock. Robert Anderson was encouraged to travel to Minnesota to survey the opportunities there. He found land there readily available, purchased 160 acres, and arranged for a log cabin to be erected while he returned to Galena to fetch Mary Jane.[9]

In both of these cases, family connections encouraged staged migration to the new farmlands of Minnesota. While this was the experience of most early Irish settlers, a minority traveled direct from Ireland. In May 1852 the *Minnesota Democrat Weekly* reported the arrival of "two respectable and intelligent Irish families," who had crossed the Atlantic and made straight for the extensive farmlands of the state. The new arrivals told the newspaper more Irish could be expected soon, a prospect it very much welcomed: "They say that the people of Ireland are also beginning to learn something about the new state of Minnesota, and expect a substantial immigration of the most substantial class of Irish farmers within the present season."[10] Whether the expected settlers subsequently arrived is uncertain; in either case, they did not initiate a substantial wave of direct migration from Ireland to Minnesota.

There were also elaborate settlement schemes, even in the early years. The best known of these was the Shieldsville settlement, initiated by Tyrone-born James Shields. Shields immigrated to the United States in 1822 at the age of sixteen and worked in a variety of occupations before his election to the Illinois legislature in 1835. He was subsequently commissioned as a general in the Mexican-American War and then, after a term in the United States Senate, selected land in Minnesota as reward for his career of government service. According to one county history, Shields "was so favorably impressed with the country that he decided to go east and organize a colony of Irish Americans to settle on the soil of Rice and Le Sueur Counties, of whose fertility he had learned while Commissioner of Federal Lands in Washington."[11] Shields set out a village, Shieldsville, in Rice County, then left to recruit Irish settlers in Saint Paul. Further Irish immigrants were attracted to the district by advertisements placed in eastern newspapers. The response to Shields's appeal was enthusiastic, and Shieldsville soon spawned the neighboring township of Erin where, according to one account, "there were none but the descendants of the emerald isle to be recorded in the pages of its early history."[12] However, relations between the settlers and Shields eventually deteriorated amidst accusations of fraud.

By the mid-1850s, then, a substantial Irish presence was clearly evident in Minnesota. Saint Patrick's Day had been enthusiastically celebrated from at least 1852, and by 1854 the demand from the immigrants was such that a Roman Catholic priest was preaching in Irish. The Sons of Saint Patrick Benevolent Society was active, and on Saint Patrick's Day 1856 it mustered three hundred members to march in Saint Paul in celebration of the national feast. By 1857, the Irish presence was so pronounced that stories of Irish political influence and voting irregularities were already in circulation. The *Daily Minnesotan,* well versed on nativists' anxieties, hoped "to gracious that none of the paddies will hear where St. Paul is. We consider those now here can poll a large enough vote provided they vote often enough." And it is clear that by this time, in addition to the many Irish settled on farm lands, significant numbers of Irish laborers were arriving in the state capital to undertake building and construction work. In July 1856 Irish laborers were reported to be on strike in Saint Paul, parading around the streets and adding to their number any compatriots found working in the city.[13]

Several important characteristics of this strong Irish settlement in mid-nineteenth-century Minnesota stand out. First, the immigrants almost invariably entered the region in a staged process—the numbers who settled direct from Ireland were very small. As one historian noted, a common pattern of transit for the Irish "included arrival in New York or Canada, and one or two subsequent moves over a period of years to Pennsylvania, Ohio, Illinois, Indiana or Wisconsin, then to Minnesota."[14] Sometimes American-born children accompanied their parents into the West. Michael J. Boyle was born in 1856 in Allegheny City, Pennsylvania, and settled with his parents in Minnesota as a young child, acutely conscious of his Irish heritage. On Saint Patrick's Day 1876, at age twenty, he attended High Mass "in honor of Ireland's patron saint and mine."[15] In many other cases this movement took more than one generation, and the second-generation Irish ventured along these migratory paths alone. Other Irish settlers in Minnesota came via much more circuitous routes. Francis Logan, born in Ireland in 1825, lived first in New Hampshire, then ventured to Illinois and California before settling down in Tyrone township, a "well settled part of [Le Sueur] county [that] has many scores of valuable, well cared for farms." Around him were other townships (Derrynane and Kilkenny) and organizations such as the Catholic Order of Foresters and the Ancient Order of Hibernians, all testimony to the strength of the Irish presence.[16] These, indeed, were examples of immigrants and their descendants on the move in search of opportunity and advancement.

The second important characteristic of Irish settlement in Minnesota was that many of the immigrants entered farming communities in which they appear to have had—at least initially—strong familial or communal ties. Minnesota's Irish were clustered in particular farming localities, a trend reflected in the wide variations in the Irish percentage of the population in different counties. In 1870 eleven counties boasted Irish-born populations in excess of 10 percent of the total population, the highest figure being 28.1 percent Irish-born in Pine County. In contrast, nineteen counties within the state had Irish-born populations of less than 2 percent—nine of these had no Irish-born residents at all. This clustering was particularly evident in the southeast of the state, and by 1870, 72.5 percent of Minnesota's Irish-born population lived in 20 counties of the southeast.[17] This concentration of the Irish presence in specific localities served to ease newcomers into unfamiliar surroundings. Moreover, numerically strong and confident in their new environment, the Minnesota Irish seem to have been subjected to less sectarian or national conflict than their compatriots further east. This was a theme emphasized by John Ireland, the archbishop of Saint Paul, who, when celebrating the fiftieth anniversary of the Catholic Church in the northwest, remarked that "there are few places where religious freedom has so reigned as in Minnesota and its two neighboring states."[18]

Third, Minnesota's Irish indisputably took to the land with enthusiasm. In 1870, 58 percent of Minnesota's Irish listed in the census as employed were farm workers or farm owners, a figure higher than that of the native-born population but consistent with that of other European-born immigrant groups. Most Irish were individual farmers or planters rather than agricultural laborers, and they showed a keen appreciation of the opportunities available to them in Minnesota. In 1857 Lewis Doyle, a native of County Carlow, settled in Kilkenny township in Le Sueur County, in that southeastern portion of Minnesota so favored by the mid-nineteenth-century Irish. In January 1873, after a period of twenty years in the United States during which he maintained little contact with Ireland, Doyle resumed correspondence with his cousin John Doyle in Carlow. By the time he wrote home, Lewis Doyle owned a farm of eighty acres, though almost two-thirds of the land was still wooded. His wife had recently died giving birth to their eleventh child, nine of whom were still alive. Despite her death, he remained optimistic about life in Minnesota and positive about the opportunities it promised for future immigrants from Ireland. "There is thousands of acres of vacant land here of the very best quality and can be bought for 1 to 2 pounds per acre. . . . We grow here the very best kind of wheat, oats, barley, rye, potatoes and all kind of fruits and vegetables without any manure for several years. . . . The largest part of this state is Prairie looking as level and as nice as a gentleman's domain in Carlow but no timber in sight for several miles."[19] Modestly successful on his own farm, Doyle believed the long Minnesota winter was the only drawback of his life on the land. His only wish was to be sent a new wife from Ireland, a "safe match," chosen from "some good young widows or old maids . . . because I know her and I could get along together." He could, he assured his cousin, give a new bride "all the tea and coffee and pork she can possibly get out of sight."

The fourth important characteristic of Irish settlement in Minnesota was that it initially outstripped the advance of the Roman Catholic Church, and Irish clergy in particular. Writing in 1882, Philip Bagenal, an advocate of western settlement by the Irish, portrayed the model scheme of Irish rural placement to be one where the "first person to enter the colony is the priest, selected with a special view to his knowledge of country life, who is to be the pastor of the flock. He is on the ground to receive the first family, who find at once in him a friend and help."[20] However, the reality of mid-nineteenth-century Irish movement to the West was far removed from Bagenal's model. The initial Roman Catholic clerical presence in Minnesota was French and the church grossly underresourced—in 1849, there were only two priests stationed in what was later to become the diocese of Saint Paul. This was to change quickly under the leadership of Bishop Cretin, and in less than a decade the Roman Catholic Church could proudly boast of the establishment of twenty-nine churches and five convents as well as the presence of twenty priests—an achievement Archbishop John Ireland later compared to the coming of Saint Patrick to Ireland.[21] The crucial point, however, is that Irish settlers in mid-nineteenth-century Minnesota could not and did not make settlement choices on the basis of the strength of religious infrastructure or the comforting presence of a parish community—these came only later. Immigrants' settlement was motivated by the availability of land and work and the need to seize the best chance while opportunities in the region were at a premium. Formal religious matters were attended to when economic security was secured.

*

Irish settlement in southwest New South Wales also exhibited these important characteristics, though the immigrants' presence in this Australian region originated in very different circumstances. The initial impetus for Irish settlement in the southwest came from land grants awarded to emancipated convicts by the colony's governor, Lachlan Macquarie, in the late 1810s and early 1820s. Encouraged by the Irish convict surveyor, James Meehan, his compatriots actively sought landholdings to the southwest of Sydney.[22] From this starting point, settlement spread rapidly in the 1830s and 1840s, forging a southwest axis that became the key line of Irish settlement in the colony. This was the direction to which large numbers of Irish convicts gravitated when their period of servitude was completed, and subsequent immigrants, too, were attracted to this region of heavy Irish settlement.

By the 1830s this pattern of inland settlement was clearly visible to friends and foes of Irish settlement alike. The English Benedictine bishop, John Bede Polding, appealed to the Protestant Irish governor, Richard Bourke, for the provision of additional resources to the Roman Catholic Church, stressing the particular shortage of clergy in the southwestern areas of the settlement. Conversely, an alarmed Judge W. W. Burton decried unchecked Irish concentration in the southwest and expressed considerable alarm at the strength of Irish Catholics "in disseminating their doctrines and establishing churches."[23]

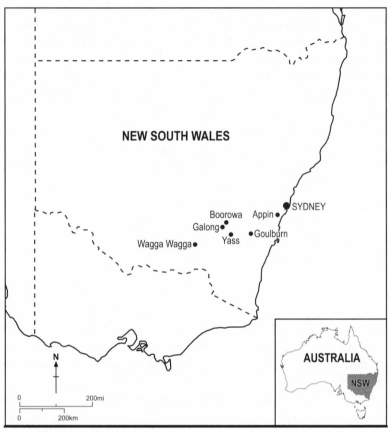

Map 3. Southwest New South Wales

However, the initial Irish presence in the southwest was not exclusively Catholic but was remarkable for both its religious and regional diversity. Early arrivals in the region included Anglo-Irish settlers such as Henry and Cornelius O'Brien, who disembarked in New South Wales via India intent on establishing themselves on the land. Henry O'Brien was one of the first Europeans to venture onto the extensive tablelands of the southwest and acquired substantial landholdings. As early as 1816, the O'Brien brothers' uncle, William Browne of County Galway, wrote to an acquaintance that there were greater opportunities for advancement in the colony than his family would ever have enjoyed in Ireland. He believed that his nephews were "comfortably situated, and satisfied with their situation, and [I] have only to regret that my poor old mother did not live to enjoy the satisfac-

74

tion it would give her to see her family so eligibly situated." Four years later he expressed delight at the "flattering prospects of certain prosperity which this new and fine country holds out to such of them as may not be able to establish themselves eligibly elsewhere." Thomas Pope Besnard of Cork, later appointed as overseer on a government chain gang in southern New South Wales, also saw in his new life the chance to distance himself from the limited opportunities and restricted freedom that he had known as a young man in Ireland. In the old country, he wrote, "I was then with kind friends, leading the life of an idler!" Now, in New South Wales, he was achieving independence. Moreover, Besnard believed, this autonomy was available to all Irish immigrants willing to work. Appealing to the Irish working class to consider emigration to the colony, he described Australia as "a country wherein every honest, industrious man can be sure of reaping a reward for his labor."[24]

Immigrants from Ulster were present, too, among the most prominent of whom was Henry Osborne. A native of Dromore parish in County Tyrone, Osborne emigrated from Ireland to New South Wales in 1829 at the age of twenty-six years. His family, among the wealthiest in his home locality, provided him with a sum of £1,000 to finance his endeavors. Osborne settled initially in the coastal Illawarra district with his two brothers, where he received two substantial land grants from the colonial government. However, in the 1840s he turned his attention inland and began to acquire land in the southwest between the Murrumbidgee and Murray Rivers. By 1854 Osborne's landholdings totaled approximately 261,000 acres, and he also acquired mining interests along the New South Wales coast. A man of considerable influence, Osborne's power was attributed by one writer to his "policy of tenanting his large holdings in the district by bringing from Ireland the families and friends of most of those who were in his employment."[25] Such behavior ensured that Irish settlement in the rural southwest was largely self-perpetuating: not surprisingly, immigrants were attracted to those localities where they encountered other immigrants of like mind and behavior. Further evidence of the presence of clusters of Ulster settlers is provided in the reminiscences of Samuel Shumack. Shumack's father, Richard, brought his family to New South Wales, probably as an assisted immigrant, in 1856. Soon after the family arrived in Sydney, Richard Shumack was met aboard ship and offered immediate employment at Charles Campbell's property, Duntroon. Duntroon was then widely recognized to be the center of Presbyterianism in the southwest—in the 1841 census almost all the Presbyterians present in that county resided at the one large sheep-grazing station. The presence of Presbyterian Irish in southern New South Wales was further confirmed by the clergyman John Dunmore Lang who, while touring near Braidwood in 1862, wrote that he "had no idea of finding such a little knot of Presbyterian families (all from Scotland and the North of Ireland) in such a locality."[26]

By midcentury, the Irish presence in New South Wales was a strong and varied one indeed, the Irish-born accounting for one-fifth of the total population. A major weakness of the Australian census data is that no comprehensive information exists on the employment patterns of the major nativity groups before the end of the nineteenth century. However, through the second half of the nineteenth century agriculture remained the mainstay of the colonial economies, and the qualitative evidence indicates strongly the Irish propensity for farm work and adaptability to life on the land. Through this period, as a leading historian of the Irish in Australia observed, the image and the reality of Australia's Irish was that of a predominantly rural people engaged in modestly successful farming.[27]

The diversity of the Irish population evident in the early years of European settlement was to a considerable degree maintained through the second half of the century. Clare, Limerick, Tipperary, King's County, Kilkenny, and areas of south Ulster were significantly represented in southwest New South Wales, with clusters of Tipperary-born and Limerick-born settlers attracting particular comment from contemporary observers.[28] However, given the overwhelmingly greater scale of the American migration, and the fact that in any case "Australia's Irish were drawn to some extent from all counties and from scattered localities within counties," it seems much more

Figure 4. Farm work in neighboring Victoria. Digging and bagging potatoes, Warrnambool (*Illustrated Sydney News*, 12 March 1881). National Library of Australia.

than place of birth is required to explain the Australian Irish rural departure from America's often-emphasized urban focus.[29]

As in the case of Minnesota, several crucial features stand out in the process of Irish settlement in southwest New South Wales. First, the migration was a staged one, where the Irish gained substantial opportunity to adjust to the conditions of New World farming. The period of convict servitude, in particular, was influential for many early arrivals in the region. They had served as laborers on farms and had gained familiarity with the conditions of the land—some, indeed, had served as overseers or farm managers for their masters. In addition, this period of servitude enabled the convict workers to acquire a sum of capital sufficient to sustain their first endeavors when they moved to the rural margins of the society. In 1830, at the end of his fourteen-year sentence, Tipperary-born Edward Ryan listed his assets as fifty head of breeding cattle, a team of oxen, two hundred bushels of wheat, £250 in cash, and sundry agricultural implements. Ryan's wealth at this time, like his later land acquisitions, was exceptional. However, many Irish convicts completed their period of servitude with a tidy sum of capital that would finance their attempts to settle on the land.[30] The convict period provided other Irish with the opportunity to participate in expeditions into the inland, this travel revealing favorable locations for future settlement that might then be followed up when the opportunity became available.

This pattern of staged adjustment was repeated among subsequent free arrivals too. Large numbers of immigrants—assisted and full-fare-paying—entered this rural region only gradually, advised by those in place before them about opportunities available and strategies for settlement. When James Gormly arrived in New South Wales from Roscommon in 1840 his parents were advised by acquaintances, including the colony's attorney general, John Hubert Plunkett, not to venture inland with young children but to settle in the southern coastal districts. Then, having adjusted to the rhythms of life in their new society, they ventured inland to search for farmland. Others went in search of paid employment in order to accumulate a sum that would enable them or their children to take to the land.[31]

The second important feature of Irish settlement in southwest New South Wales was that the concentrated Irish presence ensured that settlers entered into a region in which strong networks of family and kinship existed and where those connections ensured the maintenance of a remarkably confident and assertive rural immigrant community. There exists ample documentation of the strong patterns of migration that bound the Clonoulty district of County Tipperary to the New South Wales district of Boorowa. In 1862,

John Dunmore Lang passed through Boorowa, about 250 miles from Sydney. Lang, a strident opponent of Irish Catholic immigration to New South Wales, was alarmed by the religious imbalance of the population in the town. He believed Boorowa to be "one of the most thoroughly Roman Catholic districts in New South Wales," warning that it was dangerous for any place to be "of so one-sided character. . . . As everybody in the Duke of Argyle's county at home is called Campbell, so everybody in and around Burrowa is called Ryan. This, at least, is the general rule, although there are particular exceptions. Burrowa, in short, is the headquarters and paradise of the Ryans, and might almost be supposed to be a veritable slice of the county Tipperary."[32]

The strong Irish presence in this locality was fostered by the ex-convict Edward Ryan and his son John, who purchased numerous parcels of freehold property and sought to induce hard-working tenants, most of whom were Irish, to occupy the farms.[33] The concentration of Irish settlers continued to gather strength after the passage of land reform legislation by the New South Wales parliament in 1861. Those reforms, which aimed to break down extensive holdings of pasturage and encourage small-scale settlement, offered recent Irish arrivals an unprecedented opportunity to try and secure a stake on the land. It was a chance they seized enthusiastically. A local politician, James Tobias Ryan, later recalled attending the weddings of two women named O'Rourke to young Irish fellows, reporting that the newlyweds quickly joined the ranks of Irish immigrants gravitating toward the Boorowa district. "The O'Rourke girls got married, and after the Free Selection Bill passed the whole of them cleared out to Burrowa; therefore, it is not likely the name of O'Rourke will die out in that part of the country where they now reside. The Daseys, Daleys, Shadeys, O'Rourkes, Ryans and Hogans will be found in every nook and corner of Tom Slattery's electorate, bequeathed to him by John Nagle Ryan, who introduced a great many relations, and placed them all over that beautiful country."[34] Throughout the parishes of Boorowa in King County and Geegullilong in Monteagle County, both of which bordered the township of Boorowa, extensive amounts of land were alienated in the names of Edward and John Nagle Ryan, John and Patrick Hurley, and numerous other members of the Dwyer and Corcoran families, all these offering opportunities to hopeful Irish settlers. The overall picture is of a district in which a great many of the owners and occupiers of land were bound together by common familial ties and long-established relationships. A strong sense of community and mutual support was engendered by this settlement pattern.

If Boorowa was the most renowned Irish locality of the southwest, there were many other examples, too, some well known, others now scarcely visible in the surviving written sources. Catholic Irish settlers gathered around John Dwyer, the son of the Wicklow chieftain Michael Dwyer, near Lake George; the colonial politician Terence Aubrey Murray's Yarralumla homestead had a strong Roman Catholic population closely tied to Limerick. A knot of Irish settlers, also with roots in Limerick, gathered near the small town of Tumut. In 1850 Thomas and Anne Quilty wrote from Tumut to their daughter Ellen in Shanagolden, confidently asserting the prosperity and security of the rural region in which they lived: "If ye exert yourselves ye will get a passage out here as well as other people, and we shall do all we can to make you comfortable here, in fact it is our fond wish that you be here with us, your brothers and sisters who are all doing very well. . . . You cannot want for anything here you have got too many friends before you to secure you from that."[35] Moreover, partly by virtue of their strong numerical presence, Irish settlers—Roman Catholic and Protestant— actively and successfully sought to minimize religious tension in their new homeland and to ensure generally harmonious community relations: here there was no repeat of the fierce nativism of the American East Coast. As the Australian writer Mary Durack noted of her rather exceptional ancestors' experiences in the southwest, "Despite all that is said of increasing prejudice against the Irish our family had at least as many friends in the Scottish, English and Jewish sectors of the community."[36]

The third important feature of early Irish settlement in southwest New South Wales was that, as in Minnesota, it was remarkably unaffected by the influence of the Roman Catholic Church. The English Benedictine hierarchy of the fledgling church seems to have in no way discouraged settlement on the land, nor did the immigrants allow the absence of priests and churches to inhibit their economic judgments—these seem to have been remarkably pragmatic and generally sound. Irish-born clergy did come later, embarking on an impressive campaign of church building and encouraging devotions, but lay responsiveness to clerical demands seems always to have been tempered by their own assessments of their secular and immediate material interests.[37]

At midcentury, then, strong similarities may be observed in the Irish settlement of these two rural regions. In both cases the immigrants who ventured inland, armed with considerable knowledge of their prospective new homes and usually possessing sufficient capital, made pragmatic assessments of the opportunities available. They showed a determination to seize the opportunity presented by large amounts of affordable land; on the available evidence they seem to have farmed no less successfully or persistently than settlers of other nationalities; and they viewed acquisition of the land as a positive thing—a source of pride and security.[38] Samuel Shumack, who left Ireland with his parents in 1856 and settled near Canberra, acquired a small land holding in 1865. He expressed sentiments surely held by many Irish in the New World when he wrote, "We called our selection Springvale. We now had an object in life—to secure a permanent home. . . . In February 1865 I built a bark gunyah [hut] on my selection, in which I took up residence until I could build a permanent home."[39]

There also seems to be little evidence among early Irish settlers in either region that the relative isolation of their new environments was a deterrent to their lives on the land. Of course, it might be argued that evidence of a need for attachment to gregarious neighbors and parish communities should not be sought amongst those who took to the land, but is more likely to be visible among those who actually remained in urban areas. However, the very point that such numbers of Irish did in fact settle in rural locations in both the United States and Australia tellingly refutes the assertion that the Irish necessarily found frontier life uncongenial. In the Australian case, of course, the convict system imposed constraints on the freedom of movement of Irish prisoners, but the persistence of so many Irish in the region in the decades after the termination of convict transportation suggests at the very least a fair level of satisfaction with the economic opportunities and social life available to settlers.

*

If, at midcentury, settlement in both regions exhibited several similar characteristics, the latter decades of the century saw a significant change in the pattern of entry of the Irish-born into Minnesota. Increasingly, schemes of group migration came to dominate Irish settlement on the land. Inspired by the writings of advocates such as Thomas D'Arcy McGee, and later Philip Bagenal, who forcefully argued that the salvation of the Irish lay in America's western lands, various schemes were initiated to assist poor and destitute Irish to take advantage of "the homes and fortunes, still to be made, by honest labor in America."[40] Such schemes received the support of Irish American newspapers on the eastern seaboard too. The Boston *Pilot,* for example, was distressed to see "scores of respectable farmers sons and daughters" consigned to "the inferior rank of Irish 'Paddies' or 'Biddies'" in the cities. It believed the establishment of an immigrant aid society to encourage settlement in Minnesota was highly desirable: all that was required was for "men of influence, practical ability, and capacity, to lay hold of the matter in good earnest, and put the ball in motion." The *Pilot* maintained that, "if there existed well organized societies, whose members looked upon immigrants through a just and friendly medium, and understood all the phases of Irish character and Irish life, employments suitable to the character and capacity of each might be procured."[41]

In response to such appeals, several schemes were initiated in the period from the mid-1870s to the 1880s. Best known are the settlements initiated by John Ireland, a long-time advocate of Irish movement to the West, who from 1875 acted as an agent for railway companies and sold land on favorable terms to Roman Catholic settlers. Ireland's schemes especially targeted Irish immigrants already resident in cities on the eastern seaboard of the United States, and some there responded with very great enthusiasm to the opportunity for rural settlement. Annie King Lacore recorded the excitement with which her parents, Patrick, a native of Cavan who arrived in the United States in 1872, and Mary, who emigrated from Roscommon in 1873, heard of the bishop's colonization scheme while at Mass in Pleasantville, New York. For this young couple the opportunity "loomed large" and they "realized a dream . . . their own home on [160 acres of] land" in the village of Adrian, in Nobles County.[42] Yet despite successful examples such as this one, Ireland's program is best remembered for the unfortunate experience of "the Connemaras," a group of 309 settlers transplanted directly from Galway to Graceville in Big Stone County. These immigrants quickly showed themselves unable or unwilling to adjust to life in Minnesota, an associate of the bishop's writing candidly that "they would ruin the prospects of any colony into which they would find entrance."[43] The failure of the Connemara immigrants not only served to temper John Ireland's enthusiasm toward other settlement proposals but also generated considerable negative publicity for such schemes.[44]

The other major sponsor of settlement in Minnesota was the Irish-American Colonization Company, which released its prospectus in April 1881. The company, whose managing director was John Sweetman, sought to raise £150,000 for the purpose of facilitating Irish settlement on the land. The company maintained that while in states such as Minnesota "vast tracts of magnificent tillage land" were still unoccupied, large numbers of Irish immigrants were unable to take advantage of these available opportunities due to a want of capital. The company's plan was to surmount this difficulty:

to "purchase land in suitable localities and place settlers on it, providing them with houses, farm implements, and other suitable necessaries which the Directors may consider they require for a fair start."[45]

Despite the optimism of its early years, the colonization company was later judged by Sweetman to have failed in its aim of assisting Irish immigrants to settle on the land in America. Following the termination of the company's activities, the numbers of Irish-born arriving in Minnesota declined, so that by 1920 the Irish-born population in Minnesota numbered just over 10,000, less than 0.5 percent of the state's total population. Though the settlement schemes left some residual clusters of Roman Catholic settlement in the Minnesota countryside, the Irish flavor of the communities was quickly to pass.[46]

The generally unsatisfactory results of these Minnesota settlement schemes have done much to contribute to the deeply entrenched notion that the American Irish were unsuited to life on the land. In contrast, several other planned Irish settlements on the land in the nineteenth century have been judged to have enjoyed at least moderate success, including schemes elsewhere in the American Midwest, the recruitment plan initiated in the eastern Australian colony of Queensland in the 1860s by Bishop James Quinn, and the 1875 settlement of Ulster migrants at Kati Kati in New Zealand's Bay of Plenty.[47] Given the strong Irish presence in Minnesota's earlier decades, equally clear evidence of the Irish propensity for rural life in southwest New South Wales, and other international case studies of successful group settlement, the question arises as to why these particular projects fared so poorly?

Three principal explanations stand out for the impermanence of later Irish settlers in Minnesota. First, the colonization schemes tended to subvert the gradual processes by which the Irish had initially settled both rural regions under examination. Staged movement, assisted by family and kin, was replaced by rapid transplantation to a new environment. The planning, skills, knowledge, and economic judgments that underpinned the arrival of early settlers were replaced by inexperience and reliance upon the determinations of others. The schemes encouraged the movement inland of many who were ill prepared and ill equipped for their new lives. Additionally, they tended to depart from the successful pattern of Irish settlement that had evolved in both southwest New South Wales and Minnesota from midcentury. Whereas earlier Irish arrivals in both locations had tended to concentrate in distinctive local clusters, the new, organized settlements were for the most part located in counties that lacked established Irish populations. Murray County, site of the Irish-American Colonization Company's Avoca settlement, had only one Irish settler in the 1870s; neighboring Nobles County, site of the Adrian settlement, contained no Irish settlers at all. In short, the schemes may have transplanted groups of Irish settlers, but they positioned them in locations their compatriots had previously avoided.

Second, the settlement schemes encouraged the undercapitalized, or those unduly dependent on the capital of others, to move onto the land. The pastor of the Sweetman colony in Murray County, the Reverend Martin Mahony, was a frequent correspondent to newspapers such as Boston's *Pilot.* Mahony's letters repeatedly emphasized that immigrants should bring at least $500 to finance their establishment on the land, preferably more.[48] However, in their enthusiasm to encourage expansion and provide salva- tion for destitute immigrants, the promoters of the schemes sometimes waived the requirement for a sound capital base, or bore the risk them- selves—often with dire consequences to their own finances. Hence, where earlier Irish settlers on the land in both Australia and Minnesota moved onto the land only when they acquired sufficient capital, and then risked their own savings, for later Minnesota settlers the stakes were much lower and the commitment to the land correspondingly reduced.

Finally, the schemes to settle Irish on the land occurred at a time when fundamental changes were occurring in the economic structures of both societies—where the Irish, like their neighbors, were increasingly part of an urban drift. By 1891, 33 percent of the Australian population were city dwellers: no other society had massed its urban population in so few cities. While for many observers this was undesirable—an encouragement to an unhealthy lifestyle, crime, and poor public health as well as detrimental to happiness—some observers took a rather different view. The American soci- ologist Adna Weber saw the pattern of development as a sign that Australia was "the newest product of civilization"; it was the model that the rest of the world would follow.[49] In the United States, too, the Irish were at the fore- front of the urban movement.[50] For some immigrants this trend encouraged the abandonment of life on the land in favor of greater opportunities in America's cities. James Middleton, born in Ireland in 1833, arrived in the United States in the 1840s and took up land in Washington County, Min- nesota. A diligent farmer and family man, Middleton was prominent in his local community before being elected to the state legislature in 1876. How- ever, soon after, he was on the move, taking up real estate sales in Saint Paul. Middleton's departure from the land was not an indication of a lack of farm- ing ability—his diary testifies to his industriousness—but a sign of greater economic opportunities elsewhere, of pragmatic choices made on America's urban frontier. Just as Middleton seized the chance in Saint Paul, it is little wonder that later immigrants forsook the opportunity for life on the land offered by the colonization schemes to try their luck in the state capital.[51]

*

This chapter set out to compare Irish settlement in two New World rural regions and, through a process of comparison, to illuminate the diversity of life in Ireland's new worlds and evaluate the validity of prevailing explanations for the failure of Irish immigrants to settle on the land. In the process, several points have become clear. First, on the basis of existing evidence, the Irish origin of the immigrants seems in itself an inadequate basis to account for differential patterns of settlement across the regions or for explaining variations in Irish performance in the United States. More surprising, perhaps, is the extent of similarity in aspects of Irish rural settlement in the two regions under review at midcentury. Successful Irish settlers in both locations seem to have followed analogous strategies in their process of adaptation to life on the land, and the patterns of their local concentration seem also to bear resemblance. In both societies Irish settlers took advantage of the favorable economic opportunities that arose from their time of arrival in frontier communities, and as a result of their pragmatic desire to acquire readily available land, they fared well in farming. By virtue of their strong presence in the regions, they enjoyed generally harmonious and supportive relationships with their fellow settlers, a condition that made for stability and prosperity. The Irish in Minnesota and southwest New South Wales in the mid-nineteenth century were not worlds apart.

However, Minnesota's late-nineteenth-century experience of Irish group settlement marked a significant departure from the earlier experiences of both regions. While these schemes certainly drew publicity for Minnesota as a point of destination for the Irish, their limited success tended to contribute to American perceptions of the Irish as a group ill suited to the land. But, as this chapter has argued, the inadequacies and failures of those schemes should be explained in terms of their conceptualization, operation, and timing rather than by attributing responsibility to characteristics allegedly peculiar to the Irish. When viewed in such an international comparative context, Minnesota's experience suggests the need for the abandonment of stereotypical assertions about what the Irish did not do (or could not do) on the land. To achieve a more balanced assessment, greater emphasis should be placed on the specific experiences of rural settlers in Ireland's new worlds.

4

The Pacific Irish
California and Eastern Australia

IN THE SIXTY YEARS SINCE THE PUB-
lication of Oscar Handlin's *Boston's Immigrants,* most historical writing on the
Irish in the United States has focused on the lives and experiences of those
immigrants who settled in cities along the northeastern seaboard. In the
main, historians have concentrated their attention on the Catholic Irish who
settled adjacent to the Atlantic coast between the onset of the Irish Famine
and the 1880s, frequently portraying these immigrants as unfortunate newcomers whose purported cultural disabilities and prior experiences left them
ill equipped for life in their new society. Only in the latter decades of the
nineteenth century, most accounts concur, did a combination of acute political skills, intense Roman Catholic faith, and a strong sense of community
diminish Irish estrangement and enable the group to move gradually toward
middle-class respectability.[1]

This eastern model constitutes a powerful, but only partial, representation of nineteenth-century Irish America. In other regional settings,
immigrants' experiences and local communities' interactions departed
significantly from that eastern mold. California stands out as one location
where in the mid-nineteenth century Irish immigrants encountered conditions markedly different from those faced by their East Coast compatriots,
and they responded with vitality to carve out a distinctive niche in West
Coast society. The rapid expansion of California's population from the time
of the gold rush cast Irish newcomers into an environment where social
and economic structures were extremely fluid. Present from the outset, the
West Coast Irish prospered in this more open society in a way unmatched in
most other parts of the country. Yet, to date, the experience of California's

Irish has registered only slightly in national narratives of the Irish American experience.[2]

Historians on the West Coast, concerned at the homogenizing power of the national narratives, have attempted to assert their own distinctive voice in the historiography of the American Irish. In the main, their strategy has been to contrast the experience of California's Irish with that of their compatriots who settled in the major cities of New England and the mid-Atlantic states, highlighting the more favorable standing of the Irish who settled adjacent to the Pacific Ocean. Regrettably, those efforts have done little to date to reformulate the dominant account or appreciably alter popular understandings of nineteenth-century Irish American life.

An alternative strategy is to invoke a cross-national perspective and compare the experiences of California's nineteenth-century Irish immigrants with their compatriots who settled on Australia's eastern seaboard. The absence of such a strong, comparative, trans-Pacific dimension is understandable in its historiographical context. However, its ongoing omission from present-day studies of the Irish in both California and Australia is surprising given the close connections that existed between Irish immigrants in the two societies in the second half of the nineteenth century. Indeed, California and eastern Australia, together with neighboring New Zealand, were for much of the later-nineteenth century part of a Pacific Irish emigrant world—locations separated by the vast distances of the Pacific Ocean but unified by complex exchanges of peoples, information, and goods. At present, these connections remain uncharted, while parallels in the Irish immigrants' experiences have until now been scarcely surveyed.

In order to explore the rich diversity of experiences encountered by the Irish in these societies, this chapter engages in a specific comparison of California and the east coast Australian colonies of New South Wales and Victoria. It indicates that the societies on the two Pacific coasts shared a range of common characteristics—demographic, economic, and social—that contributed to very similar receptions and opportunities for Irish immigrants. In both, the immigrant experience deviated from the experience of the Irish in the northeastern United States.

*

In the second half of the nineteenth century, California and the eastern Australian mainland colonies of New South Wales and Victoria were frequently identified to be among the most favorable of all destinations for Irish emigrants. "Give me the South aye any part of it in preference to any of the northern abolitionist fire eaters but above all give me California the land of speculation," wrote James Riordan to his sister in New Orleans in 1859, sounding a note of optimism and enthusiasm that is resonant in numerous other observations of Irish life in the Golden State.[3] For example, in 1868, after an extensive tour of the United States, the Irish journalist and politician John Francis Maguire wrote glowingly that "there is not a state in the Union in which the Irish have taken deeper and stronger root, or thriven more successfully, than California, in whose amazing progress—material, social, and intellectual—they have had a conspicuous share."[4] Maguire's enthusiastic assessment was endorsed a decade later when the Reverend Hugh Quigley published his book, *The Irish Race in California,* an immense catalogue of Irish men's achievement in California's public life in the three decades after 1849.[5]

A wide range of evidence indicates that the Australian colonies were perceived in terms broadly similar to California—as an advantageous destination for Irish emigrants. From the enthusiastic testimonials of Irish settlers collected by the pro-emigration campaigner Caroline Chisholm in the 1840s to the fervent observations of visiting Irish nationalist politicians in the 1880s, the historical record supports the judgment that conditions in the colonies were mainly beneficent to newcomers.[6] Australia's Irish did not consider themselves subject to hardships and privations on a scale at all comparable to those present in the northeastern United States or Great Britain but for the most part celebrated their new homeland as one of opportunity and reasonable prosperity. Though the judgments of contemporaries on both sides of the Pacific that conditions were relatively advantageous might now appear unduly impressionistic, nineteenth-century Irish immigrants in both locations were in fact keenly interested in, and well informed about, the progress and affairs of their compatriots elsewhere across the Irish diaspora. Roman Catholic newspapers and immigrant letters in particular were of crucial importance in bridging the vast distances that separated the Irish worldwide and facilitated pragmatic assessments of the most favorable destinations for settlement.[7]

Many historians have concurred with positive nineteenth-century judgments about the merits of life on the two Pacific coasts. In San Francisco, the Irish heartland in the West, the immigrants were, in Robert Burchell's assessment, "comparatively successful and fortunate." His later analysis of the situation in southern California confirms much the same picture, while other writers have extended the assessment to the Californian Irish in general.[8]

Evaluating the historical record in Australia, the distinguished Irish historian Oliver MacDonagh concluded that Irish "diffusion, geographically, socially and even occupationally" was the outstanding characteristic of the Australian settlement. David Fitzpatrick made much the same point but differently: rather than experiencing particular disadvantage, Australia's Irish were "unique in their ordinariness."[9]

The wide difference between these assessments of Irish immigrant life along the Californian and eastern Australian coasts and the more arduous experiences of their compatriots in New England or the mid-Atlantic states poses the question, what factors were distinctive or unique about the two regions of more recent European settlement? At least four factors may be identified as contributing to the more benign experience of the Irish in California and eastern Australia. These are the immigrants' time of arrival; the backgrounds and prior experiences of the Irish in the two Pacific regions; the cosmopolitan characters of both host societies; and the presence in each region of significant non-European immigrant populations.

Paramount among the factors that delineate the experience of the Irish on both sides of the Pacific from the eastern model is time of arrival. As Patricia Nelson Limerick wrote of the American West, "In a society that rested on a foundation of invasion and conquest, the matter of legitimacy was up for grabs, and it remained up for grabs as long as a large sector of the population continued to be migrants from other regions and nations."[10] By virtue of their early presence in California, the Irish secured a position of legitimacy in a society where the nascent political, economic, and social structures were fluid and keenly contested. Even before the Mexican War, the Irish were present in significant numbers in the small Californian population. The discovery of gold in 1848 provided the impetus for a rapid expansion in the territory's population and drew large numbers of gold seekers, including many Irish, to the American West Coast.[11] The Californian population increased dramatically in the wake of the gold find, rising from around fourteen thousand in 1848 to nearly ninety-three thousand in 1850. Within this novel society, the Irish were strongly represented, accounting for 11 percent of the overseas-born population. Moreover, this figure takes no account of large numbers of second- or third-generation Irish who were present among the native-born population that journeyed to the West Coast, a group whose presence was undoubtedly significant in shaping the tenor of life in California but who are rendered nearly invisible by the absence of census data on ethnicity. The Irish influx into California in the decades immediately after the discovery of gold was so pronounced that by 1870 the

Irish-born were the largest overseas-born group in the state, accounting for a quarter of all foreign-born residents in California and almost 10 percent of its total population. Thereafter, despite an increase in absolute numbers until 1890, the Irish-born proportion of the state's population gradually declined until 1920.[12]

Early time of arrival was also a key feature of Irish settlement in mainland Australia. Irish convicts were shipped to eastern Australia from the commencement of European occupation in 1788 until 1840, and the vast majority of these men and women then remained as part of the ex-convict (emancipist) population following their period of servitude. From the late 1830s the Irish also figured prominently within the ranks of immigrants assisted to migrate to the colonies.[13] By 1851 the Irish-born constituted approximately 15 percent of the total population in New South Wales and Victoria, a remarkable figure compared with other locations across the Irish diaspora.

As in California, the discovery of gold fundamentally transformed the demography of European settlement and with it the profile of the Irish component. Following gold finds in New South Wales and Victoria in 1851, over one hundred thousand Irish immigrants arrived in the decade 1851–1860, though that great inflow led to only a small increase in the Irish share in the population of these eastern Australian colonies, from 15.4 percent in 1851 to 16.0 percent in 1861. In the 1860s and 1870s, as rural Ireland was transformed in the wake of the Irish Famine, eastern Australia became an increasingly attractive destination for the Irish, both in absolute and relative terms. Thereafter, as was the case in California, the number of Irish-born in the population declined throughout the period until 1920.[14]

For the Irish who settled in California in the years immediately after 1848, the openness of their new society offered substantial opportunities for social and economic advancement. The immigrants were, from the outset, full and assertive participants in a society Hubert Howe Bancroft described as "a gathering without parallel in history."[15] Certainly, measured against the less satisfactory standing of their compatriots elsewhere in America, Irish achievements on the West Coast were impressive. Contemporary accounts, including Quigley's *Irish Race in California,* provide page upon page of effusive detail of Irish successes in the state and clearly indicate substantial Irish penetration into the fields of commerce and government from early on. That advancement was not confined only to Irish men. Irish women also achieved positions of prominence in California's public sphere in the second half of the nineteenth century. For example, Mary McHenry, native-born but of Irish Catholic descent, was the first woman to graduate from the Hastings

School of Law and soon publicly contested the diminishment of women's status within the patriarchal family. Kate Kennedy, born in Meath in 1827, led the campaign for women's promotion within the state's education system and for equal pay for female teachers.[16] Though the wider dimensions of Irish women's experiences on either Pacific coast have as yet received only limited scholarly attention, future research may well support the hypothesis that for women, as well as men, California offered far superior prospects than the alternatives of life either in Ireland or on America's eastern seaboard.

By 1870 Irish immigrants and their descendants were widely dispersed across California, though as at midcentury their presence remained strongly centered upon San Francisco. Indeed, 62 percent of the state's Irish-born population was resident in San Francisco and the five neighboring counties of Alameda, Contra Costa, Marin, San Mateo, and Solona. San Francisco itself was by far the most heavily populated Irish county in both absolute and proportional terms: 48 percent of California's Irish lived there. Indeed, one in every six of the city's residents was Irish-born. Elsewhere, Irish immigrants were present in their greatest concentrations along an axis running northeast from San Francisco to the Nevada border and in coastal districts to the north and south of San Francisco. Relatively few Irish then lived in Southern California: Los Angeles County, for example, was home to only 471 Irish, or 3.1 percent of that county's population.[17]

Across California, the Irish-born were from the outset an integral part of the labor force in the rapidly expanding economy. This was particularly evident in the 1860s as the Civil War disrupted economic production in the East, causing the West Coast's economy to experience a decade of sustained growth. Large increases of capital investment and a fourfold rise in the value of manufacturing production were accompanied by a tremendous expansion in the size of the state's work force, especially in San Francisco.[18] The 1870 census reveals the Irish-born to have been major participants in this period of economic, industrial, and urban growth. While the proportion of Irish-born employed in agriculture was lower than that of most other immigrant groups, the most notable feature was the heavy concentration of Irish immigrants employed in the provision of personal and professional services. The large number of Irish in this category reflected very strong Irish concentrations in the categories of laborer and domestic servant, both consistent with the group's strong presence in urban San Francisco. Elsewhere, the Irish were overrepresented in the ranks of the military in California, constituting 33 percent of the United States army stationed in the state at a time when they comprised only 10 percent of the population. Twenty-nine percent of California's stable keepers and hostlers and a quarter of its boarding house keepers were also Irish.

For those who arrived later, as class lines solidified, prospects were less rosy. Within the rapidly expanding urban frontier beyond the Mississippi River, class divisions were present and proved critical, the working-class Irish consigned often to the most menial work and deep-rooted socio-economic disadvantage. But there are nevertheless strong grounds for distinguishing California, part of that region of explosive colonization that in the last third of the nineteenth century engulfed the New World from Chicago to Melbourne, from the Atlantic-coast experience. Whereas the Irish in the East confronted intrinsic hostility and deep sectarian animus, those further west seem to have encountered emerging societies more fluid and reflexive in their appreciation of newcomers from Ireland. The result was an occupational profile that, while setting to rest any notion of California as a land of unbridled opportunity, also refutes the notion that the group was chiefly disadvantaged above any other. As Burchell demonstrated in his study of San Francisco, "taking first and second generations together, the Irish community was experiencing considerable mobility. If parents were disappointed in their own progress, they could take satisfaction from that of their children." Subsequent studies have tended to confirm this view.[19]

*

Like their Californian counterparts, historians of the Irish in eastern Australia assert the primary importance of time of arrival as a determinant of the group's experience, emphasizing that the immigrants entered a society where economic structures were more fluid, less resistant. Oliver MacDonagh argued (overlooking California) that "full participation in the earliest developments of the new nation and the maintenance for so long of this participation on a very considerable scale, render Australia unique in Irish terms."[20] His general emphasis upon the benefit of early arrival is justified, but in terms of the comparison of the two Pacific coasts, it requires an important qualification. The period of the greatest Irish inflow to Australia, during the years 1850 to 1870, came more than half a century after the establishment of the British penal colony at Sydney and translated into slightly different stages in the development of the eastern Australian colonies under study.

In New South Wales (the foundation colony) the predominantly rural-based economy was not open to all comers. Vast areas of pastoral land were by then concentrated in the hands of a small elite, and this was a source of enormous resentment for many newly arrived Irish immigrants. Indeed, some newcomers drew parallels between the situation encountered in the colony and the concentration of wealth in so few hands in their homeland. A correspondent to one newspaper, "Irish Laborer," wrote angrily to his fellow immigrants: "You have been compelled to fly from your native lands to escape the galling yoke of a merciless despotism in the shape of monarchy, and its blasphemous attendant an Aristocracy. And when you expected to find a new home in this new land, capable of supporting millions of your fellow men, you can no more secure an acre of land unless at fifty to one hundred times its value, than you can secure it in the domain of the Duke of Norfolk, Devonshire or Northumberland."[21] The introduction of land reform legislation in New South Wales in the 1860s ultimately did little to satisfy the aspirations of the new arrivals.

In neighboring Victoria, the southernmost mainland colony, the situation was initially more fluid. However, in 1847 pastoralists in occupation of Crown lands were granted fourteen-year leaseholds, which provided more secure tenure for landholders. As a result, the free-for-all atmosphere previously evident slowed: landholders now had greater incentive to erect permanent dwellings and improve the land.[22] Weighed against this consolidation on the land was the instability that followed the discovery of gold. Employment opportunities were initially available in the major town, Melbourne, as gold fever drew workers away in search of fortune, and in this environment Irish immigrants were well placed to gain a foothold.[23] However, for those unable to do so, and for those who arrived in subsequent decades, opportunities were limited. In other areas of the economy, too, the Irish faced a measure of exclusion. In Melbourne, many Irish workers struggled unsuccessfully during the 1870s and 1880s to move beyond the ranks of the unskilled.[24] Yet against such pessimistic accounts may be found conflicting evidence. In parts of the Victorian countryside Irish farmers seem to have been as successful as their English, Scottish, or Australian-born neighbors, while numbers of Irish-born lawyers, doctors, and academics, mostly graduates of Trinity College Dublin, achieved positions of status and privilege within Melbourne society.[25]

There was, then, just as in California, a range of experiences for Irish immigrants in Australia's east coast colonies. However, the crucial point is that, even though many Irish immigrants in the second half of the nineteenth century did enter areas where resources and opportunities were subject to considerable competition, other Irish—whether ex-convicts or free settlers—had been there from the outset. As a result, the legitimacy of the Irish presence in eastern Australia was well established: there were few structural impediments that worked very much more severely against the Irish than other European immigrant groups. There was, in other words, an openness about society, and the Irish role in it, that much more closely resembled the American West Coast than the East Coast. And within this less constrained society, Irish achievement in the fields of politics and business were visible and proudly proclaimed, just as they were in California.

The first state census to cross-tabulate Irish nativity and occupation in eastern Australia was taken in New South Wales in 1901. It highlights the significant structural differences that existed between the economies of California and eastern Australia. In 1901, despite strong industrial growth in the 1870s, 36.7 percent of male breadwinners in New South Wales were employed in agriculture or the rearing of animals. In contrast, as early as 1880 the proportion of California's working population engaged in all forms of agriculture had declined to barely one in five.[26] In 1901, pastoralism, agriculture, and dairying together contributed 20 percent of the value of Australia's gross domestic product; manufacturing was of less importance and accounted for barely 12 percent of the total.[27] In New South Wales and Victoria, where industrial development was weaker and delayed compared to the Golden State, the Irish exhibited a markedly different employment profile to that of their American-based compatriots. The most striking aspect of the Australian situation is in fact the close similarity in the profiles of all overseas-born groups in the colony. The Irish were spread across all employment categories and in proportions closely aligned with the English, Scots, and German-born. The Irish presence in farming work was marginally greater than among the other immigrant cohorts, and in this respect the Irish profile most closely mirrored that of the colonial-born population.

More distinctive is the occupational profile of Irish women. Though the majority of women in paid employment in each nativity group found work in personal or professional service, a greater proportion of the Irish were employed in these occupations than any other group. A sizeable number of Irish were engaged in what was classified as religious and charitable work, while over 4,000 Irish women also derived incomes from the provision of board and lodging. The other striking feature is the lower level of Irish women's participation in manufacturing industries compared to the other major nativity groups, perhaps reflecting Irish women's receptiveness to clerical warnings about the moral and health threats posed by factory work.[28]

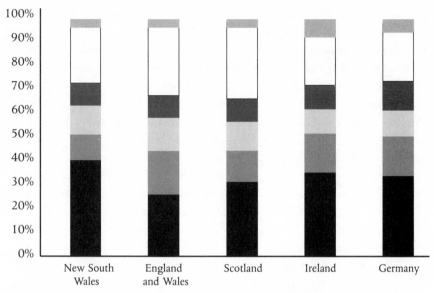

Graph 1. Male occupations by nativity, selected groups, New South Wales, 1901

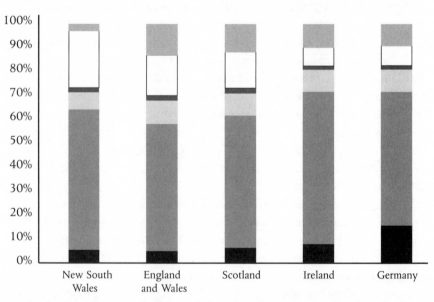

Graph 2. Female occupations by nativity, selected groups, New South Wales, 1901

■ Cultivate land or rear animals   ■ Transport and communications

■ Total service (personal and professional)   □ Manufacturing and construction

■ Retail (sales and dealing)   ■ Other

Source: T. A. Coghlan, *Results of a Census of New South Wales (1901)* (Sydney: Government Printer, 1901), 770–85.

Despite such points of distinction, however, the weight of evidence on Irish participation in the New South Wales labor force at the end of the nineteenth century supports the conclusion that Irish-born men and women were by then well established participants in the labor force. They were dispersed across the different fields of employment in proportions not very different from those of the other major immigrant groups. There is little evidence that Irish immigrants in general were locked into a narrow band of disadvantageous occupations or consigned disproportionately to the bottom rungs of the occupational ladder.

*

Historians justifiably identify time of arrival as the paramount factor that contributed to the superior standing of Irish immigrants adjacent to both Pacific coasts, though it was certainly not the only one. Critical, too, were the immigrants' backgrounds.[29] Though little data exist on the home-county origins of California's Irish-born population, their pre-Californian backgrounds are noteworthy in one important respect. In contrast to the East, only a small proportion of newcomers came directly from Ireland to the West Coast. For example, in 1852 only 7 percent of San Francisco's Irish-born immigrants identified their previous place of residence as having been in the British Isles. Instead, California's Irish-born arrived on the West Coast after periods of residence elsewhere and were, in the main, experienced New World settlers by the time they reached the Golden State.[30] Unsurprisingly, the largest number had previously resided elsewhere in the United States. In 1852, 45 percent of San Francisco's Irish-born population had previously lived in the East, most in either New England or the mid-Atlantic states, but smaller numbers in states further west.[31]

The other main source of Irish immigrants to California was Australasia. In 1852 the number of trans-Pacific Irish resident in San Francisco was almost identical to the number who had relocated within the continental United States. Within Australasia, by far the greatest number of Irish came from Sydney or gave Australia as a generic label for their previous place of residence. In contrast, less than 1 percent of the immigrants indicated that they were previous residents of New Zealand.[32] This eastward migration of Irish to California is intriguing and has attracted only limited attention from historians. Most of the Irish arrived as part of the group known as the "Sydney Ducks," gold seekers who met an adverse reception upon arrival in San Francisco due to their purported criminality (some were undoubtedly ex-convicts) as well as their reputation for gambling and excessive drinking. On account of their negative image, the "Ducks" became a particular target of the Committee of Vigilance in 1851. However, despite their reputation, the immigrants from Australia were not in fact primarily young, single, reckless men. The most careful demographic study to date shows that these trans-Pacific migrants frequently arrived as part of family units. The average age of the men and women who disembarked in San Francisco was significantly above that of California as a whole, and the sex ratio of the group (152 men for every 100 women) far more closely approximated that of the entire United States (105 in 1850) than California (1,214 in 1852). Irish immigrants arriving from Sydney in 1852 were represented across all major occupational categories, though like their English-born counterparts the majority were concentrated in laboring work.[33]

Overall, these statistics make clear that California received very few immigrants directly from Ireland, and those who did arrive without interludes elsewhere defy simplistic categorization as impoverished Roman Catholics escaping famine or poverty at home. The well-documented case of the Louth-born Protestant Thomas Kerr, who arrived with his brother-in-law in 1848 to seek his fortune on the gold fields, is suggestive of the diversity in class and regional backgrounds to be found among California's Irish-born population at midcentury.[34] In general, those who arrived on the West Coast were seasoned New World citizens, adaptable, experienced, worldly, and possessed of some degree of skill and savvy, men and women eager to seize the main chance.

Their ambition was nurtured by the presence of strong and effective community leadership. Through their involvement in business, public service, or the broader social life of the West Coast, California's first generation of Irish leaders guaranteed their compatriots a voice in the shaping of the community, publicly asserting the right and responsibility of the Irish to full and effective civic participation. Some, such as James Phelan, built family dynasties, culminating in his son's service as United States senator for California from 1915 to 1921.[35] But there were many others too: Garret McEnerney, John Francis Neylan, and Kate Kennedy in law and public education; Frank Roney, the labor organizer—these few in San Francisco alone.[36] Historians are rightly wary about placing too much significance in individuals and obscuring the lives of the majority. However, the lives of California's Irish population were undoubtedly shaped by the extent to which their leaders—of all classes, dispositions, and political persuasions—engaged with their fellow citizens, as indeed those engagements were circumscribed by the broader soundings of Irish life in their new homeland. That characteristic of effective community leadership also proved to be a feature of the Australian scene. Numerous studies have shown the important roles played by Irish leaders there—Roman Catholic and Protestant, clergy and lay—and the conflicts and competition between them, in shaping the social relations of the Irish and their fellow colonists.[37]

Much more is known about the specific regional origins of the Irish-born population on Australia's east coast. While newcomers were drawn from across the entire island, clear concentrations arrived in mid-nineteenth-century New South Wales and Victoria from a band of south midland counties— Clare, Tipperary, Limerick, and Kilkenny—and from south Ulster.[38] In contrast to the situation in California, the great majority of Irish immigrants settling on the Pacific Ocean's western shore arrived directly from the British Isles, either embarking in Ireland or putting to sea after a short interlude in England. Significantly, though, most arrived with the benefit of state assistance. In Australia, less familiar, further from Ireland, and more expensive to reach, the various colonial governments were compelled to recruit actively, sponsor, and embark the immigrant labor necessary for economic expansion. A variety of assistance schemes operated through most of the nineteenth century, and despite sustained criticism from Protestant church leaders and sections of the colonial press over the size of the Irish component, the schemes continued, the Irish embracing them with enthusiasm.[39]

The greater level of direct settlement in eastern Australia marks a significant difference from California. Most of the West Coast's Irish newcomers arrived after a transitional period in which marketable skills or disciplines suitable to California's industrializing economy could be acquired. In contrast, most of Australia's Irish had no such opportunity to up their skills. However, staged arrival was arguably rendered less necessary for the smooth adjustment of the colonies' Irish immigrants by the operation of the assisted immigration schemes. These diminished the imperative of gradual adjustment to the New World because they provided a predeparture filter on the composition of the immigration stream. One study of literacy levels among government-assisted emigrants from the United Kingdom to Australia in the period to 1860 found the newcomers were "significantly more literate than their peers that stayed at home." It substantiated the view that "government emigrants were enterprising, self-selecting individuals who took advantage of a scheme that allowed them to improve their employment prospects abroad."[40] This assessment of the temper of the assisted immigrant schemes, which parallels much Australian historical writing about the quality of the gold rush immigrants of the 1850s, has resonance with the informal selection processes through which a minority of the Irish in the United States deliberately relocated to California.

Yet, if differences in regional origins and variety of presettlement experience did not greatly affect the relative prosperity and well-being of the Irish on either side of the Pacific, it is likely that they did contribute to the immigrants' preparedness for the particular economic conditions they encountered in their new host societies. California's Irish population, many migrating onward from New York, Massachusetts, or Pennsylvania, was familiar with the routines and disciplines of urban life and came with skills learned in years of residence in those states. This interlude in the eastern states helps explain their propensity for settlement in the Bay Area; it also provides some of the strongest evidence for David Doyle's categorization of the Irish as America's urban pioneers.[41] Yet in eastern Australia, the Irish revealed no such tendency. Most of east coast Australia's Irish, drawn heavily from the ranks of displaced rural laborers of the postfamine period, had no such urban schooling. Without that background, and cast into an economy that was considerably less developed industrially than California's, they displayed little compunction about moving out from urban centers to the Bush. For them, unlike the archetypal Irish immigrant in so much of the eastern American literature, the Great Famine left no indelible scarring to prevent new ventures on the land.

*

A third critical feature distinguishing California and eastern Australia from the eastern model was their more favorable ambience. California was from midcentury set apart by an elusive quality that Bayard Taylor long ago termed the "cosmopolitan cast" of life in the West.[42] Commentaries on the diversity of city life in antebellum America are ubiquitous in contemporary writings, and the power of such rhetoric certainly proved advantageous to the Irish in California. As early as 1855 Frank Soule wrote that in San Francisco, "English, Scotch and Irish immigrants were also numerous, but their characteristics, although somewhat different, were less distinguishable from those of Native [born] Americans than were the manners and customs of other foreigners." He went on to suggest that "since the common language of the Americans and British [including Irish] is English, and their customs and habits of thought are generally the same, there seems no impropriety in calling them all in California simply Americans."[43]

To some extent, this process of Irish inclusion rested upon the society's perception of itself as something new and different. On the West Coast, numerous contemporaries remarked, the feverish arrival of newcomers during this period of explosive colonization and the conditions of life they encountered worked to diminish the differences between national groups and instill common characteristics. "Our population, selected from the choice young men of all the most active nations of the world, has not been thrown together into the vast alembic of society, without developing many qualities, whose existence was hitherto latent," wrote Casper T. Hopkins in 1854.[44] Admittedly, the notion that the force of the environment would produce common behavior was not always applied consistently, and criticisms of the Irish did occur. However, despite painful slippages into old prejudices—whether these were imported directly from the Old World or products of life back East—the belief that the materialism of the West would forge a new people was widely shared, and the position of the Irish was never so seriously challenged as on the Atlantic seaboard.[45]

In a remarkably similar manner, writers on Australia's east coast frequently invoked ideas of egalitarianism and openness as the principal defining characteristics of colonial society. Moreover, as in California, the novelty of the society was a key ingredient in the way in which the European population in eastern Australia defined its identity, marking itself as different from the Old World. In both places the arrival of large numbers of people in so few years demanded the rapid creation of new community identities, and in both the processes were similar, though the redefinition, the establishing of distinctiveness, was struck against different parents—for eastern Australia, the imperial center; for California, the East Coast. But both societies, through their assertion of difference, paved the way for fuller participation of the Irish than existed elsewhere across the diaspora, and the immigrants celebrated this difference enthusiastically.

One aspect of this ambience that proved advantageous for Irish settlers was the presence of a far greater degree of religious tolerance than characterized society either in the eastern United States or Great Britain. This does not imply that sectarianism was absent or insignificant, or that religious affiliation was unimportant in shaping the various life experiences of Irish men and women. In the nineteenth century, and for most of the twentieth, religious bigotry was indeed an endemic feature of the lives of Irish Catholics on both sides of the Pacific. However, there were critical points of distinction with the Atlantic coast. In California, the prior presence of Roman Catholicism and the diversity of faiths present after midcentury ensured that there was less fertile ground for the nativism Irish immigrants confronted in the East. The Catholic newspaper the *Monitor* recognized the absence of religious enmity that distinguished life in the far West: "Our countrymen need not fear that they will have to encounter prejudices against their race or religion, that are such drawbacks to their settlement in many parts of the Eastern states. . . . Irishmen have made themselves a position here fully equal to any other nationality in our cosmopolitan population, and newcomers of the same race will find no prejudice to bar their advancement, unless what any fault of their own may rise [*sic*] against individuals.[46]

The Roman Catholic Church, less besieged in this environment, grew vigorously to provide an important institutional affiliation for the state's Irish Catholics and stimulated fraternal organizations that eased the path of immigrant adjustment.[47] However, unlike the situation in many cities on the eastern seaboard, where the church responded stridently to the rising tide of evangelical Protestantism, the character of California's Roman Catholicism was not especially belligerent in support of an oppressed laity, but took on a rather different and more accommodating character. Reflecting this less intense environment, Hugh Quigley asserted that the clergy in the state "generally defend their own creed if attacked, but seldom, if ever, do they assail what they consider to be the errors of those who differ with themselves."[48] This is not to say that religious tensions were absent. The controversial campaigns of the Roman Catholic priest, Father Peter Yorke, including his attack on the unrepresentative composition of the Board of Regents of the University of California, provide ample testimony to the presence of the sectarian edge.[49] However, these overt public confrontations tended to be sporadic affairs, with religious bigotry cast more in the recesses of community life rather than at the forefront.

In the second half of the nineteenth century eastern Australia closely resembled California in the extent to which the Roman Catholic Church faced less vehement opposition than in the eastern United States. This had not been the case initially, and in the first decades of the convict settlement official suspicion of Catholicism and the absence of clergy restricted religious practice among Irish prisoners. But after this bitter and unpromising beginning, religious tensions in New South Wales gradually diminished. A key factor was the decision in 1836 of the Anglo-Irish governor, Richard Bourke, to provide state funding to all religious denominations. Reinforcing that tendency, the English Benedictine leadership that controlled the Catholic Church in Australia presented to Protestant critics a more palatable and less confrontational alternative than American nativists recognized in

New York's Archbishop John Hughes. From midcentury on, anxieties increased. There was awareness and considerable sensitivity among Irish Catholic leaders in Australia to the eastern American experience, and concerns about the threat of "Know-Nothingism" were sometimes expressed.[50] But in the main, religious difference was not too dominant a feature of colonial life, and opposition to Roman Catholicism never enjoyed the currency it attained in the more hostile environments of Boston or New York. The Australian historian Hilary Carey best captured the temper of the colonial scene when she wrote recently, "Australians lived in a sectarian environment in the nineteenth century. . . . However, the sectarian tensions of colonial Australia remained a pale imitation of rival tensions in northern England, Ireland and Scotland or in other settler societies, including the United States."[51]

*

The fourth feature critical to the experience of the Irish on both sides of the Pacific was the presence of substantial non-white immigrant populations against whom community antagonism was directed. Where California's English-speaking Irish were from midcentury viewed within an assimilatory frame and considered to have much in common with other new arrivals from the British Isles, the substantial Chinese population was not. Generalization here is dangerous, but on the whole the Irish on the West Coast seem to have been less fearful of, and insecure about, their standing as white insiders than was the case among their compatriots elsewhere in the United States. For example, the Irish in the West were notably less antagonistic toward abolition than their compatriots on the East Coast or in the South, and as a result California's Irish were spared much of the legacy of bitterness that resulted from the Irish American resistance to the antislavery cause.[52] This security did not translate into any special affinity with, or concern for, the plight of the state's Chinese immigrant population. Denis Kearney, Irish-born president of the Workingman's Party, was a forceful opponent of the Chinese presence and one of the foremost campaigners for legislation to ensure their exclusion. His profile was one factor that prompted Mary Roberts Coolidge to believe that the high proportion of the Irish in the Californian population was "a cause of the anti-Chinese movements there [and that the] preponderance of Irish names in the leadership of mobs, anti-coolie clubs, persons arrested for attacks upon the Chinese, and also among legislators and municipal officers, bears witness to the rapidity of their assimilation."[53] Certainly, not all Irish in the West sympathized with the pervasive anti-Chinese sentiment of the late-nineteenth century. The labor leader Frank Roney, born in Belfast in 1841, declared he was hostile to the more virulent opponents of the Chinese presence. However, irrespective of such individual Irish responses, the crucial point is that the Chinese presence served further to mark the Irish as mainstream players in their new society.[54]

The Chinese presence was also a factor that contributed to the Irish position as insiders in Australia's east coast colonies. However, its importance was less pronounced than on the American West Coast because of the half century of European presence before the discovery of gold, a period of time during which the Irish had done much to carve their niche in colonial society. For Australia's Irish, the presence of the Chinese mainly served to reinforce a preexisting tendency toward inclusion, but it did provide the Irish with a further issue on which to publicly articulate their demand for full participation in society. Ill feeling toward the Chinese, which gathered strength during the gold rushes of the mid-1850s to early 1860s, was to be a feature of Australian (and Irish Australian) colonial life for the remainder of the century. "'Australia for Australians' will be a principal plank of our platform," declared the *Irish-Australian* newspaper in its first editorial in 1894, its demand mirroring the radical *Bulletin* magazine's famous masthead "Australia for the Australians." "We shall advocate it on generous lines, offering a hearty welcome to all who would become Australian by unreservedly casting in their lot with us [but] while doing this, we shall champion the claims of Irish-Australians to perfect essential equality with their fellow citizens," the newspaper explained.[55] That the Chinese did not fall within this privileged group was soon apparent when the *Irish-Australian* commenced a campaign against the "Chinese and other inferior European races" who, it claimed, had "usurped the public market places." The newspaper demanded action by civic authorities to control the non-white population and noted the hearty congratulations it had received from readers for its campaign.[56] While such attitudes were widespread in the Australian press at the time, and the campaign by the *Irish-Australian* was certainly less vociferous than the anti-Chinese hysteria found in many other newspapers in the late-nineteenth century, the point remains that the Irish were then strongly positioned on the privileged side of the color bar that increasingly dominated Australian national life.[57]

*

As this chapter has demonstrated, the experience of the Irish in California and the east coast Australian colonies of New South Wales and Victoria in the period 1840 to 1900 was similar in many respects. Both Pacific coasts played host to large and dynamic Irish communities that experienced less troubled adaptation to the New World than confronted their compatriots in the eastern United States, and in each location the immigrants achieved satisfactory levels of prosperity within a generation. In both locations, similar forces can be identified as contributing to this outcome: early time of arrival that ensured Irish legitimacy and access to resources; the immigrants' preparedness for their new environment; the openness and diversity of the new society; and the presence of other immigrant groups against whom intense hostility was directed. However, significant differences existed across this matrix of factors, reflecting variations in time of settlement and organization of the migration process, the comparative development of each society's industrial economy, and the differing propensities of the immigrants for urban and rural settlement.

This comparison of California and the Australian east coast indicates that historians of Irish migration would do well to move beyond the constraints imposed by national narratives and utilize subnational comparison as well in exploring immigrants' experiences. Such an approach will not enable all lines of possible inquiry to be exhausted, as national ideologies and nationwide developments also undeniably affected the experiences of immigrants across the Irish Diaspora throughout the nineteenth century. Nevertheless, through transregional studies such as this one, historians will find confirmation of the presence of other well-adjusted and generally successful Irish communities and will be able to bring more sharply into focus the specific and distinctive features of Irish settlement in their own regions.

5 New Worlds Converge

Immigrants, Nationalisms, and Sectarian Cultures

THE AMERICAN CIVIL WAR CHAL-
lenged Irish immigrants and those of Irish descent to demonstrate their
overriding loyalty and commitment to their new society. The rallying call
was answered on both sides of the terrible divide, and Irish soldiers fought
with valor and distinction in the armies of the Union and the Confederacy.
Through their display of heroism on the battlefield, the Irish won a short-
term reprieve from the extreme nativist hostility of the 1850s, though
wartime sacrifice did little to ameliorate the unfavorable economic position
of Irish immigrants across the nation. Indeed, in the next two decades,
antagonism toward the Irish continued to be a feature of American life, and
many within the immigrant group remained mired in positions of acute
material disadvantage. Confronted with this predicament, America's Irish
entered the era of Reconstruction eager to establish once and for all their
right and proper standing as full participants in American life and to secure
a greater measure of economic well-being. They were roused and fortified
in these objectives by a new and popular version of Ireland's recent history, a narrative of their homeland's brutal subordination and genocidal
treatment at the hands of a merciless Great Britain. This account of Ireland's
history, widely disseminated and increasingly accessible in print, took root
and flourished in America in the two decades after the Civil War, endow-
ing the Irish with a fierce desire to achieve vindication in their new society and a determination to bring to its knees the implacable enemy of the
Old. In contrast, in the 1860s and 1870s Australia continued to provide bar-
ren ground for such pointed nationalist sentiments or vituperative attacks on
the British administration of Ireland. As in previous decades, the colonial

context continued to provide the framework for the actions and reactions of the Irish in Australia, and the vast distances and remoteness in time between the Old World and the New continued to prove near insurmountable obstacles to the generation of any militant Irish national consciousness. Yet despite these constant factors, the prevailing mood of Irish Australia began to shift markedly in the mid-1860s, becoming much more cautious and uncertain. A volatile sectarian environment emerged in the colonies to disrupt the placid atmosphere of the 1850s, the shift fuelled by controversies over education, fears over the threat posed by militant Irish nationalism, the imposition of a more rigorous version of Roman Catholicism on Australian soil, but most importantly, by the commencement of a process of sweeping economic change. Irish Australia was transformed under the weight of these factors into a more insular and defensive immigrant group, and its experiences came more closely to resemble those of the American Irish than had been the case before. This chapter examines these changing contours of the immigrants' experiences in Ireland's two new worlds from the 1860s to the 1880s, emphasizing the significant convergence in the experience of the Irish in each society as wider economic and social transformations affected the United States and the Australian colonies.

*

When John Mitchel prepared to depart from Greytown for New York City on 18 November 1853, he reflected upon his expulsion from Ireland, his detention in Australia, and the prospect of life in America. "How can I expect to find men in New York, though they be banished Irishmen, too; or in Ireland, though they be unhappy in not being banished—so full of these thoughts as I am? Six years, that have been ages and centuries of bitterness to me, have been to them six years of work and of common life. I know that, let exile be as long as it will, the returning wanderer is apt to take up his life again, as it were, at the very point where he quitted it, just as if the interval were a hasheesh dream, wherein men spend years, and lead weary lives in a second of time."[1] Mitchel's question was soon answered; his ruminations put to the test. Despite the anguish of his forced exile in Tasmania, John Mitchel arrived in the United States ready and eager to take up life where it had been interrupted in 1848—in the bitter denunciation of Great Britain and British influence in Irish life. Like other fervent advocates of an independent Ireland, he understood very clearly that the United States constituted the most fertile ground for the resumption of the nationalist project. Indeed, only six months before Mitchel's arrival, his fellow antipodean exile, William Smith O'Brien, had visited New York to a rapturous welcome.[2] O'Brien's reception offered Mitchel ample reason to believe that he, too, would quickly secure a place of eminence in the hearts and minds of Irish Americans.

Shortly after Mitchel's arrival in New York, his determination to continue to struggle for Irish nationhood was evident. He launched a newspaper, the *Citizen,* declaring that he desired "to awaken again the natural spirit and ambition of Ireland."[3] He also initiated a new Irish nationalist organization, the Irishmen's Civil and Military Republican Union, which drew together the bedraggled remnants from the old 1848 activist groups to seek Russian support for a rising in Ireland. However, Mitchel's proposals received little encouragement from Tsarist diplomats in the United States and, with its members' enthusiasm at low ebb, the movement quickly foundered. At the end of 1854 Mitchel left New York and, after a brief flirtation with farming, settled in Knoxville, Tennessee, where he opened another newspaper, the *Southern Citizen.* Yet Mitchel remained restless, and returned to Europe before traveling again to America to reside in Richmond, Virginia, where he became an advocate of Southern secession. Unsettled, wandering, and absent from the major Irish immigrant concentrations in New England and the mid-Atlantic states, John Mitchel thereafter failed to secure the position of distinction he sought in Irish American life.[4]

However, if in person John Mitchel made only a modest impact in America, his writing was to prove of profound importance, bequeathing an enduring legacy to Ireland and Irish America. Mitchel's *Jail Journal,* first published in serial form in 1854, *The Last Conquest of Ireland (Perhaps),* serialized in the *Southern Citizen* in 1858, and his *History of Ireland from the Treaty of Limerick to the Present Time,* published in 1868, together constituted the nineteenth century's most intense denunciation of British policy in Ireland. Mitchel's writing on the famine—flawed and remote from the historical record as it was—proved especially influential and quickly assumed the place of objective history in Ireland and among the Irish abroad. His account of the hunger imbued nationalist discourse with a searing antipathy toward Britain and provided thousands of Irish famine emigrants in the United States with the staple explanation for their departure from Ireland and their continued suffering abroad.[5] Acerbic and uncompromising, the works of John Mitchel would set the tone of Irish America for decades to come.

*

In the wake of John Mitchel's departure from New York, nationalists struggled on, their ambitions frustrated by internecine divisions. The Emmet Monument Society was formed in New York in March 1855; later that year the Irish Emigrant Aid Society was established in Massachusetts to recruit insurgents for service in the liberation of Ireland. Neither organization achieved distinction. The Aid Society convened a national convention in New York, but rivalries and intrigues soon dissipated the activists' energies. So parlous was the state of affairs that prominent Irishmen were inclined to dismiss Irish American nationalism as nothing but veneer. John O'Mahony, soon to rise to prominence as leader of the Fenian movement in the United States, complained to his compatriot James Stephens in 1856, "I am sick of Irish Catholics in America. I am sick of Yankee-doodle twaddle, Yankee-doodle selfishness and all Yankee-doodle-dum."[6]

Out of the mire of personal rivalries and confusion, a more coherent and formidable force did eventually arise. Under the leadership of O'Mahony, a Young Irelander who fled from Dublin to Paris in 1848 before he migrated to the United States, the Fenian Brotherhood was established in New York and spread up and down the Atlantic coast. The fledgling American movement received much-needed encouragement when James Stephens, head of the Irish Republican Brotherhood, toured the United States in late 1858 to solicit funds. A further fillip for the revolutionary cause on both sides of the Atlantic came in January 1861, following the death of a former Young Irelander, Terence Bellew MacManus, then living in poverty in San Francisco. Informed of the veteran nationalist's death, James Stephens arranged masterfully for the return of MacManus's remains to Dublin, after an interlude in New York where the body lay in state in Saint Patrick's Cathedral. The return to Ireland of MacManus's corpse seized imaginations in the United States and Ireland and refocused popular attention on Ireland's predicament as no event had done since 1848. When MacManus's body did eventually arrive in Dublin for burial, a crowd of more than twenty thousand, including an official delegation of prominent Irish Americans, witnessed its interment in Glasnevin cemetery. The ardor and spirit of nationalism in both Ireland and the United States lifted appreciably as the nationalist hero was finally returned home.[7]

Despite encouraging signs of a nationalist awakening on both sides of the Atlantic, Fenian leaders remained uncertain about how best to build and activate their organization. Tentative plans for insurrection in Ireland were concocted, but the outbreak of the Civil War in America thwarted hopes for any immediate action. However, the war proved a mixed blessing, for the convocation of Irish regiments in both the Union and Confederate armies created unparalleled opportunities for the Fenian movement to enlist new recruits. Northern antipathy toward Great Britain, which intensified during the course of the Civil War, added further momentum to Fenian efforts to mobilize Irish Americans. In 1863, as the movement's popularity grew, John O'Mahony and his supporters organized a convention in Chicago to publicize Fenian achievements and generate plans for the future. An ancillary organization for Irish American women, the Fenian Sisterhood, was also inaugurated at this convention. The Chicago gathering proved timely in raising the Fenians' profile, and the movement's membership increased significantly in the succeeding months. By January 1865, when a second Fenian convention was held in Cincinnati, the strength of the brotherhood had risen dramatically: 348 delegates attended that conference, representing groups from the Atlantic coast to the Pacific. Fenians everywhere then looked forward with anticipation to the end of the Civil War, to the moment when the latent energy of the movement would be unleashed against Ireland's implacable enemy.[8]

The Cincinnati convention, however, was to prove the high point for the Fenian Brotherhood in the United States. Through the latter half of 1865, just as its prospects seemed most promising, the movement splintered. Disagreements emerged over the control of its finances and the deployment of its resources. But at the root of the matter was a deeper division between Irish and Irish American perspectives of the future. For the founder, John O'Mahony, and his followers, Ireland was to be the principal setting for action—the liberation of the homeland was, after all, the Fenians' *raison d'être*. However, others, mostly men of longer standing in Irish America, urged a more circuitous route to address Ireland's grievances. A rival faction led by William Roberts and Thomas Sweeny challenged the Ireland-first strategy and urged instead an invasion of Canada by ten thousand armed men. Any blow struck against British interests, they maintained, was a blow struck for Ireland, no matter the setting. Amidst personal bitterness and growing enmity, rival Fenian conferences were convened, first by O'Mahony in New York in January 1866 and then by Roberts's faction in Pittsburgh in February. At odds over leadership and future strategy, grassroots support for the movement dissipated rapidly.[9]

In an attempt to salvage respectability and secure prestige, the two groups commenced separate actions against Canada in 1866. In April, against their leader's better judgment, a contingent from O'Mahony's faction launched a raid on Campobello Island in New Brunswick. Within days the armed incursion degenerated into farce. Their plans thwarted, many of the Fenian raiders gratefully took advantage of free tickets provided by the United States government and boarded trains home. The futile raid severely damaged O'Mahony's credibility and threatened to drive his disaffected supporters into the ranks of the rival faction.[10]

James Stephens visited the United States in May in an attempt to heal the rift between the warring factions and reassert his standing at the head of the transatlantic Fenian movement. However, the course of events quickly moved beyond his control.[11] On the night of 31 May, Roberts's faction launched its own northward assault, when nearly one thousand men marched from Buffalo, New York, across the border into Canada. This second incursion made more progress than its predecessor, and the invaders inflicted a number of casualties as they skirmished with squads of hastily recruited Canadian volunteers. But with few reinforcements at hand and woefully short of supplies, the Fenian army was soon forced to retreat. United States authorities, eager to put an end to their acute embarrassment at the Fenian Brotherhood's activities, detained nearly seven hundred men at the border.[12]

The abortive Fenian invasions of Canada provoked mixed reactions among native-born Americans. In general there was little sympathy for the Irish invaders, and the humiliating failure of the expeditions was widely interpreted as confirmation of Irish haplessness and mischievousness. At the same time, though, many who had supported the Union during the Civil War felt a residual antipathy to Canada and took delight in their northern neighbor's temporary discomfort. The increasingly irascible George Templeton Strong agreed the Canadians would be well justified in hanging Fenian prisoners but maintained that the "fright and worry and expense that Fenianism is inflicting on our northern neighbors are a just retribution for their treatment of us during the war. . . . A specially comforting feature of the present case," he added derisively, "is that this 'invading army' of outlaws and land-pirates appears to have been officered by ruffians formerly in the confederate service, and therefore beloved of all Canadians two years ago."[13]

When the botched Fenian incursions into Canada incurred derision, postwar Irish America responded not with regret or apology, but with defiance. Hostile press attacks, the Boston *Pilot* asserted, were motivated "not from what they know upon the subject, as from their prejudices and party opposition to the Irish-Americans as a race." According to the *Pilot,* the raids demonstrated that "from the Irish people, scattered over the four quarters of the globe, England has nothing to expect but enmity—bitter, unquenchable and undisguised—ready to be organized in array against her whenever a fair opportunity shall present itself."[14] With these words the *Pilot* expressed well the dominant tone of America's Irish in the late 1860s, replete with strong elements of persecution and defiant resolve—both characteristics found in abundance in the writings of the nationalist John Mitchel. However, the *Pilot* erred in its analysis in one important respect. It failed to recognize the partial and distinctively Irish-American hue of its perspective on Irish and Irish immigrant affairs. In its remonstrations, the *Pilot* saw Ireland and Irish issues only through the filtered glasses of post–Civil War America, wherein with increasing frequency Ireland was an allegory for local Irish American grievances. But as the former Young Irelander Thomas Darcy McGee soon pointed out, the *Pilot*'s was not the only way of comprehending Ireland, nor was Ireland useful as allegory for the experiences of all its emigrant sons and daughters. In a letter from his new home in Canada, McGee wrote to the *Pilot* declaring his delight at the greater freedoms and opportunities available to Irish Catholics in Canada compared with the United States. He protested over the immorality of the Fenians' private war against those who chose to live freely within the bounds of the British Empire and enjoy its more benign environment. "I do not look upon these men—these American Fenians—as enemies of England, for in that light they are contemptible, but as enemies of Ireland, and in this capacity they *are* formidable," he warned.[15] Many Irish immigrants in Australia would have equally shared McGee's distaste for crude and blinkered attacks on Britain and its empire.

The Fenian misadventures in North America in 1866 foreshadowed the future of the movement in Ireland. In December, James Stephens was deposed as leader of the Irish movement, replaced by a more militant Irish-American clique. Thomas J. Kelly, a former Confederate army officer now described as "acting chief executive of the Irish Republic," led the new Fenian executive that sailed from New York in January 1867 to prepare for armed insurrection in Ireland. When the much anticipated rising did commence it proved a dismal failure, and Fenian plans for action in Britain were foiled. However, though the movement's failures in 1867 far outweighed its successes, Fenianism gained worldwide notoriety in a series of dramatic events. The rescue of Colonel Kelly and a fellow Fenian from a prison van in Manchester, the trial and execution of the men who staged the rescue, and the bombing of Clerkenwell prison in London, instilled in the minds of the populations of Britain and its colonies an unprecedented fear of Irish insurgency.[16]

*

While America's Irish resumed their quest for social recognition and economic advancement, in Australia the quarter of a century after 1860 saw
much of the amity that had previously characterized relations between the
Irish and their fellow colonists diminish. In particular, controversies over
education and the course and effect of Irish nationalist politics promoted
highly visible divisions along national and religious lines, producing what
one historian accurately described as a "consolidation of sectarian subculture" in Australian life.[17] The education question came to the forefront from
the 1850s, as the inadequacies of the existing denominational system (state
funding to churches to provide schools) became more and more apparent.
Inadequate funding, poor facilities, the presence of large numbers of
untrained teachers, and low levels of pupil attendance prompted reformers
to advocate a shift from the denominational system to one that was (in their
terms) secular, compulsory, and free. As one advocate of reform boasted,
"This is with us not a question of sentiment but of political wisdom and pru-
dence. Such education as is thought amply sufficient for the working classes
in old countries, where men rarely change their social position, will not do
for Australia."[18] Commencing in South Australia, successive colonial governments moved to diminish funding to denominational schools and exert
greater state control over the provision and organization of education.

Australia's Roman Catholic hierarchy steadfastly denounced the mounting
attacks on denominational education. At their 1862 provincial council the
bishops criticized as "persecuting sectarianism" the tide toward state-controlled education. The pressure of their opposition increased through the
1860s as the character of the Roman Catholic Church in Australia was recast.
The arrival of a succession of Irish bishops, ardent supporters of Paul Cardinal Cullen, introduced a new, more abrasive edge to the church's engagement with society at large and ensured increasingly strident opposition to
public schooling. The bishops' presence fanned the sectarian embers in colonial life: as Patrick O'Farrell observed, "The new bishops were, from their
arrival, notably—and censoriously—interested in colonial politics, and dis-
posed toward the adoption of a belligerent Catholic sectarianism."[19]

In line with this more militant mood, the 1869 provincial council of the
Australian Catholic bishops reaffirmed its determination to oppose the introduction of secular education and insisted on the teaching of Roman
Catholic doctrine in Catholic-run schools. Though Protestant leaders in the
colonies were themselves far from acquiescent toward the principle of state-

funded secular education, the unwavering Roman Catholic position was quickly represented by its opponents as one of exclusiveness and intransigence—as a demonstration of that Church's overriding commitment to foreign rather than local Australian precepts. The issue came to a head most visibly in Victoria in 1872, when in a bitter election the government of the former Young Irelander, now moderate colonial Irishman, Charles Gavan Duffy, was defeated. The new Victorian government, emboldened with its success at the poll, moved to abolish state aid to denominational schools. The education controversy in Victoria foreshadowed conflicts that would occur across colonial Australia, though with varying degrees of intensity and bitterness. But the general situation was clear: the worlds of Australia's Irish Catholic and British Protestant populations were becoming more separate and insular.[20]

The bitter controversy over education coincided with increasing concerns throughout the British Empire at the course of Irish affairs. In the latter half of 1867 the Australian colonies watched with trepidation the rising tide of Fenian violence in the British Isles. It was hardly surprising, then, that the British government's announcement of a plan to send a contingent of Fenian prisoners to Western Australia aroused intense alarm. Complaints against the scheme proved ineffectual, however, and in January 1868, 62 Fenian prisoners and 217 other convicts arrived in Western Australia aboard the *Hougoumont.* The rebels' presence incited real concern, but the isolation of Australia's western colony was not the only factor that aroused disquiet. The arrival of the Fenian prisoners was given particular poignancy by the coterminous visit to Australia of Prince Alfred, the Duke of Edinburgh, the first member of the British royal family to tour the Australian colonies.[21]

The prince arrived in South Australia on 31 October 1867 and received an effusive welcome from the local population. His party subsequently moved on to Melbourne, in tone the most Irish of Australian cities in the nineteenth century. Melbourne's Irish Catholics showed a measure of defiance to the royal visit, rallying outside the city's Protestant Hall, where a provocative illumination recalling the Battle of the Boyne had been erected. Shots were fired from the hall toward the protestors, and a Catholic youth was killed. A brawl ensued and an Orangeman was arrested. Though this incident possessed no definite Fenian overtones, it provided a stark indication of sectarian tensions then on the increase throughout the Australian colonies and a chilling foretaste of the violence that would soon engulf the tour.[22]

From Victoria the prince traveled north to New South Wales where, as elsewhere in Australia, he was greeted with enthusiastic displays of affection. The *Sydney Morning Herald* attempted to explain the colonial rapture when it wrote on 21 January 1868: "There is in the colonies a large reservoir of loyalty long pent up. [The] colonies have had few opportunities to exhibit their love [and these] demonstrations in honour of Prince Alfred are its overflow."[23] Sydney's Roman Catholic newspaper, the *Freeman's Journal,* likewise wholeheartedly endorsed the royal visit and made no attempt to disguise its relief that the prince's arrival in the city had proved incident free. "So far, at all events, we may congratulate ourselves that the royal visit has been marked by no incident distressing to anybody. All things being taken into consideration our freedom from accident has been most remarkable." Its editorial comment, though, betrayed nervousness about the days ahead, an air of fearful anticipation engendered at least in part by the shadow of Fenianism.[24] It did not take long for those fears to materialize. In Sydney the prince agreed to attend a picnic to raise funds for a new sailors' home. On 11 March, while attending the event in the pleasant harbor-side suburb of Clontarf, an Irishman named Henry James O'Farrell shot Prince Alfred in the back. The would-be assassin was wrestled to the ground, arrested, and saved from the vengeful crowd.[25] But even before the culprit had been publicly identified, all attention focused on the assassin's nationality and his political motives.

As news of the assassination attempt spread, the *Freeman's Journal* feared the worst. Its weekly edition, forced to press before the gunman's identity could be confirmed, admitted "the prayer which was fervently uttered by thousands of our countrymen on their learning of the sad affair was 'Pray, God, that he is not an Irishman.'" Should the culprit indeed prove to be Irish, the newspaper avowed, "then Irishmen must bow their heads in sorrow, and confess that the greatest reproach which has ever been cast on them, the deepest shame that has ever been coupled with the name of our people, has been attached to us here in the country where we have been so free and prosperous."[26] Too late for the newspaper's editor—but soon enough for the colony's Irish Catholic population—the awful truth was known: the culprit was indeed an Irishman and a Fenian connection was strongly suspected.

Despite O'Farrell's cry at the time of the shooting—"I'm a Fenian—God Save Ireland"—most historians discount the possibility that he was truly a Fenian. He was, instead, an unbalanced young man, recently cast out from a seminary.[27] But the prospect that the perpetrator had Fenian connections, coupled with the recent arrival of the nationalist prisoners on Australian soil, incited a wave of anti-Irish, anti-Catholic hysteria the like of which had not been seen in the Australian colonies since the early convict days. Local politicians, most notably the colonial secretary, Henry Parkes, inflamed passions with allegations of conspiracy, with the result that the cloak of suspicion fell heavily upon the entire Irish Catholic population. Sleuths scoured the countryside, bounty hunters seeking payment in return for uncovering evidence of the diabolical Australian Fenian connection.[28] The colonial parliament, mortified at the attempt on the life of the monarch's son, enacted a treason felony bill. The New South Wales premier, Cork-born Sir James Martin, declared in parliament that should Fenianism be found in the colony, "it would be met with a vigour and determination which it had not encountered in the mother country." Membership of the Loyal Orange Order in the colony doubled by the end of 1868 as outraged and fearful Protestants enlisted their support in defense of queen and country. Across the land, anti-Irish bigotry and sectarian animosity escalated to levels scarcely imaginable a decade before.[29]

Irish Catholics responded to this upsurge in two ways. Most heeded the advice of the *Freeman's Journal* to "obey the law of the land and patiently wait till the good sense of the people returns."[30] Underpinning this counsel was a confident belief in the generally tolerant circumstances of colonial life and recognition of the presence of freedoms and liberties far exceeding those experienced in Ireland. Firm in those convictions, Irish Catholics cast their opponents as bigots, men and women out of touch with the true tenor of Australian life. As Melbourne's *Advocate* remarked welcoming the New Year in 1869, those who perpetuated sectarian division in the Australian colonies were "out of date and out of place. . . . The wretched days [of] idiotic nervous no-popery are now passed for ever," it asserted all too prematurely, before prophesying better times ahead for Ireland. "For the first time in history those who have an influence on English opinion seem to think that the wishes of Irishmen should count for something in the government of their native land."[31] In line with that optimism, most Irish Catholics initially eschewed open conflict with the Protestant majority.

However, a minority of Irish reacted to the taunts with a greater measure of defiance—or, at least, a show of fight. Most famously, drunken gold diggers in New South Wales, worse for wear after the excitement of the Saint Patrick's Day races, yelled at local townspeople "We're bloody Fenians! Come On! We'd soon kill a man as look at him!" Others joined in, too, if less dramatically and more ambiguously, to assert and defend their own stake in Australian society. A resident of the township of Goulburn was brought before the magistrate's court after declaring that the shooting served the prince right for "he had no business in the country." Influenced by such incidents, the New South Wales governor, Lord Belmore, reported to the parliamentary undersecretary for the colonies, "Rumors of a spirit of Fenianism [are] abroad, particularly in the country districts."[32] But concerns also existed about the likelihood of a radical nationalist presence in the towns and cities. W. A. Duncan, a prominent Scots-born member of Sydney's Roman Catholic community, spoke publicly to deny the presence of organized Fenian groups, but admitted that "there were a few hot-headed young men who could not keep quiet, . . . hot-headed youths who talked very foolishly." Where once such expressions of bravado would have attracted little notice, now they were sufficient to sound the alarm that violent Irish nationalist activity would surface in Australia and served to intensify the fires of national and sectarian animosity then burning throughout the colonies.[33]

Among Irish Protestants, reactions were similarly complex and multilayered. Geographic origin in Ireland, denominational adherence, occupation, and region of residence in the colonies were all factors that worked to mold individual reactions to deteriorating intergroup relations. Two main lines of response were available: join hand in hand with the most militant opponents of the Irish Catholic presence in the colonies and vigorously assert loyalty to the Crown, or fade as unobtrusively as possible into the colonial mainstream, neither denying Irish heritage nor overtly drawing attention to it.

Events in the neighboring colony of New Zealand added further to the Fenian commotion. In 1867 a new arrival on the South Island's west coast, John Manning, founded a newspaper, the *New Zealand Celt*. Manning's journal was provocative and uncompromising and soon found a strong following among the large number of Irish immigrants on the region's goldfields. The substantial population of single Irish men present on the west coast proved especially receptive to the *Celt*'s enthusiastic promotion of Irish national consciousness. In line with the affirmation of that new and assertive Irish identity, on 8 March 1868 the Irish in Hokitika staged a mock funeral for the Manchester martyrs. Led by a Roman Catholic priest, Father William Larkin, a funeral procession wound its way to the local cemetery where a Celtic cross was erected. This overt display by Irish gold miners caused consternation among local loyalists, and when news of the attempted assassination of Prince Alfred reached New Zealand, hostility was further aroused. Soon after, when Father Larkin made a provocative speech in which he expressed sympathy with Fenianism, local authorities reacted. Manning and five others were arrested. Rumors of Fenian activity in the west coast mining community abounded, and the colony's Anglo-Irish governor, Sir George Bowen, dispatched troops to reinforce local volunteers. All Australasia then seemed vulnerable to the tentacles of radical Irish nationalism.[34]

On both sides of the Tasman Sea, the Fenian threat was grossly inflated—in fact, as best one can tell, invented. But isolation, remoteness, and colonial fragility bred fear and paroxysm. By the late 1860s, Australia's Irish Catholic population confronted more strident opposition than had existed for decades, and all groups in society endured a more hostile sectarian environment. In 1869, with the assassination attempt of the previous year still fresh in the colonial mind, renewed attacks were made on the level of Irish immigration to Australia. In a debate in the New South Wales parliament on administrative changes to the assisted immigration program, opponents of the Irish decried the threat posed to the colony by the twin evils of Romanism and Irish pauperism. Henry Parkes, who had exploited the O'Farrell affair to inflame sectarian passions, now advocated greater restriction on Irish entry to Australia and quoted Sir Charles Wentworth Dilke's observations on the allegedly deleterious effects the Catholic Irish were having upon American life to support the case for immigration restriction. "Through drink, through gambling, and other vices of homeless, thriftless men, they are soon reduced to beggary; and moral as they are by nature, the Irish are nevertheless supplying America with that which she had never possessed before—a criminal and pauper class."[35] Though political and economic conditions in Australia and the United States were different in numerous ways, by 1870 the image of Australia's Irish was increasingly influenced by local (Australian) interpretations of the Irish experience in North America, not just by negative stereotypes of the Irish at home. And though the reaction of Australian Irish Catholics was in degree nothing so defiant or abrasive as that evinced by their American counterparts, they, too, would exhibit a decidedly sharper, brusquer exterior to their opponents through the 1870s. In November 1872 a new newspaper, the *Irishman,* was founded in Melbourne. Opposed to the maintenance of sectarian predilections and resistant to party allegiances, the newspaper ceased publication within four months. Its blandness, the insipidness of its Irishness, won no support in the more contentious times after the Fenian scare.[36]

*

As the Irish in Australia struggled to come to grips with the more volatile scene after 1868, vast numbers of their compatriots endured deprivation at the margins of American life. Patrick Ford's recently established *Irish World* newspaper captured their sense of ostracization when it declared in November 1870, "Our lot is cast among a people who hate our nationality." Ample evidence supported the *World*'s pessimistic assessment. During the previous July bitter political rioting had taken place between Roman Catholics and Orange defenders of Protestantism on the streets of New York; July 1871 would see the violence repeated, culminating in 162 civilian casualties, almost two-thirds of them among the Irish-born. Both bouts of rioting highlighted the extent to which the postfamine Irish immigrant population was proscribed from the mainstream of American life.[37]

It was not only the persistence of ethnocentrism and racism that set the Irish apart. With increasing frequency, Irish immigrants articulated concern at their continuing economic impoverishment within industrializing America. Anxiety over the immigrants' deprivation was particularly evident in Ford's newspaper, which articulated the most pointed critique of the Irish American predicament in the Gilded Age and soon became the leading voice of the Irish working class. "The misfortune of our race has been to the advantage of capitalists and the country at large," wrote Ford

GRAND TURNOUT OF THE "APES" AND "ORANG-OUTANGS,"
NEW YORK, JULY 12, 1871.

Figure 5. "Grand Turnout of the 'Apes' and 'Orang-Outangs,' New York, July 12, 1871" (*Irish World and American Industrial Liberator*, 12 August 1871).

on 27 January 1872. "While the Germans, the English and the Scotch, are working for themselves, we have been, and are yet, toiling for others. . . . Of course, here and there an Irishman holds some civic office, or shines in some of the professions, and a few acquire riches; but the immense majority of our race constitute the telling mass." In the *World*'s home city, ample evidence testifies to the extent of the Irish disadvantage. In 1858, for example, the Irish constituted fractionally over 25 percent of New York's population but 44 percent of admissions to the lunatic asylum, 65 percent of admissions to the alms house, 56 percent of prison commitments, and 72 percent of admissions to Bellevue Hospital.[38] Ford's shrewd analysis of the condition of the people and his demand for economic and social reform, which grew more passionate and coherent in subsequent years, struck a chord with thousands of America's Irish laborers that was reflected in the *World*'s high circulation at the time.[39]

Nationwide census data confirms the challenges confronting Irish immigrants. In 1870 the Irish-born comprised 4.8 percent of the total United States population. The distribution of the immigrant population in that year's census mainly confirms trends already evident two decades before. Compared to the total United States population, the Irish-born were overrepresented in New England and the mid-Atlantic states, not only in the places of first disembarkation but in the adjacent states as well. At this time, twenty-six of the fifty most populous cities in the nation were located in these two regions, and in all these urban centers the Irish presence was substantial. Irish immigrants were also present in significant numbers in a band of Midwestern states, especially Minnesota, Illinois, and Wisconsin, and nearer the West Coast in California, Nevada, and the Wyoming and Idaho territories. In contrast, the Irish continued to be underrepresented across the South and the Sun Belt states.

The 1870 census has featured prominently in historians' debates about whether the Irish in the United States ought most accurately to be classified as a rural or an urban people. Taking issue with Donald Akenson's critique of Irish American historiography, David Doyle argued that the fact that only 40 percent of the Irish-born population resided in the 30 major cities in the nation does not permit the presumption that the remainder were rural dwelling. Based on an examination of 1,090 counties in the twenty states with the largest Irish populations, he concluded that 74 percent of the Irish resided in counties that were urban or mining based, with only 26 percent of the immigrants dispersed across rural counties.[40] Notwithstanding difficulties implicit in Doyle's process of classification, his analysis of the state of affairs in 1870 is fairly persuasive. It shows that the Irish-born, more rapidly than native-born Americans, accommodated to the rise of urban society, and in doing so, his analysis challenges conventional perceptions that the Irish were actors with little agency in industrializing America.

The principal results of Doyle's survey are confirmed by an examination of the detailed data on nativity and employment gathered in the 1870 census. At the time of the census, 14.6 percent of those Irish-born in the United States in paid employment were engaged in some form of agricultural work. However, that bald figure disguises tremendous regional fluctuations. In Wisconsin, Minnesota, and Iowa, well over half of all Irish workers were engaged in agriculture, most often as farm owners but with a significant minority employed as farm laborers. In ten other states and territories, mainly in the Midwest but also including Mississippi and Arkansas in the South, more than one-quarter of the Irish workforce were agriculturalists. Not surprisingly, the number of Irish engaged in farming was markedly lower in the New England and mid-Atlantic states, and in those locations of longer-standing settlement (though not New York State) the Irish were more likely to be employed as farm laborers rather than owners of farms.[41]

In contrast, in 1870 by far the largest proportion of Irish men and women, 44.9 percent, were employed in the provision of "personal and professional services." The two leading occupations in this category were laborer and domestic servant, and in both, Irish workers were found in large numbers right across the nation. However, at a local level, diversity is once again apparent. Dakota, Arizona, New Mexico, Wyoming, and the District of Columbia recorded the highest proportions of Irish in the category of personal and professional, but in the outlying territories the high Irish representation was invariably due to their presence in local army garrisons. In New Mexico, for example, 270 out of the 347 Irish recorded as employed in providing personal and professional services were soldiers. In contrast, in the District of Columbia, four-fifths of the Irish employed in this category were laborers and domestics. A similar pattern was repeated in Maryland, New Jersey, Delaware, and Louisiana, where high proportions of Irish workers were concentrated in low-skill occupations.

The distribution of Irish immigrants who were employed in manufacturing and mining provides the least surprising aspect of this analysis. In 1870, one-fifth of the Irish-born men and women working in manufacturing or mining found employment in just five states—New York, Massachusetts, Pennsylvania, Connecticut, and New Jersey. In New England, employment in textile mills was crucial to the Irish, with the result that

in Massachusetts the Irish-born constituted a quarter of the state's mill operatives. Large numbers of Irish were similarly employed in New Hampshire
and Rhode Island. In the mid-Atlantic states the picture was more diverse.
Pennsylvania's Irish-born population was employed in large numbers in
the state's textile and steel mills but was also prominent in mining. Across
the continent, Irish immigrants were strongly concentrated in manufacturing and mining employment in Nevada and in the Idaho and Montana territories. Crucial here were the strong Irish mining communities: in Montana,
three in every five Irish workers was a miner.[42] Meanwhile, the lowest proportion of Irish workers, a mere 12.6 percent nationwide, was employed in
the census grouping of trade and transportation.

Overall, this analysis confirms that by 1870 the Irish-born were firmly
positioned as an urban people in the United States. On a nationwide basis
the Irish recorded the lowest proportion engaged in agriculture of any of the
major national groups and the highest level in the census category that
included unskilled laborers and domestic servants. Only a meager proportion of Irish were employed in manufacturing and mining, higher than that
of the native-born and Scandinavian populations to be sure, but well below
that of English, Scots, Canadian, or German immigrants. Yet despite its clar-
ity on the situation in 1870, the census data leaves unresolved key questions as to the spatial and occupational distribution of the multigenerational
Irish population in the United States as well as to the propensities of the
Irish-born to undertake rural settlement in the half century prior to 1870.[43]

Taken as a whole, the strongest impression generated by an analysis of
Irish employment patterns in the 1870 United States census is the sheer
diversity of the immigrants' engagement with the nation's economy. It was
enormous in its geographical range and wide-ranging in its local shades and
nuances, and it demonstrates the Irish presence across all grades and manners of American life. The data is suggestive, not of immigrants inherently
retarded in their capacity to cope with industrializing America, but of men
and women who were active agents, adaptive and adapting, but in intense
competition with the educational and mechanical skills possessed by their
competitors, both native-born and from elsewhere in the Old World. Eager
for betterment, Irish immigrants, like all newcomers, carved niches where
they could, marking some regions and localities with an indelible Irish presence, leaving others only lightly trammeled.

Irish Americans at this time badly required strategies to facilitate their
incorporation into mainstream American life. In accordance with similar
attempts earlier in the century, immigrants and those of Irish descent

endeavored to establish and propagate their own version of American history and through the power of their narrative to demonstrate and affirm their credentials as citizens. In the late 1860s and 1870s, immigrant newspapers and community leaders frequently reiterated the significant Irish contribution to the success of the revolution and contrasted their eighteenth-century predecessors' wholehearted support for the achievement of national independence with the position of English loyalists. They also emphasized the long-standing Irish contribution to the work of nation building, a role, they contended, that was graphically demonstrated both in the Irish preponderance within the American population and in the great capital works of the nation. Tremendous pride was invested in these measures of the Irish commitment to America, so that when J. A. Froude, despised as an English apologist by Irishmen across the world, crudely assessed the total multigenerational Irish population in the United States in 1870 at four million, the *Irish World* indignantly increased the estimate threefold. Froude's lower estimate, the *World* maintained, was nothing but another English connivance to denigrate the standing of Irish Americans.[44]

Yet however frequently made and sincerely put, assertions of loyalty and declarations of commitment to the new nation were burdened by the heavy millstone that was Ireland's failure to measure up to the American example of independent nationhood. The degree to which Ireland's position within the United Kingdom adversely affected native-born perceptions of the Irish is difficult to ascertain. Though for some Americans Ireland's plight was proof of Irish failings and fecklessness, in others it aroused a good measure of sympathy and compassion. But more significant, arguably, was the impact of the unfulfilled national aspirations on the Irish themselves. Overall, it seems likely its effect was to generate an acute degree of self-consciousness, and this proved to be a persistent tribulation that played on the collective mind of the immigrant group and hindered its capacity to engage fully with American life. Indeed, in its most extreme form, Ireland's continued political subordination was interpreted as a form of emasculation, and Irish American leaders frequently asserted that only the proud pursuit of independent nationhood could make the Irish immigrant man equal in virtue and stature to his New World neighbors. Speaking on the West Coast in 1870 the Fenian leader John Savage declared:

> I am thoroughly American in my ideas, and believe that no Irishman in America is so good a Fenian as he who is a good citizen. While the most individual of men, individually and collectively, Americans are also the most law abiding, naturally taking to discipline and organization. It is this wonderful

fact, not always acknowledged by superficial observers, which makes their far-off settlements habitable, their enterprises successes, and their progress irreversible. My appreciation of these manly characteristics fills me with the desire that the Irish would keep pace with the Americans in respect to their personal independence which gains strength from discipline and in organization, even as the states, individually independent, gain strength and dignity within the union which is the reliance and boast and defense of all."[45]

Savage's association of the collective goal of nationhood with the virtue of individual manhood was not unique. On Saint Patrick's Day the following year, the *Irish World* asserted, "On this one day in the year an Irishman is *a man*. On this one day he attains his full height. . . . He does not slink into a corner; he does not conceal himself in the shade, lest people may think he is Irish, but he goes abroad in the plenitude of his stature, and he bears himself aloft, the equal head and shoulders, of the proudest in the land."[46]

Irish American women's responses to the call of nationalism remain as yet less well understood. Hasia Diner suggested that in the postfamine period Irish women, in contrast to men, accumulated greater power and influence after immigration to the United States. Within the family, through their involvement in the paid workforce, and by means of their participation in parish and community organizations, Irish women transformed their formerly precarious standing to become the more secure and confident of immigrants. "From scattered autobiographies, from the fragmentary evidence of letter collections of Irish immigrants, one can see that Irish men endured a harder process of adjustment to life in America and demonstrated less emotional flexibility in learning to cope with their new home than did Irish women."[47] If Diner is correct, this greater adaptability may have channeled many women's energies into avenues that made active engagement in the pursuit of Irish nationalist causes less imperative than appears to have been the case for many men. Nevertheless, the existence of organizations such as the Fenian auxiliary and, later, branches of the Irish Women's Land League, indicates a persistent if less visible level of nationalist activity among Irish immigrant women.

Support for one of the numerous Irish American nationalist movements was a path by which some Irish immigrants worked toward alleviating the burden of unfulfilled aspirations and securing a niche in middle-class Anglo-America.[48] However, following this route to middle-class America placed constraints on expressions of allegiance to the old homeland. Paramount loyalty to the United States was an essential requirement for acceptance, and American sensibilities demanded the abandonment of measures that compromised their nation's interests or otherwise invited reproach. The American career of the Fenian John Boyle O'Reilly illustrates well the manner in which American conditions tempered radical proclivities and encouraged other, more palatable modes of response. O'Reilly arrived in the United States in November 1869 after his escape from penal custody in Western Australia. Welcomed enthusiastically by Irish nationalists, O'Reilly enlisted in John Savage's faction of the Fenian movement, joined the secretive Clan na Gael, and secured employment as a journalist for Patrick Donoghue's *Pilot* newspaper in Boston. When in May 1870 Fenians attempted a third invasion of Canada, O'Reilly was appointed a commander in the Fenian army and was briefly detained by American authorities. However, the invasion, which like its predecessors in 1866 was both a dismal failure and an acute embarrassment, profoundly affected O'Reilly's feelings toward radical expressions of Irish nationalism. He resigned from the Fenian movement in the wake of the debacle, writing to John Devoy in January 1871 that he now hated the name Fenianism. "Had we been called Republicans or United Irishmen or aught else we would have retained respectability—but that meanly sounding word, with its associations of defeat, dissension, and trickery has been a millstone on the neck of our nationality for years."[49] Thereafter O'Reilly, who was appointed editor of the *Pilot* in mid-1870, became a force for moderation among Boston's Irish and was acknowledged nationwide as an advocate of accommodation and conciliation. When, following the bitter New York riots of 1870–71, journals including the *Irish World* railed against the intrusion of Orangeism into American life, O'Reilly argued instead in support of the Orangemen's right to assemble and condemned the Catholic rioters. This response to the riots, and O'Reilly's concern for the plight of African Americans, typified the former Fenian's broad social policy until his death in 1890.[50] His legacy, a commitment to the creation of a less parochial and more enterprising Irish presence in America, proved enduring and foreshadowed the gradual elevation of the immigrant group's socioeconomic standing in the latter decades of the century.

O'Reilly's moderate nationalism and broad social concerns represented only one mode of engagement with American life, however. Its timidity proved unpalatable to a large number of Irish Americans. Across the country and through a range of industries, Irish workers were active trade unionists, with the Irish-born and the children of Irish immigrants fulfilling critical leadership roles in the Knights of Labor.[51] Moreover, for many immigrants during the Gilded Age, Irish nationalism also served as a pathway not into a dominant middle-class culture but into a strong, oppositional working class. To these workers, important parallels existed between the oppressive conditions of postfamine Ireland and their own plight in industrializing America. Their campaigns served not only to loosen the shackles of their own oppressive conditions but also helped narrow the gap between themselves and the native-born working class.[52] At least until the 1920s the nexus between the Irish working class and the American labor movement, as well as between the Irish and radical politics, remained a powerful one.

The diverse motivations and aspirations of Irish Americans were reflected in the rampant divisions and mediocre achievements of so many of their nationalist groups. In early 1871 two contingents of Irish activists arrived in New York, the *Cuba* Five, and another group aboard the steamship *Russia*. After an enthusiastic reception the newcomers launched the Irish Confederation, an organization designed to heal the destructive rift between the warring Fenian factions. This promise of a new beginning attracted initial euphoria in New York; however, prudent observers were skeptical. John Boyle O'Reilly wrote to the recently arrived John Devoy, describing himself as a changed man since Devoy had known him as "a careless, reckless light dragoon," and warning Devoy he would find the mood of Irish America very different outside the hothouse atmosphere of New York. He advised Devoy to settle first into America before launching a nationalist crusade: "No matter what organization you join, you have a right, a duty, to make your means of living a primary consideration. . . . Go into business as soon as you can." Irish Americans, O'Reilly explained, "held aloof heretofore because they saw dissension, and chicanery, and impulsive rather than well-considered determined action," and would need much persuasion as to the confederacy's merits.[53] But despite O'Reilly's injunctions, the newcomers persisted, and their movement soon faltered. Their aims and outlooks were in most cases inherently different from those of their Irish American members, whether middle or working class. As Kerby Miller rightly pointed out, hard-core Irish nationalists had no real interest in assimilation; their status as embittered exiles precluded attempts to settle in and conciliate with the host society. Ireland, not America, was their spiritual abode.[54] In contrast, for those of longer standing or more settled disposition, Irish American nationalism was first and foremost a vehicle for American ends, and Ireland's liberation, a desirable step in the fulfillment of broader individual and group goals. This tension, starkly evident in the failure of the Irish Confederation, would continue to disturb relations between Irish and Irish American nationalists until the onset of the Irish Civil War.

For one other group of immigrants Irish nationalism remained no effective path to assimilation—the group of new arrivals, mostly drawn from the west of Ireland, who felt no strong sense of shared communion in an Irish nation. Several microhistorical studies, notably those of Victor Walsh for Pittsburgh and Kevin Kenny for the Pennsylvania anthracite region, have emphasized the presence in the United States of newcomers from those regions least touched by the influence of anglicization. For immigrants drawn from the westernmost counties, among whom Gaelic persistence was most widespread, local identities and associations frequently remained of paramount importance. Only gradually would these older and more nuanced identities wear down; then, in the crucible of American society, Irish American nationalism might emerge as another layer of identity.[55]

*

Through the 1870s, Australia witnessed the continuing polarization of the majority Protestant population and minority Irish Catholic population. On the Protestant side, doctrinal differences were subsumed as new, politically active, pan-Protestant organizations emerged. The Protestant Political Association, formed in 1872, provided one forum for moderate Protestants to lobby against the extent of Roman Catholic influence on colonial life. Protestant social and fraternal organizations also experienced strong growth. Membership of the Loyal Orange Order, which had risen sharply in the immediate wake of the 1868 assassination attempt on the Duke of Edinburgh, continued to increase at an extraordinary rate through the 1870s. One study suggests its membership in New South Wales rose from fewer than three thousand in 1869 to as many as nineteen thousand members in 1876, while the number of affiliated lodges rose from 28 to 130 in the same period. By the late 1870s, as many as 15 percent of Protestant males over sixteen years of age were members of the organization.[56] This expansion in membership of the Orange Order was accompanied by a diminution in its Irish orientation. Gradually, inexorably, the movement expanded to become one more reflective of Australian Protestantism at large than of its specific Irish antecedents. Its impetus drew more heavily on the growing influence of evangelicalism and its associated reform campaigns such as temperance than of matters Irish. Though the movement encompassed diverse denominations and social backgrounds, its cornerstone membership in 1870 was clear enough: lower-middle-class and respectable working-class men of ambition, frustrated in their yearnings, and often insecure in disposition.

Protestant fraternity offered such men security, ritual, prestige, connections, and the hope of social mobility. Some were fortunate to secure that upward movement, too, if the gradual elevation in social status among the movement's leadership by the end of the 1870s is an accurate guide.[57]

A new level of discipline and vigor among Roman Catholics matched this increased level of mobilization within Australia's Protestant population. This was largely attributable to the arrival on Australian shores of Ireland's so-called "devotional revolution," particularly as the ranks of the Australian episcopacy swelled with relatives and protégés of Cardinal Cullen. However, the Australian scene lent a particular urgency and purpose to the introduction of that model of religious reinvigoration. In Australia, a society renowned for its apathy and indifference to religious matters, a strong institutional framework—particularly one instilled with heavy Irish practice, tone, and rhetoric—offered the best hope for the Roman Catholic Church to consolidate and strengthen its position.[58]

Historians in Australia have debated the question of which group was most responsible for the worsening climate of sectarianism that affected colonial life in the 1870s. In a detailed study of developments in New South Wales, Mark Lyons identified the attitudes and desires of Australia's Irish Catholic population as the paramount cause of worsening relations: "The real impediment to Catholic assimilation came from the Catholics themselves." On this reading of events, the greater politicization and heightened national consciousness present among Irish immigrants of the "forties' generation," in conjunction with militant Roman Catholic intransigence on matters such as religious education, terminated the amicable relations that had characterized colonial life in the preceding decades. However, Michael Hogan strenuously contested Lyons's view, arguing that Protestants bear at least equal responsibility for the deterioration in relations, and that the roots of sectarianism in Australia could in any case be identified much sooner than the 1860s. This is of course true, but neither approach establishes persuasively the specific forces that caused the flame of sectarian hatred to burn so bright in Australia at this time.[59]

Comparison with the United States provides important insights into the wider forces that influenced Australian developments and brought about signs of convergence between the experiences of Ireland's two new worlds. The greater sectarian animus in Australian life in the final quarter of the nineteenth century is resonant of the bitterness and division that was so pervasive in American life in the second quarter of the century, as the unnerving impact of the market revolution was felt. In Australia, the 1870s marked the beginning of a first wave of major manufacturing expansion. Though statistical data for the decade are limited and imprecise, two major studies point to a virtual doubling in the number of Australians employed in manufacturing between 1870 and 1880.[60] With the expansion in manufacturing employment came an increase in the proportion of the population resident in the largest urban centers. Whereas in 1871, 46 percent of the population of New South Wales was resident in urban areas, by 1881, 58 percent of the colony's population lived in the major cities or towns. Most of that increase occurred in the capital city, Sydney, where the population increased by nearly 300 percent between 1861 and 1881. In Victoria the proportion of the colonial population resident in urban areas had increased quite substantially in the 1860s, and the population of Melbourne continued to increase despite some decline in the size of smaller urban centers. Smaller Australian cities also experienced growth: Adelaide, for example, doubled in size between 1861 and 1881.[61] Together, these factors of industrial expansion and accelerating urbanization generated increasing levels of uncertainty and insecurity, conditions ripe for worsening intergroup hostility and religious and racial bigotry.

The more feverish sectarian atmosphere in Australia in the 1870s also coincided with growth in the influence of evangelical religion, a conjunction that had occurred in the United States during its earlier period of economic transformation. This point ought not to be overstated: the strength of the movement in the Australian colonies was never as powerful as in America. Nevertheless, from the appearance of the revivalist William "California" Taylor in Victoria in the mid-1860s, the arrival of overseas preachers became more common, and their messages seem to have been favorably received by the sizeable crowds who attended their meetings.[62] Among these visitors were Irishmen, including the Reverend George Grubb, whose style prompted one historian to observe that "Australian evangelism owes much both in tone and in potency to Irish Protestants."[63] In line with this development of the Protestant side of the divide, the Roman Catholic Church in Australia encouraged a similar series of visitations, a tendency best exemplified by the visit of the globe-trotting Irish missionary, Father Patrick Hennebery.[64]

Concomitant with this sea change in Australia's settlement pattern and the soundings from the first tremors of modern industrial society was renewed unrest on the land. After the introduction of universal male suffrage in the major colonies in the late 1850s, pressure had mounted on the various colonial administrations to address the vexed question of land occupation. If in mid-nineteenth-century America myth continued to extol the infinite untapped opportunities of the frontier, many immigrants in Australia viewed the situation exactly in reverse.[65] Specifically, the colonial legislatures were impelled to constrain the power and privilege of the group of landholders who held large tracts of land under a system of license and to unlock and redistribute land so that a new and prosperous yeomanry might be created. The vision of a class of small proprietors with secure tenure over the land has had deep roots and an enduring appeal in Australia and was certainly embraced by large numbers of Irish immigrants used only to uncertain tenure and exorbitant rents. It was endorsed, too, by leading Irishmen in the colonies, including Charles Gavan Duffy, who became an influential figure in the design of land reform legislation in Victoria. Indeed, it was a vision Duffy imagined had come to fruition when in 1877 he campaigned in rural regions of that colony. "All the unaccustomed toil of a long journey was repaid by the pictures I had imagined long ago realized under my eyes, the picture of happy homes possessed by a free, manly, yeoman proprietary," he told an audience in the town of Sale.[66]

Despite the initial optimism that accompanied the various land reform proposals (and in spite of significant regional variations in outcomes) most historians adjudge the schemes enacted by the colonial parliaments failures. Flaws in the legislation enabled the existing occupants to secure the most fertile and productive sections of their landholdings and to pursue, through a variety of other strategies, conduct that thwarted the aspirations of smallholders. Confronted with land of marginal quality, compelled to undertake backbreaking labor to make it viable, and faced with crippling costs to transport produce to market, the dream of free selection had by the mid-1870s faded to despair for many settlers.[67]

In 1878 the disillusionment of the free selectors, and their resentment at the oppressive power wielded by powerful landholders and the police, seized Australia-wide attention when the outlaw Kelly Gang undertook a campaign of crime in northeastern Victoria. Following the shooting of three police troopers on 26 October 1878, a massive manhunt ensued for Edward (Ned) Kelly, his brother Dan, and their accomplices Joe Byrne and Steve Hart. All four were young single men of Irish descent and came from a close-knit community where resentment toward authority ran deep. For twenty months, police sought to apprehend the Kelly Gang as it engaged in a campaign that some historians have viewed as a form of social banditry.[68] No doubt the Kelly outbreak had clear Irish overtones: indeed, to some colonial conservatives, the affair was a demonstration of Irish agrarian outrage transported to Australian soil, hideous and unwelcome.

This was taking matters too far—none of the gang had ever visited Ireland, and the principal stimulus to their criminality was their conviction of the injustice of Australian conditions. But neither should the Irish connection be downplayed. The language of Ireland's oppression permeated the rhetoric of the gang's leader. To Australian-born Kelly, Ireland was synonymous with injustice, its persecutors embodied now in the forces of authority against which his own campaign of violence was directed. And to Australians (including many Irish Australians) Kelly became a symbol of defiance, of resistance, and of pride in difficult times. Ireland's oppression was demonstrated metaphorically, too, when Kelly was tried, convicted, and sentenced to hang by a member of the Victorian establishment, the Anglo-Irish judge, Sir Redmond Barry.[69]

*

News of severe economic distress in Ireland reached the United States following the poor harvest of 1877, and the deteriorating conditions in the Irish countryside provided the impetus for renewed political activity among nationalists in America. In August 1878 Michael Davitt, recently released from Dartmoor prison, made his first trip to the United States, where in collaboration with John Devoy, he planned what was to become known as the "New Departure." In essence, the arrangement committed the secretive, nationalist movement Clan na Gael to support the Irish Parliamentary Party, led by Charles Stewart Parnell. In return, the Irish Party pursued the twin goals of an independent parliament for Ireland and peasant proprietorship of the land. This agreement, coalescing radical and moderate nationalist ambitions and means, proved an attractive one to Irish America at large. Devoy secured John Boyle O'Reilly's endorsement for the new program, while Patrick Ford's New York *Irish World* was a keen and influential supporter of the New Departure.

Parnell assumed the presidency of the Irish National Land League following its inauguration in October 1879 and soon after commenced a fundraising tour of the United States. During his visit, which included an invitation to address the House of Representatives, Irish nationalists exhibited a degree of unanimity and resolve that had seldom before been evident. Not only were tremendous sums of money subscribed to support the new political strategy, under Parnell's leadership the league attained a level of respectability that far surpassed previous nationalist endeavors. By the early 1880s, a new level of optimism and vitality seemed visible among Irish Americans.[70]

*

If the mood of Irish America was brightened by Parnell's success, by the beginning of the 1880s the tenor of life in Australia had been transformed markedly, and the colonies now offered a less secure and accommodating destination for Irish newcomers than had been the case two decades before. Sectarian animosity, fears of Irish militancy, and the presence of pervasive racial stereotypes now challenged the standing of Irish Australians. In 1881, the essayist A. M. Topp argued in the *Melbourne Review* that Ireland's population was fundamentally different from that of other regions in the British Isles. Whereas the Welsh and Scots merged naturally with the English, he believed, the Irish were irreconcilably set apart. "It is only with regard to them that the question of race becomes important. Only as to them can any doubt arise concerning the loyalty and benefit to the empire of any of the races that have acquired the English tongue and are allowed the rights and privileges conferred on its people by the institutions of the English people." To Topp, the prevalence of Roman Catholicism in Ireland was an evil and menacing by-product of Irish racial inferiority, a subordinate status that threatened to undermine the future of the whole of the empire in just the way it had been "sapping the vitals of the great republic." A crisis was fast approaching, Topp apprehended, not just for the colonies abroad but for Great Britain itself.[71]

In fact, little on the Australian scene lent credence to Topp's fears. The increasing pulse of political activity in Ireland that so alarmed Topp was much delayed and then scarcely felt in the colonies, where it seemed most Irish were intent on trying to shore up their eroding position within the social mainstream. In the 1870s Isaac Butt's campaign had attracted little attention in Australia, and awareness of, and support for, the New Departure did not reach levels at all comparable with those in the United States. Instead, the best-known Irish organizations were those engaged primarily in the provision of welfare and the arrangement of convivial social activities. The most prominent of these groups, the Hibernian Australasian Catholic Benefit Society, was active in the provision of benefits within the Roman Catholic community and annually convened a dinner and sports carnival in celebration of Saint Patrick's Day. Other groups, such as the Irish National Foresters, fulfilled similar roles. In general, the attitude of most of Australia's Irish toward the old country was "basically sentimental or nostalgic." Until the mid-1880s, organizations that did profess any more explicit political purpose were invariably small, unstable, and isolated within the broader currents of Irish Australian life.[72]

Strong Australian interest did persist in the welfare of the Irish population at times of economic distress, however. When news of harvest failure in Ireland reached the Australian colonies in December 1879, a relief appeal was quickly established. The fund-raising campaign, in which middle-class Irish Australians were to the fore, proved a remarkable success. In quick time, nearly ninety-five thousand pounds was subscribed for the Lord Mayor of Dublin's Mansion House fund. Especially striking was the breadth of support: the response was one of "warmth, generosity and spontaneity [that transcended] religious, political, national and class barriers." This was because, in Australia, the relief of hunger and distress at home was almost universally recognized as acceptable—and, indeed, appropriate—behavior for the privileged subjects of the New World colonies, fair that the bounty of their good fortune should be bestowed on those less fortunate.[73]

In the wake of the relief campaign, and as news of Irish developments slowly filtered in, signs of greater politicization gradually became apparent. A campaign to raise funds for Parnell's party was initiated, though compared to the relief effort it received only a lukewarm response. Land League branches also began to appear. But on the whole, the nationalist movement remained weak and directionless, deprived of leadership by a middle-class Irish population whose primary interest lay in local affairs and who were concerned that their involvement might prove disadvantageous on the local scene. That privilege of aloof detachment was soon to be challenged, however, with the arrival in Australia of John and William Redmond, delegates from the Irish Parliamentary Party. Their 1883 mission to Australasia, and its attendant controversy, would compel Australia's Irish to pay greater attention to political developments in the United Kingdom, force the issue of Home Rule to the forefront of Irish associational life, and strengthen diasporic ties between Irish immigrants in Australia and the United States.

6

Call of the New
Irish Worlds in the Late Nineteenth Century

IN THE PERIOD OF TWO DECADES, from 1841 to 1861, Ireland's population fell by nearly 30 percent, from 8.2 million to 5.8 million. However, to the dismay of Irish nationalists, the end of the Great Famine did not halt the decline of the population, and in the following half century the number of people residing in Ireland continued to fall. By 1911 Ireland's population was 4.4 million, about half the number present on the eve of the famine. Although the famine decade constituted the greatest concentrated exodus of Irish men and women, in fact more Irish departed their homeland in the fifty years that followed than during the decade of most acute distress.[1]

The emigration of four million Irish men and women in the period 1850–1914 occurred within the context of far-reaching economic and social change in Irish society. Within the agricultural sector, the consolidation of landholdings underpinned noteworthy (though, by wider European standards, modest) increases in farm productivity. Between 1861 and 1911 the number of small holdings of one to five acres fell by more than one-third, while those of five to fifteen acres fell by one-quarter. These changes increased the amount of land under pasture, a process encouraged by export demand for livestock and dairy produce. Irish agriculture also benefited from changes in technology and improvements in farm management. For farmers with substantial landholdings, the period after the famine was mostly one of increasing prosperity, interrupted by downturns in the 1860s and 1880s. However, the rewards of restructuring and improvements were not evenly shared. Simultaneous with the reforms of the postfamine period, the number of agricultural laborers in Ireland fell by two-thirds. To this group, the price of reform in Ireland was the excision of their own direct stake in its future.[2]

Change was also occurring in other sectors of the Irish economy. The number of people living in towns increased, promoting a greater measure of commercialization. However, in Ireland's case, the movement to town life was not accompanied by any substantial expansion of manufacturing. Except in the northeast, the postfamine decades were ones of lackluster industrial performance, especially compared to Great Britain. If Irish workers were to find industrial employment they had to look further afield, and this they did in large numbers, providing an essential labor force for the expansion of manufacturing in Great Britain and the northeastern United States.[3]

Especially conspicuous in this period was the high level of emigration among Irish women, to the point where in the late nineteenth century the rate of departure of females exceeded that of males. This characteristic distinguished Ireland's experience from patterns of emigration elsewhere in Europe. Whereas in the 1860s the ratio of female to male emigrants from Ireland was approximately 800 to 1,000, by the 1890s this had reversed to 1,150 to 1,000.[4] A variety of factors contributed to the predominance of females within the Irish emigration stream in the late nineteenth century. Reform in the rural sector and the absence of significant industrial development meant few opportunities existed for paid employment for women. In addition, the shift from partible to impartible inheritance, a rise in average age at first marriage, high rates of permanent celibacy, and the constraining atmosphere of the postfamine years all encouraged large numbers of single women to seek wider horizons elsewhere. Though the precise motives and aspirations of women who left Ireland have been the subject of considerable speculation, it is indisputable that for many Irish women emigration offered opportunities for economic independence and satisfying personal relationships that could not be realized at home.[5]

Despite the tardiness of Ireland's industrial performance, the half century after the famine was, by the numbers game at least, one of gradually rising prosperity and improving standards of living in Ireland. Yet while average incomes rose threefold between 1845 and 1914, those who continued to embark for new lives abroad determined that the economic and personal rewards to be gained by emigration exceeded those that could be obtained at home. Gradually, though, the gap between Irish living standards and those on offer elsewhere diminished. According to one recent study, Irish real wages increased from 43 to 53 percent of United States real wages by

1913, and had reached near parity with real wages in Britain by World War I.[6] Beyond this economic context, a range of less quantifiable and more personal motives for seeking life abroad also entered into emigrants' decision making. The rigorous intensity of post-1850 Irish Catholicism, frustration and loneliness caused by demographic shifts toward less frequent and later marriage, and tales of the novelties and adventures of life abroad all undoubtedly played a part in shaping Irish attitudes. Emigration was, everywhere, an inescapable fact of postfamine Irish life.

Emigration in the second half of the nineteenth century was, as before, overwhelmingly destined for America, the vast wave of departures feeding off voracious industrial expansion and a renewed demand for labor in the United States. Though the momentum ebbed in 1861–62, from then to the end of the century the annual number of emigrants destined for the United States fell below twenty thousand per year only briefly, when depression struck in 1876–78. That short-term decline was reversed in the early 1880s, when Irish emigration to America again exceeded eighty thousand per annum. A gradual tending downward occurred after this time, until the First World War caused the stream to run dry for a time.

In Australia, it was not industrial development but the discovery of gold that first promoted Irish immigration after the famine. Gold finds in the eastern colonies of New South Wales and Victoria in 1851 brought about a massive increase in the small Australian colonial population. Between 1850 and 1860 the population of the colonies almost trebled from 405,000 to 1,145,000. However, Australia's importance as a destination for the Irish peaked later, in the 1860s and 1870s, when over 10 percent of Ireland's emigrants traveled to the Australasian colonies. The newcomers came, supported by government assistance, to the encouragement of friends and relatives already there. As one historian noted recently, "Chain migration appears to have been responsible for the overwhelming gravitational pull, rather than pulsating economic cycles, or even gold rush fever."[7]

Just as late-nineteenth-century Ireland was in the midst of a period of profound transformation, so the United States and Australia, both homes to large, multigenerational Irish populations, were experiencing their own far-reaching processes of change. Industrial development and urbanization were in train in both societies, transforming landscapes, creating more volatile economic conditions, undermining old ways of life, and nurturing radical new modes of thought. For Irish immigrants and those of Irish descent, two immediate consequences arose in these New World settings. First, the rapid pace of social and economic change brought forth fervent demands in both societies that immigrants become quickly indistinguishable in outward trappings and inner ideals from the host population. Second, running counter to the call of the New World, the global power of nationalism provided the motivation and opportunity for Irish immigrants and those of Irish descent to argue more assertively in support of Irish national aspirations. As the turn of the century approached, the populations of Ireland's new worlds worked within their own particular political and ideological settings to resolve the dilemmas posed by these competing challenges.

This chapter, then, examines Irish immigrants' lives during the momentous decades of the *fin de siècle,* as the Australian colonies federated to achieve nationhood, as Americans wrestled with the fear that diversity threatened the very fabric of their nation, and as Ireland moved to the verge of self-government, only to be frustrated once more. It highlights, in particular, the ways in which the two distinctive New World settings generated different reactions toward Ireland and Irish national aspirations.

*

Through the 1880s and 1890s, the pace of change in the United States was frenetic. The nation's economy moved roller-coaster-like through periods of strong economic growth, interspersed with troughs of depression in the years 1884–86 and 1893–94. Despite its erratic path, the effervescence of the American economy was remarkable. National income rose strongly, increasing by 50 percent in the 1890s, while transport and communication networks across the nation were revolutionized. However, it was in the principal cities that the most profound changes in American life were apparent. Whereas in 1880 one-quarter of the United States population consisted of urban dwellers, by 1900 four in every ten Americans lived in urban settlements of over twenty-five hundred persons. By 1910, the three most populous cities, New York, Philadelphia, and Chicago, each exceeded one million inhabitants, and together these metropolises housed 10 percent of the nation's population. The fifty largest cities in the United States then accounted for 22 percent of the total population.[8]

Much of the dynamism and uncertainty of late-nineteenth-century and early-twentieth-century American life was born of the combined effects of this relentless urbanization and the large-scale immigration of the so-called "new" immigrants, drawn from nontraditional source countries in southern and eastern Europe. The transformation in the nation's immigration base was remarkable. The number of immigrants from Italy rose exponentially, from fifty-six thousand in the decade 1871–80 to more than two million in the decade 1901–10. Increases of a similar magnitude occurred from the Austro-Hungarian Empire and Russia. At the same time, annual arrivals from traditional source countries in northern and western Europe declined. Thus, where newcomers from Great Britain, Ireland, France, Switzerland, Scandinavia, and the Low Countries accounted for 73.6 percent of reported immigration to America between 1871 and 1880, in the first decade of the twentieth century, immigrants from these countries together constituted barely one-fifth of new arrivals. To observe this shift in the immigrant base is not to assert a total disjunction between the old immigrant streams and the new, for similarities and differences existed across the span of "old" and "new" immigrants as well as within each particular group. Yet the reorientation of the immigrant stream was undeniably of great perceptual importance in American life. It sharply refocused conceptions of what was new and different on the streets of the nation and in a short space of time rendered what was formerly remarkable now hardly conspicuous.[9]

The confluence of frenetic immigration and the rapid expansion of cities posed an array of social problems. Poverty, overcrowding, poor sanitation, and disease all sounded alarms. Indeed, to some critics, the ills seemed so severe as to threaten the very foundations of American life. As New York's *Nation* noted in 1882, "the unprecedentedly heavy stream of immigration . . . seems to alarm timid citizens with serious apprehensions as to whether this mass of humanity, consisting of people wholly unacquainted with American life, can be safely absorbed by the body politic."[10] Contemporary observers, including the photographer Jacob Riis, documented powerfully the growth of the great new urban conglomerations and the immigrants' plight within them. In doing so, they aroused fears that the mobility and opportunity so central to nineteenth-century Americans' vision of their society would soon give way to a more rigid and oppressive class structure. They made conspicuous, too, the squalid living conditions of America's urban immigrants and in doing so inadvertently brought down the wrath of nativists upon the "unworthy poor"—men and women whose plight was attributed to "race" or class failings and individual faults rather than systemic failures.[11]

The Irish were center stage in this process of urban augmentation. In the crowded cities of the eastern seaboard, they continued to be the recipients of habitual attacks. Nativists criticized them vehemently for their Roman Catholicism, their drinking, and their indigence. Though conditions proved slightly more favorable in other regional settings, across the nation anti-Irish sentiment was prone to upsurges in temper. Yet at the same time, an increasing number of signs pointed toward a significant transformation in the Irish station in American society. Widely dispersed across the socioeconomic scale (though with a persistent clustering near its lower reaches) the Irish-born, and the second and third generation of Irish descent, were a more confident, settled, and imperious force in American life than at any time since the 1820s. In the political sphere, Irish Catholic mayors were elected for the first time in New York in 1880, Boston in 1886, and Chicago in 1893, while across the nation in San Francisco the Irish continued the tradition of powerful political influence initiated by David C. Broderick in the 1850s.[12] In economic terms, too, there were grounds for optimism that the disadvantage of previous decades was gradually being eroded. By the early-twentieth century the Irish-born had nearly obtained occupational parity with native "white" Americans, the proportions of the Irish-born male workforce in middle-class, lower-middle-class, and unskilled laboring now close to those of their American-born neighbors.[13] In 1910 one-third of the United States working population was engaged in agriculture, and this group was dominated by the native-born. The Irish ranked low among nativity groups engaged in agriculture, but by virtue of their concentration in the manufacturing heartland of the nation were employed in industrial work in the same proportion as the nation's workforce as a whole. Most significant, however, was the presence of a large number of Irish males in finance, insurance, real estate, and public administration. In spite of regional variations, the Irish-born ranked strongly in such occupations, their employment profile broadly in line with the British- and Canadian-born populations. The data provides strong evidence of significant Irish men's mobility into white-collar occupations and the professions by the eve of World War I, the result a far cry from the more pessimistic future that confronted their forbears who arrived to escape the ravages of the famine sixty years earlier.[14] In contrast, Irish women continued to figure strongly in the field of domestic service, their concentration in this category mirroring the Australian pattern of the time.

This trend was replicated in the diffusion of Irish immigrants through many of the great urban centers. Analysis of the 1910 census shows that across ten major cities the Irish-born experienced only moderate levels of ethnic clustering, their position broadly on par with English, Canadian, and German immigrants. Most segregated in the early-twentieth century were the newer immigrants groups—Italians, Poles, and Jews—as well as African Americans and French Canadians. There were observable differences between cities—the Irish were less isolated in New York, Boston, or Philadelphia than in Chicago or Cleveland—but aggregate analysis of the residential patterns of the Irish-born suggests a considerable degree of integration into the American mainstream.[15]

Reflecting their improved standing, prominent Irish leaders described a marked diminution in the strength of nativist opposition and observed with pleasure the increasingly assured step of their countrymen and women. In 1897 Baltimore's James Cardinal Gibbons, a leading figure on the liberal wing of the Roman Catholic Church, noted, "In the older states the social and religious dislike that once operated to the detriment of the Irish is disappearing rapidly, owing to several important reasons, chief among which is the ease with which the Irish immigrant merges into the political and social life around him." Competence in the English language and a remarkable political adeptness, Gibbons believed, were key factors in Irish immigrants' rapid adjustment. Outside the major cities, where the accommodation of newcomers from Ireland had been a more congenial process, the situation continued to be favorable, and the Irish enjoyed "a high degree of consideration."[16] Though it is too optimistic to assert, as John Higham did, that by the early 1880s the Irish in America were "generally well regarded," evidence of the gradual elevation in the immigrant group's material and moral standing in this period is widespread and largely unequivocal.[17]

*

In the Australian colonies, too, the 1880s witnessed the continuing expansion of manufacturing and the growth in size of urban centers. By the end of that decade, one-third of Australia's population of nearly four million people lived in cities or towns of over ten thousand people. The rapid rate of urbanization was particularly striking to contemporary observers and prompted the American sociologist Adna Weber to characterize Australia as the likely model for developments elsewhere across the globe.[18] The capital of Victoria, "Marvelous" Melbourne, was then unquestionably Australia's premier city. In 1891, it was the world's twenty-second-largest city, and its population of 473,000 represented 41 percent of that colony's population. Both Melbourne, and its chief rival Sydney, then a city of 358,000 people, ranked among the ten largest cities in the British Empire.[19]

Within Australia's cities, the Irish presented a diverse portrait. Marchamp Longway, writing as the boom years came to an end in the late 1880s, believed Australia's Irish-born to be "a very numerous and a very respectable portion of the community. All the learned professions are full of them. Many are schoolmasters, rate collectors, customs house officers and not a few are well-to-do farmers and horse breeders."[20] However, the affluence and influence Longway observed, though real enough in itself, represented but a part of the Irish Australian scene. In late-nineteenth-century Melbourne, while Irish-born professionals rubbed shoulders with the colony's elite, their compatriots were simultaneously overrepresented among the ranks of the city's unskilled laborers compared to the wider pool of overseas-born. The Irish-born also constituted a disproportionate share of the inmates of colonial asylums and prisons. Their literacy level was lower too. In 1901, nearly 10 percent of the Irish-born in the state of New South Wales aged five years and over were reported to be unable to read, compared with 7 percent of the Australian-born, 4.5 percent of Germans, 3.6 percent of the English-born and less than 2 percent of Scots.[21] And while sprinklings of Irish immigrants were found residing in the affluent suburbs, other areas of Irish residential concentration attracted unsavory reputations. That pattern of solid overall Irish integration into society and a residual clustering at the lower end of the socioeconomic scale seems on the available evidence to have been characteristic of the wider Australian scene.[22]

Late-nineteenth-century Australia, therefore, closely resembled the United States in its tendencies toward dense urbanization, expansion in manufacturing, and the incidence of volatile economic conditions. It shared, too, the experience of strong Irish participation in labor activism. In the United States, with its tradition of Irish involvement in the Knights of Labor, the first decades of the twentieth century saw leadership positions within American Federation of Labor–affiliated unions disproportionately filled by the Irish-born or American-born men of Irish descent. That commitment to labor activism was matched in the Australian colonies, where class-conscious Irish workers soon established themselves as cornerstones upon which the trade union movement and the parliamentary Labor Party were built.[23]

However, a major point of contrast between Ireland's two new worlds was the relatively homogeneous composition of the colonies' immigrant streams. In the 1880s and 1890s, Australia experienced no large-scale arrival of continental European migrants comparable to the torrent that so disturbed American nativists. Only a trickle of newcomers from southern or eastern Europe then chose to undertake the long-distance voyage to the colonies, and it was not until after 1945, when Australia was faced with acute labor shortages and defense concerns, that the nation departed appreciably from its traditional reliance on newcomers from Great Britain and Ireland. As a result, there was no great surge of newcomers that, by its very presence, served to push the Irish further mainstream.

Though the diversity of Australia's immigration remained slight compared to America's, anxiety over the threats confronting Australia and its emerging national ethos was as intensely felt as in the United States. Due in large part to Australia's geographic location, animosity was directed toward the Chinese, whose presence was perceived to threaten the evolving Australian "national type" and jeopardize the core values of society. Virulent hostility toward the "Yellow Peril" that was first witnessed during the midcentury's gold rushes now revived and quickly fulfilled an analogous role to the American attacks on the new immigrants. From the mid-1880s, as the Australian colonies embarked upon the final stages of the road to federation, concern over the effects of the Chinese presence in Australia and fear of the threat posed by large-scale immigration from Asia would increasingly dominate Australian life. The Irish stood shoulder to shoulder with their fellow colonists as perpetrators of this sharp intensification of bigotry and, through their complicity in the imposition of a rigid color bar in Australian life, facilitated further their positioning as privileged white insiders.[24]

In both societies, the intense chauvinism directed at groups who were believed to threaten national cohesion culminated in demands for legislation to restrict immigration. America's nativists, alarmed at the problems posed by rampant urbanization, amended the focus of their campaign from appeals for the naturalization of newcomers to demands for outright immigration restriction.[25] At the same time, the Australian colonies and New Zealand embarked on a series of legislative measures that would drastically curtail non-white immigration. The result of that movement came in 1901, when shortly after federation, the Australian parliament passed the Immigration Restriction Act implementing a notorious dictation test based on the Natal model and heralding the creation of a "White Australia."[26]

*

In the early 1880s, concern with Irish affairs took on a wholly new momentum in the Australian colonies. In 1883 John Redmond, accompanied by his younger brother William, arrived in the colonies to commence a tour on behalf of the recently constituted Irish National League. Recently elected to the House of Commons and a man who, in Michael Davitt's assessment, "had already made his mark . . . as an eloquent and able debater" by the time of his arrival in the colonies, twenty-six-year-old John Redmond soon found it necessary to muster all his skills to defend his cause against ferocious attacks from the colonial press.[27]

After an initial meeting in Adelaide, Redmond traveled to Sydney where he arrived on 19 February to prepare to launch the mission proper. However, reports of the Adelaide meeting preceded Redmond's arrival in the city and provoked a battery of criticism.[28] An acerbic mood, made more intense by revelations relating to the murders of Lord Frederick Cavendish and his undersecretary, T. H. Burke, in Dublin's Phoenix Park the previous May, prevailed as Redmond prepared to hold his first meeting in Sydney. One member of the New South Wales Legislative Assembly urged the government to prohibit the lecture, arguing that press reports had led him to conclude that the address "would not have a good effect on our people."[29] Responding to the political furor, directors of the Masonic Hall refused to allow Redmond's lecture to be held, forcing the meeting to be hastily rescheduled to the less salubrious surroundings of the city's Academy of Music.

John Redmond attended his first Sydney engagement to find deep division within the city's Irish population. Unsurprisingly, in a colony with little track record of support for Irish nationalist movements, the visitors were regarded with great caution, especially by the middle-class Irish. Redmond's lecture attracted few of Sydney's prominent Irish laymen and no Roman Catholic bishops, and a strong note of bitterness was evident in Redmond's speech of thanks to the chair at the conclusion of the evening. "Several gentlemen who occupied representative positions in the city had without being solicited come to him and promised to be by his side that evening," he was reported to have complained, but "none of them, with the exception of one gentleman [who had] been skulking at the back all night, had attended to hear the cause of Ireland defended."[30] Despite the absence of the city's leading Irish, the response to the Redmond brothers' meeting was an enthusiastic one. It provided the impetus for the establishment of a Sydney branch of the Irish National League, and a subscription fund was opened.

During his mission, John Redmond's arguments were very much tailored to the experiences and aspirations of Australia's Irish and drew considerable support from the working-class Irish in particular. Ireland's demands were articulated in ways that were readily comprehensible in the colonial context. In print Redmond vigorously reiterated the similarities between the political aspirations of the Irish and Australian peoples and defended himself and his cause from the allegation that the league's demands were extreme. "The simple truth is that the demands of the Irish people are today the reverse of extreme. They are not only consistent with loyalty to the throne but with the constitution of the empire."[31] But arrayed against the Irish delegates was a colonial press that, in Redmond's view, exceeded even England's in its hostility to, and ignorance of, Irish affairs. The *Sydney Morning Herald* conducted a prolonged and bitter campaign against the national league's representatives, describing their rhetoric as inflammatory and out of place. Unsurprisingly, given the sectarian-charged atmosphere of the tour, the Protestant press was particularly vociferous in its opposition, the *Protestant Standard* describing the delegates' mission as an attempt to "white wash that blood-stained League."[32] In reply, John Redmond strenuously denied that he was out to inflame passions or stir up strife. Yet, at least in the initial months of the tour, his energetic protestations did little to convince his critics to temper their attacks.

After a controversial tour of rural districts, during which much hostility was encountered, the Redmond brothers returned to Sydney to participate in the city's annual Saint Patrick's Day festivities. On a day when the *Sydney Morning Herald* editorialized about the evils perpetrated by the Molly Maguires in the United States, the local Irish population, aroused by the energy of the Redmonds' mission, turned out in strength for the traditional Saint Patrick's Day revelry at Botany. In his speech John Redmond announced proudly that £1,000 had so far been raised and forwarded to Ireland and that a further £1,000 would be dispatched later that same week. He was then presented with an address from "the Irish working men of Sydney," the group who, in his own words, had "saved the situation" during the early weeks of the delegates' visit.[33] Signs of a thaw in relations with the colony's more affluent Irish came later in the evening, when the Redmonds attended Sydney's Saint Patrick's Day banquet. This event drew a formidable audience, including prominent Irish and non-Irish politicians. The speeches at the banquet highlighted the strong imperial orientation of the colony's leading Irishmen, a theme to which John Redmond's address was neatly attuned. In the colony, Redmond remarked, "nothing has brought to my heart such feelings of gratification and pride as the fact [that] Irishmen have shown to the world that under a free constitution and with equal chances they can be as industrious and law abiding, and as loyal as either their English or Scotch brothers."[34]

After extensive touring in eastern Australia, John and William Redmond traveled overland to Melbourne, site of the most pronounced sectarian strains in nineteenth-century Australia. Their first public meeting, held on 9 June in Saint Patrick's Hall in Bourke Street, bore a close resemblance to the first Sydney meeting. Prominent members of Melbourne's Irish population were noticeably absent as the National League's message was promulgated to the working-class faithful. Indeed, the nonattendance of men of means once again clearly annoyed the delegates, and William Redmond forthrightly reproached the "large number of cowardly Irishmen who hadn't the common manliness to stand by their side and adhere to the principles which they professed to hold."[35] Willie Redmond's censure did not go unanswered, however. John Gavan Duffy, son of the Young Irelander Charles Gavan Duffy and one of the few courageous enough to stand alongside the visitors, delivered a firm rebuke to the Redmonds. He could well understand Irish Australians who sympathized with the league but who felt "their first duty to the colony where they lived, together as friends with Englishmen and Scotsmen."[36]

Figure 6. J. E. Redmond, MP, 1883. P1R (BM) Mitchell Library, State Library of New South Wales.

John Redmond delivered three major addresses in Melbourne. Of these, the second, "Home Rule—its real meaning," proved most significant. Patiently, Redmond developed his case for Irish Home Rule, stressing the moderation of his objective for Ireland, "a middle course between separation on the one hand and over-centralization of government on the other. . . . Here in each one of these Australian colonies, you possess and you jealously guard the principles of Home Rule. I have asked repeatedly since I came to this country, and I ask now again, for some intelligent reason why Australians should refuse to concede Ireland that which they themselves acknowledge is the source and the cause of their own prosperity and their own loyalty."[37] Redmond's reasoning posed a dilemma for Australia's liberals, who found themselves caught between their traditional suspicion of Ireland and Irish reform and the well-grounded comparison with their own system of government. As the political landscape in Britain was transformed following William Gladstone's pronouncement of support

Figure 7. "The Redmond Brothers and the cause they are begging for" (*Protestant Standard*, 17 March 1883). ML ref. MDQ205/1, State Reference Library, State Library of New South Wales.

for Home Rule, Redmond's adroit linking of Australian political achievements and Irish aspirations for self-government would gradually shift the weight of colonial opinion behind the cause of Irish Home Rule.[38]

*

Redmond and his party eventually sailed from Australia to San Francisco. They received an effusive welcome in the Bay area, home since the gold rushes of the mid-nineteenth century to a large and confident Irish and Irish American population. The Irish delegates then traveled east, attending enthusiastic meetings in Denver, Colorado, and Columbus, Ohio, before addressing a gathering of five thousand people in Chicago. Subsequent meetings were held in Boston, where John Boyle O'Reilly took the chair, and several cities in New York State.

The tone and rhetoric of John Redmond's American meetings differed noticeably from those of his Australian tour. In Chicago, in excess of three thousand eager supporters took part in a procession led by the Hibernian Rifles and the Clan na Gael Guards. Governor John M. Hamilton welcomed the Irish visitors, affirming that "America was the home of liberty" and anticipating "some day . . . to see the sons of the Emerald Isle rise up from their chains of slavery, free men in the image of their God." Redmond skillfully avoided endorsing the idea that physical force should be used to redress Ireland's wrongs and explicitly deplored "Irish crime." However, where in Australia Redmond had consistently advocated the pursuit of a parliamentary strategy to secure the same rights as the colonies themselves enjoyed, to Chicago's Irish, then trapped in unrelenting internecine divisions, his speech was more ambiguous.[39]

Eventually, Redmond's unwillingness to endorse the use of physical force, and the timidity of his vision, alienated key segments of the Irish American population. During his interlude in New York City critical press comment appeared. The *Irish World,* which had initially welcomed the delegates' mission, now implored its readers not to invest all their energy in the Parliamentary Party's campaign. Its preference was that a parallel campaign of physical force also be pursued. "The best plan, perhaps, would be for Irishmen to utilize, in educational ways, all their moral force on themselves, and to expend their physical force on the enemy," it asserted. When news of a bomb blast in London broke shortly afterward, the *World*'s editorial left its readers in no doubt as to its preferred strategy: "England is given to understand once again that the Irish race is not yet subjugated. A state of war exists, and the war will go on. It is irrepressible."[40] Redmond left New York with a measure of middle-class backing, but having won little support from the more militant working-class Irish.

The *Irish World*'s position highlighted the stark differences then existing between the American and Australian scenes. Where in the United States the republican tradition prioritized unfettered independence as the desired form of government for Ireland, and gave limited sanction to the use of force to obtain that preferred outcome, Australia's colonial setting acknowledged neither claim. Nor did the Australian scene permit on any significant scale the presence or activities of secretive Irish organizations such as the Clan na Gael. Instead, within the more timid confines of empire, endorsement for Irish Home Rule was a bold step in itself and gathered support only gradually. To the overwhelming majority of its advocates, Irish and non-Irish, support for that campaign was conditional on Ireland's expression of nationhood being framed like Australia's would be, within the broader designs of empire and through strictly constitutional processes.

*

The momentum of the nationalist movement in Australia began inexorably to wane following the Redmond brothers' departure. As had been the case throughout the nineteenth century, the burden of distance weighed heavily on Australia's Irish, who were far from the old homeland and unable to experience events in real time. The 1883 mission had brought a rare sense of urgency and immediacy to Australian involvement in Irish affairs, and after the Irish delegates' visit slow motion replays in the colonial press could never capture the magic of the patriot game.

Ireland was not forgotten entirely, however, and through the 1880s, Saint Patrick's Day celebrations in the colonies provided key opportunities for the Irish to commemorate their ancestry in a spirit of conviviality and reflect on the progress of the Irish Party's parliamentary campaign. In Sydney, the major Irish societies—the Irish National League, the Hibernian Australasian Catholic Benefit Society, the National Foresters, and the Shamrock Club—organized the celebrations from 1884 to the mid-1890s. Local appraisals of the Irish situation did much to determine the frame of mind of the annual celebrations.[41] Initially, optimism was subdued, but in 1886, after news of the Liberals' endorsement of Home Rule became known, a mood of excitement overtook the Australian scene. Patrick Cardinal Moran, influential leader of the city's Irish Catholics, anticipated the moment when the sun would "bathe with glory the emerald gem of the western world [and] bring the consolation of gladness to the sea-divided sons of Ireland." Unionists in the colonies, in contrast, felt deep shock at the dramatic *volte-face* in London and expressed apprehension at the prospect of Home Rule for Ireland.[42]

The invigoration of Australia's Irish, and the process of converting Australia at large to the Home Rule cause, resumed in 1889 when John Dillon led a new delegation to the colonies. Dillon's Australasian tour, undertaken when the Plan of Campaign was in dire financial straits, bore striking resemblances to the Redmonds' visit six years earlier. In language similar to John Redmond's, carefully honed to allay the concerns of Australians, Dillon stressed his desire that Ireland should "stand in the same relation to the Empire as you in Australia." However, the disarming moderation of Dillon's rhetoric now won substantial support from affluent Irish Australians, so that the delegation's Melbourne meeting presented a striking contrast to the Redmond brothers' feeble reception six years before: "Our chairman was an ex-premier of Victoria—an Irishman by birth and sentiment, and bearing an honored Irish name; our platform was thronged with members of the Victorian legislature, several of whom spoke for us manfully during the evening."[43] A similar response prevailed in Sydney, where leading Irish Australians believed Home Rule now to be virtually inevitable. E. W. O'Sullivan, a New South Wales politician, was of the opinion that "the logic of their common enterprise in the Anglo-Celtic empire would lead the English and Irish of all parties to a compromise. The Irish could not in fact contract out of that compromise."[44] Irish Australians' enthusiasm for Dillon and his entourage was matched by the impressive financial dividend at the end of the tour. In all, some £33,000 was raised in Australasia, a sum without which, F. S. L. Lyons noted, "the Plan of Campaign could not have been carried on."[45]

The other significant outcome of John Dillon's tour was his direct exposure to debates about the future form of the Australian nation. The Irish delegates met with an array of public figures during the course of their mission and observed at close quarters the colonies' gradual movements toward nationhood. Lyons contended that these encounters instilled in Dillon not only firm admiration for the progress of the colonies within the framework of empire but also an appreciation of difficult hurdles still to be overcome. In fact, "the longer [Dillon] stayed in Australia the more he seems to have become aware of the wider problems of imperial organization which were awaiting solution and of which Irish Home Rule was a part."[46] His interest in Australian affairs and its solutions to constitutional quandaries was maintained in the subsequent decade as Australia approached Federation, and members of the Irish Party at Westminster took keen interest in the passage through the House of Commons of the Australian Commonwealth Bill.[47]

By the end of the 1880s, a considerable body of Australians had been swayed to the view that Home Rule was not merely desirable for Ireland but bound to happen. As the *Australian Magazine* reported: "Ireland has won the day. Home Rule of some sort is inevitable."[48] But after Dillon's departure the local nationalist movement's momentum again waned, until the O'Shea divorce case and split in the Irish Party plunged it into deep uncertainty and embarrassment. The problem was never a loss of belief in the principle that Ireland should be more like Australia—few Irish in Australia doubted that— but fear of division and public humiliation. When a new newspaper, the *Irish-Australian,* appeared in 1894, it openly proclaimed its intention to campaign "that autonomy, wide as that enjoyed in the constitutions of the Australias, shall be granted to Ireland." But the colonial Irish felt themselves helpless: "All that we in Australia can do is beseech the men of Ireland to unite. We are powerless to utter one word or do one act until that is accomplished. We cannot give our opinion in safety and must perforce remain silent."[49]

The situation remained glum and confused until Michael Davitt arrived on the Australian scene. His visit to the colonies in 1895 was for the most part enthusiastically received and went some way to steering the local campaign back on course. His message, which echoed those espoused during the earlier tours of Redmond and Dillon, continued to prove attractive to Australian ears: "What was Home Rule? Home Rule was what New South Wales, Victoria and twenty-three other colonies today enjoyed."[50] But Davitt offered no longer term solution to the persistent void in the leadership of Irish Australia: his primary interest was to observe developments in the New World rather than to agitate on Ireland's behalf. In the absence of forceful leadership, the tough economic times of the 1890s ensured most Irish Australians had pressing domestic matters to attend to.[51]

*

As Irish Australians moved tentatively toward accord on the desirability of Home Rule for Ireland, Irish nationalists in the United States were undecided whether such a measure went far enough. In the 1880s long-standing disputes continued to simmer between those willing to accept the Irish Parliamentary Party's strategy, even if only as a first step, and those unwilling to entertain Ireland's voluntary enlistment in the British Empire. While those who supported Parnell's strategy pointed to seismic shifts in the land-scape of British politics, opponents of Home Rule drew succor from concerns in the United States at this time over the extent of British imperial power and anxiety at American imperial ambitions.[52] On both sides of the divide, the failure of the first Home Rule Bill in 1886 shattered any illusions of a quick resolution to Ireland's troubles. The O'Shea divorce scandal and the acrimonious split in the Irish Party added to the woe.[53]

For a time, Irish America seemed subdued, at least on the surface. However, recent scholarship has highlighted the presence of a complex, less visible series of negotiations under way within Irish American communities and between Irish Americans and their neighbors. Timothy Meagher's exemplary study of the Irish in Worcester, Massachusetts, in particular, shows the manner in which the group passed "through a chronology of change from accommodation, to ethnic revival, to the forging of a new, broader group." Meagher demonstrates that whereas in the 1880s assimila-tory impulses were to the fore, from the late 1890s a revival of nativism, harsher economic times, and a weakening in liberalism in the American Catholic Church fostered a revival of Irish ethnic consciousness in Worcester. As in the Australian colonies, Saint Patrick's Day celebrations provided a critical occasion for the expression of group identity and for negotiating terms of engagement with the broader community.[54]

In the 1890s the nuances of the American scene proved perplexing to Irish leaders who, in the wake of the Parnellite party's split, vied to use American contacts to bolster their standing at home and raise desperately needed funds. On 7 May 1891 American supporters of the anti-Parnellite faction established the Irish National Federation of America, under the presidency of Dr. Thomas Addis Emmet. In a period of a little over two years, 150 branches of the federation were established across the nation, and large sums of money were raised in the lead-up to the second Home Rule Bill of 1893.[55] Not to be outdone, in 1892 John Redmond visited the United States for the smaller grouping of Parnellite loyalists, calling on America to be "a champion of humanity and the foe of oppression all over the world." His appeal for support won solid endorsement from the New York lawyer and congressman William Bourke Cochran, who called on the British government to share the "glorious fruits of the Victorian age" with Ireland, the one "lingering stain upon the English escutcheon."[56]

The defeat of the second Home Rule Bill and the lingering divisions within Irish parliamentary ranks cast a deep pall over the American scene. However, in spite of the gloom, Irish Americans in a raft of communities continued to work out their own local identities and accommodations, finding in Irish nationalism a critical tool for engaging with the host community and defining their individual and group relationships with the nation of which they were a part.[57] Still, at a time when ideas of nation and nationhood were so strongly to the fore, deep anxiety remained about the unresolved situation in Ireland. As was the case with their compatriots in Australia, many American Irish harbored an intense desire that unity could be quickly restored to the Irish political scene, for their own as well as for Ireland's sake.

That unity eventually arrived. On 2 August 1899 John Dillon wrote to Michael Davitt, agreeing with Davitt's assessment that John Redmond felt himself cornered. Dillon sensed the need for caution, however: "You will observe that he [Redmond] is getting up an invitation to visit Boston—and whenever he thinks of going to America his game is always to pose as an apostle of unity."[58] Redmond's visit to the United States in 1899 impressed upon him that harmony was the only way to break the shackles and garner wider American support for the Home Rule cause. Reunification was achieved early in 1900 following Redmond's return, and a campaign to rally Irish America then began in earnest. At the end of March, Redmond wrote to Cochran in New York, expressing his conviction that the Irish Party was now permanently unified behind him and declaring the need for new men and new resources to intensify the parliamentary struggle. Redmond called for the creation of a fund modeled on the Hoffman House Fund that had previously been initiated to support Parnell. Cochran responded enthusiastically and embraced Redmond's leadership and vision.[59]

The following year, a new body, the United Irish League of America (UIL), was formed in Chicago to support the unified Irish Party. Modeled on William O'Brien's Irish organization, it quickly established branches across the nation. Michael Davitt visited the United States and found the situation promising, cabling Redmond that he found the Clan na Gael "less hostile than I expected." Encouraged by the goodwill of the UIL and other New York supporters, Davitt urged Redmond to announce publicly his intention to visit the United States the following year.[60] The stage set, in 1902 John Redmond, together with John Dillon and Davitt, landed in Boston at the start of a major tour to promote the recently inaugurated UIL of America and reignite Irish American enthusiasm for the parliamentary campaign. In Boston, Redmond spoke out stridently against British policy, declaring, "All the power and wealth of England are at this moment being used cruelly and remorselessly to crush the Irish peasantry, to break the spirit of the people." Tied to this severe rhetoric, Redmond identified the UIL as the lineal successor of the Land League. "Its members are the same, to some extent its leaders are the same. Its policy is the same, and the UIL is being run today on exactly the same lines, on the same policies that were adopted when Charles Stewart Parnell made the Irish movement feared and respected by every political party in England."[61] The strategy of identifying the movement's leadership with the Land League proved highly successful in the short term. Indeed, in New York it led to public meetings of almost evangelical fervor, with the tremendous sum of $10,000 being subscribed on one evening alone. However, while Ireland remained a potent issue, generational changes and the fluctuating rhythms of turn-of-the-century life made Irish America a more unpredictable phenomenon than before.

*

As turn-of-the-century Irish American communities negotiated the terms of their engagement with the host society, their compatriots in Australia were simultaneously mediating their own relationships. And as in America, the precise terms of interaction varied from city to city, town to town, and village to village, reflecting the particular composition and tone of Irish communities and the neighborhoods in which they lived. Such a process was already underway in Sydney, where in a surprisingly sympathetic editorial after the 1894 Saint Patrick's Day celebrations the *Herald* observed that the festivities no longer had the ambience of days gone by: "The procession may be long, and the picnickers many, and the exuberance as ready as of old, but there is a change."[62] According to the newspaper, the declining proportion of the Irish-born in the community was principally to blame for the alteration: it was inevitable that the feast day would be transformed from its former glories, as a more homogeneous population prevailed and "Australian nationality" came to the fore.

Though the city's *Freeman's Journal* vigorously defended the celebration from the attack of its foe, even it was forced to admit all was not well. The traditional demonstration at Botany had been disrupted by the squabbles of drunken youths; foul language had deterred families; and a bout of stone throwing outside a nearby hotel provoked a policeman to draw his pistol. Nor was the traditional evening concert at the Masonic Hall as well attended as in previous years. Fund-raising efforts by the Irish associations met with little success. In total, a mere £250 was subscribed for evicted tenants in Ireland, barely half the sum collected in the optimistic days at the beginning of the 1890s. The celebration was, indeed, "on the verge of collapse."[63]

Figure 8. "St. Patrick's Day at Botany" (*Illustrated Sydney News*, 14 April 1883). ML ref. NA 108, State Reference Library, State Library of New South Wales.

The following year saw little improvement. Proposals to shift the location of the celebrations from the traditional fields at Botany to a more staid environment and to use funds raised to commence construction of an Irish hall in Sydney rather than remit them to Ireland were rejected. Some criticized the "disgraceful" conduct of the nationalist movement in Ireland and their deep disillusionment with its influence on the local scene. The Irish societies did agree to a request from Patrick Cardinal Moran to attend High Mass at Saint Mary's Cathedral, but no such show of unity could disguise the deep divisions that prevailed among the city's Irish population.[64]

In 1896 Cardinal Moran intervened directly to reform the ailing event. The city's Catholic leader asserted control over the day's festivities, displacing the lay Roman Catholic societies and Irish nationalist groups that had previously planned the celebration. Moran's intervention was motivated by two principal concerns: a desire to emphasize the religious character of the feast and a wish to unify and represent positively Irish Australians in their engagement with the society at large. These aims, in fact, constituted Moran's broader vision for the Australian Irish: "Our citizens all united in harmony and concord, emulating one another in friendly rivalry in eagerness to promote the common good—who can doubt that a grand future must await such a land."[65] Moran's intervention drew forth a measure of criticism from Sydney's non-Catholic Irish, concerned that the greater religious emphasis turned the day from a truly national celebration to one owned and controlled by only one of Ireland's traditions. As a correspondent complained to the *Freeman's Journal*, it "will tend to estrange from the cause many who are as loyal sons of Ireland as the most unsophisticated peasant from the green hillsides of Tipperary."[66] However, Moran would brook no interference with his plans to transform the tenor of the 1896 celebrations.

In 1896 the revamped celebrations commenced with High Mass, followed by an athletics carnival held at the city's Association Grounds. A formal luncheon, attended by the colony's governor, the city's lord mayor, and an impressive array of political dignitaries ensued. With obvious pride, Cardinal Moran welcomed his guests, declaring he "regarded patriotism as second only to religion. . . . There were no more enthusiastic children of Australia than the sons of Saint Patrick." That emphasis on the "Australianness" of the celebration was recognized and applauded, even by Irish Australia's most venerable critics. The *Herald* praised the inclusiveness of the day's activities, writing that "with yesterday a new order of things was inaugurated: there was no procession, no flaunting of national predilections or prejudices."[67] Twelve years after arriving on Australian shores with the declaration that he was an "Australian among Australians," Moran's redefinition of the Saint Patrick's Day celebration moved to reconsolidate the Irish position in the mainstream of community life.

Apart from a measure of discord in 1897, when Saint Patrick's Day coincided with Cardinal Moran's politically charged decision to contest the election for a position as a delegate to the Federal Convention, the pattern of celebrations in the years leading up to Federation was much the same as for 1896. The principal theme of the celebrations was the central place of the Irish within Australian life. The colonies' dignitaries attended, loyal toasts were drunk, and patriotic speeches were delivered. Funds raised went to support worthy local projects, including the construction of an orphanage. In 1900 a public holiday was declared in New South Wales and special recognition was devoted to the courageous efforts of the empire's Irish soldiers in the war against the Boers. In the wake of the triumphant celebration, the *Catholic Press* rejoiced that "the Irish people have now won, by force of character, their true position in the country."[68]

However, the Irish attainment of their "true position" was not achieved by any one event. It was a gradual process, visible across the turn-of-the-century period, and required regular reinforcement and renewal. The centenary celebration of the United Irishmen's 1798 rebellion provided the most momentous demonstration of the Irish place in Australian life. Against the wishes of Cardinal Moran, Australia's Irish undertook to erect a monument to the rising at Sydney's Waverley cemetery and planned the reburial there of Michael Dwyer, the most renowned of Irish Australian heroes. A phenomenal crowd, estimated at over one hundred thousand people, turned out for the procession from Saint Mary's Cathedral to Waverley in May 1898. Before the eyes of their neighbors, Australia's Irish "affirmed themselves, who they were, and from whence they had come."[69]

*

The task of winning their "true position" also preoccupied many Irish men and women in the United States at the turn of the century, especially those on the make. Not surprisingly, immigrant groups of long standing wished to differentiate themselves from more recent arrivals (and each other) by establishing their credentials as venerable contributors to the nation's development. In May 1889 a convention was held in Columbia, Tennessee, at which the Scotch-Irish Society of America was inaugurated. An organization comprised principally of Ulster Protestants and American-born men of Scotch-Irish descent, the society's function was to affirm the independent identity of the Scotch-Irish "race" and make better known the group's contribution to America's history. Through a series of congresses, the organizers stimulated research on the Scotch-Irish and publicized the achievements of pioneering settlers. However, though the society generated enthusiasm in its early years, by 1901 it was moribund nearly everywhere except Pennsylvania.[70]

Another organization, the American-Irish Historical Society, inaugurated in Boston on 20 January 1897, proved more enduring. Like the Scotch-Irish society, its charter was to affirm publicly the important Irish contribution to the nation's history. "Believing that the part taken in the settlement, foundation, and up-building of these United States has never received proper recognition from historians, and inspired by love for the republic, a pride in our blood and forefathers, and a desire for historic truth, this society has met and organized. Its mission is to give a plain recital of facts, to correct errors, to supply omissions, to allay passions, to shame prejudice, and to labor for right and truth."[71] The society soon numbered four thousand members, among whom the best known was President Theodore Roosevelt. From its foundation until the First World War, the society undertook an active campaign to promote awareness of the roles of Irish pioneers and nation builders. This lent the society's journal a particular bent: as one writer noted, "The patriotic prestige associated with the revolutionary era made it inevitable that three-quarters of the articles and nearly all of the monographs brought out under its auspices dealt with the colonial or early national periods."[72]

The American-Irish Historical Society's deep interest in the revolutionary and early colonial periods was far from unique. In the late nineteenth century, America's native-born demonstrated newfound concern with the nation's heritage, while numerous immigrant groups invoked the tradition of the founding fathers to shore up their own credentials and legitimize nationalist movements in the old country. As Matthew Frye Jacobson observed, "Appeals to George Washington and the national icons of revolution became a staple of immigrant dissent, invoked under the double influence of defensive 'good' Americanism and the anxious desire that the nation remain true to its origins as a colony-in-revolt."[73] In accordance with this movement, Irish politicians consolidated their standing among Irish Americans through their recognition and veneration of the Irish role as American nation builders and by appealing for like American assistance to liberate the nation at home. In August 1904, John Redmond addressed a rally reported to be in excess of twenty-five thousand people at Philadelphia's Washington Park, shortly after he had visited Independence Hall. "There I saw the portraits of Irishmen who helped to liberate America from the yolk, but when the day shall come to erect a temple of liberty on Irish soil there will be places for the portraits of no fewer Americans who helped our cause."[74] Yet while such rhetoric touched a deeply felt desire for recognition and affirmation, especially among America's Irish middle class, not all who listened were so fervent in their embrace of Redmond's rhetoric and the Home Rule agenda. The recently reunified Clan na Gael, though anti-imperialist and prorevolutionary, wanted nothing to do with the Irish Party's parliamentary strategy, whatever the oratory.[75]

*

Australia's Irish maintained their support for Home Rule following the inauguration of the Commonwealth in 1901. An Australian wing of the United Irish League had been established in 1900, and Irish politicians toured the new nation in 1901, 1904, 1906, 1910, and 1912.[76] All but a few Irish Australians viewed the question of Ireland's future through the framework of empire, and most believed Australia's influence could be brought to bear to hasten British recognition of the justice of Ireland's claims. Consequently, following in the footsteps of the Canadian Parliament, resolutions supporting Home Rule were brought forward for debate in the Australian Federal Parliament. Most arguments in favor of the resolution stressed that Home Rule would strengthen and perpetuate the empire, though the implications of the Home Rule question for Australia's future relationship with the United States were also considered. One speaker believed relations between the two New World nations could only progress once the justice of Irish claims was acknowledged: "It would be easier to gain the friendship of savages than win that country over, so long as we refuse to do justice to the land which gave birth to about 20,000,000 [*sic*] of its foremost citizens." Though a minority of members criticized the resolution as an inappropriate transgression on the domain of the British Parliament, and others engaged in more bitter attacks on the Irish, the Australian House of Representatives and Senate eventually passed timidly worded addresses to the king requesting the granting of a "just measure of Home Rule" to the people of Ireland. The passage of the motions—affirmed thirty-three votes to twenty-one in the lower house and sixteen votes to eleven in the senate—

bestowed a sense of importance on the local scene, but proved of little wider importance.[77]

The optimistic belief in the inevitability of Home Rule was maintained in subsequent years. Orangemen in Australia fought a strenuous rear guard action against the measure, bolstered by news of resistance in Ulster. In 1912 the Reverend H. K. Mack warned Australians that "the Protestantism of Great Britain, and with that the integrity of the Empire," were under siege as continual concessions were made to the demands of the Irish Parliamentary Party. However, such arguments did nothing to unsettle the widely held public expectation that the long campaign to assure Ireland's standing among the nations of the empire was nearing its fulfillment.[78]

*

When the Irish Parliamentary Party emerged from the January 1910 election holding the balance of power, Home Rule for Ireland seemed nearer fulfillment than ever before. The delicately poised political situation in the United States at this time also presented Irish Americans with a high degree of political leverage to pressure the British government for immediate action. With a close race for the presidency expected in 1912, leading political figures energetically courted the Irish vote. President William Howard Taft attended the 1910 Saint Patrick's Day celebration of Chicago's Irish Fellowship Club, while Woodrow Wilson, campaigning the same year in the New Jersey gubernatorial race, declared that Home Rule was "now supported by the opinion of the world." Other distinguished Americans also expressed support, and former President Roosevelt met with leaders of the Irish Party during a visit to London. Influential press opinion in America also moved to endorse Irish demands for self-government and pressed the British government to act expeditiously to achieve that end.[79]

Notwithstanding the wide consensus of support for Home Rule in the United States, the legislative process in the British Parliament was painfully slow. When the Asquith government's Home Rule Bill was finally introduced into the House of Commons in April 1912, John Redmond cabled Bourke Cochran in New York seeking the speedy endorsement of prominent Irish Americans. This was given without hesitation. Fifteen leading Irishmen cabled their "hearty congratulations" to Redmond on the Irish party's "marvelous success." Behind the scenes, however, satisfaction with the measures contained in the bill was less clear-cut, and Cochran astutely avoided entering into any public discussion that might open old wounds.[80]

Much of the residual optimism then waned as the bill's passage slowed, as the fierce resistance of Unionists became apparent, and finally, as the prospect that Irish nationalists might be willing to accept partition of Ireland became known. Even previously fervent supporters, including Cochran, now expressed serious doubts about the course of events. In April 1914 John Redmond wrote to allay those fears, stating that Cochran had an exaggerated view of the difficulties confronting Home Rule and predicting that within weeks it would be achieved, never to be repealed.[81] Redmond's optimism, of course, proved woefully misplaced. Unionist intransigence did not diminish, and the Guns of August soon intervened and curtailed any immediate prospect of Home Rule. Those guns also signaled troubled times ahead for both Ireland's new worlds.

7 Casting Off Ties
1914 to the Irish Civil War

THROUGHOUT THE COURSE OF THE nineteenth century, North America and Australia were profoundly affected by the large-scale immigration of Irish men and women. However, on the eve of World War I, the great torrent of nineteenth-century emigration had slowed. The returns of the registrar general, though deeply and systematically flawed, indicate that in the period 1901–10 the level of decennial emigration from Ireland fell below half a million for only the second time since 1840. According to those figures, the United States continued to be the preferred destination for the new century's Irish emigrants—86 percent of those who left between 1901 and 1910 journeyed to America. In contrast, Australia now attracted few Irish-born, with only 2 percent of emigrants in this decade choosing to settle in Australasia. As the number of Irish emigrants declined from the highs of the mid-nineteenth century, so the proportion of Irish-born in the populations of the United States and Australia also fell. By 1910, less than 1.5 percent of the United States population was of Irish birth; in Australia in 1911 only 3 percent of the nation's population were Irish-born men or women.[1] But although the influence of the Irish-born was diminished, there remained in both societies large numbers of native-born men and women of Irish descent, New World citizens who retained strong bonds of affection for Ireland and maintained a keen level of interest in its affairs.

That concern with Irish affairs reached new levels of intensity in the United States and Australia between 1914 and 1921. When on 25 May 1914 the Home Rule Bill finally passed through the House of Commons for the third time, Ireland's protracted quest for Home Rule seemed on the verge of fulfillment. But the outbreak of war put that measure into abeyance, until Easter 1916 reoriented the course of Irish aspirations. From the Easter Rising until the signing of the Anglo-Irish Treaty, Irish immigrants and their descendants in both New World societies observed Ireland's moves toward self-rule with keen anticipation. They publicly asserted the need for an immediate and just resolution to Irish grievances and sought to obtain the support of their own governments for the attainment of that goal. However, this vocal support for Ireland was not without its own cost. In both the United States and Australia, the war years saw the position of the Irish become increasingly precarious as both nations turned inward with hostility toward immigrants, dissenters, and all who were perceived to threaten national cohesion. Mired in a period of heightened national chauvinism, subjected to assimilatory pressures, and increasingly confused about the course of events in Ireland, most Irish in both societies gradually moved to distance themselves from Ireland's affairs. Indeed, by the end of 1921, as Ireland itself split on the future, all but a few Irish in both societies turned away, confused, angry, and embarrassed, now eager to cast off ties with home and pursue their own lives abroad.

This chapter compares the main currents of Irish life in the United States and Australia in the period from the outbreak of the Great War until the onset of the civil war in Ireland. It demonstrates the persistence through the first two decades of the twentieth century of the long-standing and defining determinants of the immigrants' lives in their respective societies, the motifs of republicanism and empire. However, the pervasive pressure of settler nationalism in both societies during the first two decades of the twentieth century, in conjunction with the declining Irish-born component in each society, radically reconfigured the immigrants' orientation away from involvement in Irish affairs, so that by the end of this period the long-standing and intimate ties between Irish immigrants and their homeland were all but severed.

*

When Great Britain declared war on Germany on 4 August 1914 no one seriously doubted that Australia would go to war. Though the separate self-governing colonies had federated to form the new Australian Commonwealth on 1 January 1901, the political affirmation of nationhood had not erased Australia's bonds of colonial dependence. At the outbreak of war Australia's foreign policy and defense strategy remained firmly tied to the whims and ambitions of Britain, while the new nation's education system inculcated in young Australians a deep-seated belief in the glory and righteousness of the empire. Ties of kinship with the "Mother Country" and a racial ideology that proclaimed the superiority of "British stock" over all others further underpinned the continuing connections between Australia and the imperial center.[2]

The declaration of war coincided with the campaign for a national election. Politicians of all persuasions vied with each other to declare most wholeheartedly their support for king and empire.[3] The Australian press, impressed with the gravity of the European crisis, fully supported the British declaration of war and enthusiastically endorsed Australia's participation. "What remains for us at this end of the world," the *Sydney Morning Herald* declared, "is to possess our souls in patience, while making the necessary contributions of time, means and men to carry on the great war upon which so much depends." But more than that, as the *Herald* emphasized, the war was to be the first real test of Australia's own fortitude and worthiness for nationhood. "It is our baptism of fire [and it] will test our manhood and womanhood by an immediate local pressure," the newspaper maintained. This sentiment was echoed in Melbourne's *Age,* which believed Australians were to "undergo the first serious test to which our national spirit has been subjected."[4]

In line with these sentiments, Irish Australian leaders spoke and acted enthusiastically in support of Australia's response to the crisis in Europe. The call to arms was answered, with the families of Australia's leading Home Rule supporters amongst the first to have sons enlist.[5] At a meeting hastily convened by the mayor of Melbourne, John Gavan Duffy told the audience that Irish nationalists must cast aside their old grievances. "Justice was being done to them at the present time, and they were ready, eager, and willing to stand shoulder to shoulder, knee by knee, fighting the great battle of the empire to which they belonged."[6] The most influential leaders of Australia's Irish population, the Roman Catholic clergy, likewise supported the national commitment to war. The Archbishop of Sydney, Waterford-born Michael Kelly, quickly declared the war to be a just one and claimed it "would be blessed by God." His Melbourne counterpart, Thomas Carr, a native of Galway, was more circumspect but urged his congregation to "join heartily [in] defense of the mother country." The major Catholic newspapers, too, lent support to the decision to go to war, arguing that as loyal Australians the Irish and their descendants must step forward to defend the interests of their new homeland. Thus, the initial Irish response broadly mirrored that of the Australian community in general, though the rhetoric of the Roman Catholic

Church was invariably less strident than that of more excitable Protestant denominations.[7]

The stocks of the Irish in Australia were boosted by the early decision of John Redmond, leader of the Irish Parliamentary Party, to pledge support for the British war effort. Redmond's stand appeared as yet a further vindication of the argument put fervently in the past by moderate Australian-based nationalists that the granting of Home Rule to Ireland would in fact prove beneficial to England and the empire, as well as to Ireland itself. The major Catholic newspapers noted with satisfaction the enlistment of so many of Ireland's sons for battle and took pleasure in reporting their achievements in the field to an appreciative Australian audience.

By the end of 1914, over fifty thousand men had enlisted for service in the Australian Imperial Force. Many were motivated by a desire for adventure, others by a sense of duty to defend their nation's interest, others still went to war for a range of more personal reasons. Studies of enlistment in Australia demonstrate that the British-born were slightly more likely than their colonial-born counterparts to volunteer for service, though not by a very wide margin. Figures for the enlistment of the Irish-born are not available, but some indication of Irish Australian attitudes to the war may be gauged from the rate at which Roman Catholics—overwhelmingly the Irish and their descendants—joined up. Overall, Roman Catholics comprised 19 percent of the First Australian Imperial Force, a figure only slightly lower than their proportion in the total Australian population, recorded in 1911 at 22 percent. This shortfall is at best indicative of only a low level of Irish antipathy to the war, and the lesser level of Catholic enlistment is partly explicable on other grounds, including the somewhat greater concentration of the Irish in working-class employment.[8]

In late 1914 Australian troops departed for Egypt for training; on 25 April 1915 they went ashore at Gallipoli to engage in battle for the first time. The campaign in the Aegean, designed to open the Dardanelles Strait and force Turkey out of the war, proved to be a futile one. Ill conceived and poorly planned, the empire's troops were thwarted in their objectives by courageous Turkish defense. In December, in a concession of failure, the troops were withdrawn for rest and reinforcement prior to being posted to the bloody stalemate on the Western Front. Though a failure, the Gallipoli operation was to prove of momentous significance to Australia. Around that military campaign, the first trial of Australian troops in battle, was built the legend of the ANZAC (Australian and New Zealand Army Corps) and of the heroic Australian fighting man.

*

In March 1915, one month before Australian troops first went ashore at Gallipoli, the Irish population in that most Irish of western American towns, Butte, Montana, turned out in force to celebrate Saint Patrick's Day. The previous year, before the outbreak of the European war, Butte's celebration had featured a parade including the local branches of the Ancient Order of Hibernians, the Robert Emmet Literary Association, and the Irish Volunteers, the militia armed and in uniform. In 1915, amidst fears that the parade might be curtailed, the Volunteers gave up their rifles and the procession took a different route to the year before, marching right through the German quarter of town. Irish marchers were joined by German and Austrian townsfolk, prompting one Butte newspaper to remark, "For the first time in the history of the world, perhaps, the flags of three nations were flown on Saint Patrick's Day."[9] The contrast in attitudes to the European war between Butte's Irish population and Irish Australia could not have been starker.

At the outbreak of World War I the standing of John Redmond and the Irish Parliamentary Party (IPP) among the American Irish seemed secure. With Home Rule imminent, Redmond's demand for representation on the provisional committee of the Irish Volunteers accepted, and a successful campaign underway in the United States to raise funds for the IPP, moderate Home Rulers were in the ascendancy. Radical nationalists in the United States were on the defensive—to them, all news seemed bad news. The veteran Clan na Gael leader John Devoy declared in a letter chastising Bulmer Hobson, general secretary and quartermaster of the Irish Volunteers, that the provisional committee's decision to admit IPP representatives had "supplied [Redmond] with a club to hit us here. . . . This places us and you on utterly divergent lines of action and makes difficulties that would not otherwise exist," Devoy protested, before summarily terminating Hobson's tenure as Irish correspondent for the *Gaelic American*.[10]

However, John Redmond's response to the outbreak of war soon dramatically recast the American scene. Although most nationalists tolerated his initial pronouncements, the suspension of Home Rule and Redmond's increasing identification with the British side soon caused rupture. Following the speech at Woodenbridge, County Wicklow, on 20 September, in which Redmond declared that Irish Volunteers should serve not only in the immediate defense of Ireland but also "wherever the firing line extends," New York's *Irish World* repudiated its earlier support. Through October, the newspaper's pages were dominated by vitriolic attacks on Redmond (the "recruiting sergeant of the British Army"), Dublin's *Freeman's Journal,* and the IPP. In an editorial on 3 October, the *Irish World* railed against Redmond, invoking the powerful rhetoric of exile and noting the remarkable decline of Ireland's population through the second half of the nineteenth century, a drain of the nation's lifeblood it attributed directly to British policy: "The vicious economic system, backed up by all the power of the British Empire, in defense of which the youth of our race are now asked to shed their blood, rendered it impossible for thousands of Irishmen and Irishwomen to earn a decent livelihood in the land they loved with all the ardor of their Celtic souls."[11] Now, it emphasized, was not the time to support England in its attempt to "strengthen and expand her empire."[12]

Through the latter months of 1914, correspondents writing to the *Irish World* were vociferous in their denunciation of Redmond and his willingness to commit the Irish Volunteers abroad. Several themes emerged repeatedly in their letters: the fear that war would further depopulate Ireland so that a future self-governing Ireland would be left only "for cattle and sheep when the young men of Ireland are slaughtered," the firm resolve that England's past policies of oppression now deserved no succor from Ireland, the belief that German victory would hasten the achievement of Irish independence, and the distinctively homegrown opinion that, as Irish Americans and German Americans had no substantive differences, Ireland itself should not commit itself to one particular side.[13] Irish women featured prominently among those who voiced opposition to Redmond's stance, and several correspondents to the *Irish World* emphasized what they saw as women's particular responsibility to oppose the Irish Party's position. One writer in Brooklyn, New York, wrote that she opposed war at any time, "but I hope and pray England will suffer as Ireland did under British rule. . . . I, being a woman, can't take a man's part and fight for old Ireland, but I will never forget to tell what I have read of Ireland's sufferings." One other wrote, "if we Irishwomen sit and weep, while parliamentary leaders cajole and tempt our countrymen to leave their own shores unprotected and go to fight for our enemy, the robber empire, then we shall have to share in the great crime and guilt and shall deserve the punishment we will suffer for it."[14] While the battlefields of Europe might be the preserve of misguided Irish men, Irish women in the United States were determined to nurture and preserve the memory of Ireland's bitter past.

Gradually, Irish American leaders and their organizations moved to distance themselves from the IPP's unpopular pro-British position and to demand neutrality. James K. McGuire, former mayor of Syracuse and president of the John E. Redmond branch of the United Irish League in that city, resigned in haste, informing members: "I acknowledge the great services of John Redmond, but I cannot follow him as a recruiting sergeant for the British Army." The presidents of branches of the Ancient Order of Hibernians in Germantown, Pennsylvania, Utica, New York, and North Easton, Massachusetts, also publicly condemned recruitment for England's war, while the national president of the Hibernians, Joseph McLaughlin, wrote that "national safety does not require the surrender of nationality, and the attempt to annex the patriotism of Ireland to the chariot wheels of Empire will meet with the reprobation of all real Nationalist Irishmen."[15] For the IPP, the loss of support in America was both a moral and a serious financial blow. By 1915, the situation had deteriorated so remarkably that the pro-IPP United Irish League in America was dependent on Irish rather than American funds to continue its operations.[16]

*

In a letter to the *Irish World* published at the height of the vitriolic denunciation of the Irish Party, Hugh McGovern of New York expressed a sentiment shared by many of his compatriots in the United States: "I say that Irishmen who take the field with the allies in this war are traitors to their country." One other correspondent wrote, "No man or set of men can be British loyalists and Irish nationalists at the same time."[17] To many Irish Americans, it was inconceivable that an Irish man could entertain the notion of service in the British army in the war against Germany and still remain a patriot.

However, this was only one perspective, which privileged one emigrant version of Irish nationalism—the American—over the aspirations and deeply held beliefs of many thousands of Irish men and women at home and abroad. For there were Irish-born in Australia, as elsewhere through the British Empire, whose nationalist ideals in no way precluded service in the war. Their desire for accommodation with the empire and feeling of pride at Ireland's achievements in it, was incongruous in Irish America. On rare occasions Irish Americans attempted to come to grips with the imperial connection that circumscribed reaction to the war in Canada, New Zealand, and Australia, but invariably those attempts were masked by scarcely concealed suspicion as to the depth of British beneficence and disbelief that settlers of Irish descent could in the longer term draw satisfaction from life within the empire.[18] Yet whatever disbelief their outlook might engender among Irish Americans, in Australia only a tiny minority of Irish men or women felt inclined to rebel; while in Ireland itself, moderate nationalists rationally viewed Australia and Canada as virtuous models for future Home Rule.

*

The diminished standing of John Redmond and the IPP gave radical Irish nationalism in the United States new impetus and rekindled the hopes of its most fervent supporters that Ireland would soon be freed from imperial rule. The Clan na Gael, which had at the commencement of the war seemed moribund, was now possessed of new will and resolve, revitalized as many Irish Americans turned away from the discredited constitutional agenda.[19] With levels of enthusiasm raised, the republican movement utilized a vigorous publishing offensive to rally Irish opinion and counter the strong British influence on elite American opinion. Books and pamphlets critical of Britain's imperial policies and its influence upon American affairs enjoyed wide circulation. By January 1916, the weight of the campaign for public opinion was so strong that the British ambassador in Washington, D.C., Sir Cecil Spring-Rice, noted a "most active propaganda is going on and all the enemies of England have been marshaled against us."[20]

Despite Spring-Rice's concern, influential opinion in the United States remained firmly wedded to the British side. However, visible divisions within America over the European war, and mounting evidence of the persistence of Old World nationalisms in American life, gave weight to escalating anxieties over national cohesion and identity. Prompted first by the extensive and diverse immigration of the turn-of-the-century era, Americans now increasingly questioned the commitment of newcomers to the values of their republic. In the years preceding the declaration of war in Europe, demands had been advanced by nativist groups not only for the introduction of immigration restriction but also for the initiation of a campaign of "Americanization."[21] Part of this drive for cohesion included a strong public campaign against "hyphenism"—a charge directed at some Irish Americans by President Woodrow Wilson when he unveiled a statue of the Irishman John Barry in Washington, D.C., in May 1914. "Some Americans need hyphens in their names, because only part of them has come over; but when the whole man has come over, heart and thought and all, the hyphen drops of its own weight out of his name. This man was not an Irish-American; he was an Irishman who became an American."[22]

Subsequent events, including the increasingly frequent contacts between militant Irish nationalists and German agents in the United States, fuelled official concerns about where the primary loyalty of Irish Americans lay. Through 1915, revelations of the activities of German operatives in America, including the sabotage of shipping, the purchase of a munitions plant, and attempts to disrupt labor relations, cast a lengthening shadow over the activities of the most militant Irish nationalist groups. By the end of the year, Wilson's restrained chiding of hyphenism had turned into a full-force assault. In an address to Congress, he denounced the presence of those "who have poured the poison of disloyalty into the very arteries of our national life [and] sought to bring the authority and good name of our government into contempt."[23]

*

Where American neutrality provided considerable scope for German-born and Irish-born immigrants to debate the legitimacy of Britain's wartime ambitions and press the case for nonintervention, few similar opportunities existed in Australia. For not only were Australia's Irish more in sympathy with the empire's war effort than their American compatriots, but in any case the domestic situation precluded such open defiance. During the course of the war, the government introduced repressive measures in order to curb internal dissent. Germans and those of German descent were viewed with particular odium. Many had their employment terminated, some were interned, and German place names in Australia were erased from maps, replaced with new ones deemed more in consonance with Australia's imperial ties.[24] However, the net of repression was cast rather more widely, and socialists and Irish agitators also felt the heavy heel of state intervention during the years 1914–18. Censorship was a feature of national life during the war, when customs regulations prohibited the importation of numerous overseas newspapers and journals, including New York's *Irish World,* on the grounds that such publications were likely to incite sedition.[25]

Despite the proimperial fervor of the early war years and the force of state restriction, a thin, radical edge did exist within Irish Australia. On 21 July 1915 the Irish National Association (INA) was established in Sydney to champion the attainment of Irish independence outside the imperial framework and to promote and preserve Irish Gaelic culture in Australia. Branches were established in the other major eastern seaboard cities, Melbourne and Brisbane, with a combined membership in the low thousands. A women's auxiliary branch of the league was also established in Sydney in 1919, though it withered in the aftershocks of the Anglo-Irish agreement. Though by Australian Irish standards the INA boasted a respectable number of members, like preceding nineteenth-century Irish organizations it depended strongly on the drive and commitment of a small group of enthusiasts. The Sydney branch prospered due to the particular passion of its first secretary, Albert Thomas Dryer. Born in Sydney in 1888, Dryer's mother was an immigrant from County Clare and his father of German descent, though Dryer himself had never visited Ireland. According to Dryer's own account, in 1914 he purchased and read Mrs. Alice Stopford Green's book *Irish Nationality*, and this work sparked a fire of commitment that was to burn throughout his life, even in the face of very great personal adversity.[26]

Given that the cause of Irish nationalism in Australia was then almost uniformly understood within the narrow spectrum of Home Rule within empire, the INA and its supporters trod a rocky road. When in August 1916 the association issued a handbill at a Gaelic athletics carnival requesting donations to a fund "for the relief of those who so gallantly fought freedom's fight in Ireland," the government censor threatened prosecution. But while Albert Dryer and his cadre of INA supporters agitated, most Irish Australians took pride in the achievement of Australian and Irish troops abroad and used their example to press the case for the speedy implementation of Home Rule. In the Australian context, this was an acceptable formulation for Ireland's future and articulated a demand that enjoyed a considerable degree of popular support. Australians in general seemed well able to acknowledge that Ireland had a legitimate claim to a place within the empire, a place similar to Australia's own. However, that concession, won in the face of antagonism over preceding decades, was soon to be recontested. For many Australians, the events of Easter week in Ireland, 1916, rendered the accommodations of the previous years null and void.

Initial reaction in Australia was highly critical of the rising. In the largest cities, the major newspapers expressed condemnation, a sentiment that penetrated further across provincial Australia. In the eastern industrial city of Newcastle, for example, the major newspaper stated, "The outbreak in Ireland is unworthy even of the name of rebellion. The men who are taking part in the armed riots cannot be said to represent either of the great Irish parties who have sunk their differences for the moment with the splendid intention of fighting for the empire."[27] In chorus with general Australian attitudes, Irish Australian leaders and organizations hastily condemned events in Dublin and vigorously affirmed their loyalty to Australia, the empire, Home Rule, the IPP, and John Redmond. None, bar a tiny cell of extremists, entertained any thought of support for an Irish Republic that, according to Patrick Pearse's proclamation, professed to be allied with Germany. The United Irish League in Victoria cabled Redmond: "The Irish in Victoria view with abhorrence the outbreak at Dublin of futile and meaningless rebellion, and sympathize with the Irish National Party in its cruel struggles against the criminal efforts of an insignificant minority." Similar sentiments were expressed up and down the eastern seaboard. Even in far away Perth, Western Australia, once the billet of the Fenian exiles, the Celtic Club wrote succinctly to Redmond: "Irishmen of Western Australia regret the Dublin affair. They have confidence in you. Reply and enlighten us."[28]

The Catholic Church hierarchy and Catholic newspapers were similarly condemnatory. Sydney's Archbishop Kelly described the Easter Rising as an event of "ranking, misconceived patriotism," while Melbourne's Bishop Carr believed it must be "the result of German intrigue, or support from some Irish Americans, of hostility to the Irish Nationalist Parliamentary Party." Even Bishop Daniel Mannix, the most overtly nationalist of the Australian hierarchy, described the rising as "truly deplorable," though coupled this criticism with a firm rebuke for "Carsonite influences" within the British government. But in wartime Australia, this more ambiguous response was contentious and brought forward robust criticism. A correspondent to Melbourne's *Argus* believed it equally "deplorable" that the bishop could at this time "deliberately strive to stir up bitter feeling against the British Government."[29]

Middle-class Irish Australians moved quickly to isolate the few who espoused more radical opinions. On 29 April 1916, in an early response to events in Ireland, the Melbourne Irishman Dr. N. M. O'Donnell was reported as saying that "there was a nest of Sinn Féin men in that city, whose interests were in common with the Sinn Féin society in Ireland." The "Sinn Féiners," O'Donnell revealed, had "disassociated themselves from any activities of the Irish bodies and refused to march in the Saint Patrick's Day procession on the grounds that the processionists stopped outside Parliament House and sang 'God Save the King.'"[30] The group comprised, in the main, newly arrived immigrants: "They are what may be described as 'new chum' Irishmen, who have recently come to these shores inculcated with the violent views of the organization at home." But, acknowledged Melbourne's *Argus,* "this ideal does not in any way appeal to the huge majority of Irish nationalists in Australia, who are convinced that England and Ireland are economically interdependent."[31]

News of British reprisals against those involved in the Easter Rising caused deep surprise in Australia. A sense of injustice soon infused not only the Irish press, but many mainstream newspapers as well. Sydney's radical *Bulletin* asserted, "no shuffling or side stepping can alter the fact that the recent fighting in Dublin was primarily caused by Edward Carson and the House of Lords." It believed that while in law the executions might be just, they were "impolitic" and went "a long way to emphasize the blindness of English governments to the real nature of Ireland's quarrel."[32] However, it was the Catholic Church and Catholic newspapers that most vociferously attacked the executions, drawing parallels between the British government's response to this act of defiance and its limp reaction to Orange intransigence in 1914. According to Sydney's *Freeman's Journal*, "Whilst few could sympathize with the misguided individuals who so insanely precipitated a senseless and bloody conflict, the Irish and their descendants the world over cannot easily forget the extraordinary tenderness which the English government displayed toward the Carsonites when they were arming and drilling with open threats of insurrection on their lips." Archbishop James Duhig of Brisbane best captured the sentiments of the Australian hierarchy when he stated that the executions would "exasperate the great mass of loyal Irishmen all over the world. . . . The rebellion in Ireland might soon be forgotten," he told a luncheon of the Hibernian Australasian Catholic Benefit Society, "but the executions had created a set of martyrs who were sure to find many to cherish their memories and recall their names long after the statesmen of our day were gone and forgotten."[33]

*

First reactions to the Dublin rising proved broadly similar in the United States. The mainstream American press quickly expressed consternation at events in Dublin. According to one historian, "The American papers regarded the Rising as foolish and misguided (and largely inspired by the Germans and the contemptible Irish-American revolutionaries safe in the United States), and they hoped that, in view of the conspicuous loyalty of the majority in Ireland, the British government would heed the lessons of South Africa and deal with both Ireland and the rebels in a lenient and generous manner."[34] The wish for magnanimity was denied by the executions in the wake of the revolt. The American press reacted with disdain to British policy, while several resolutions were debated in Congress that condemned the executions and demanded that the secretary of state pursue inquiries as to the condition of American citizens involved in the rising. Even elite American opinion was angry and ostracized: the former president, Theodore

Roosevelt, wrote to Hamilton Lee, parliamentary secretary to Lloyd George, "I wish your people had not shot the leaders of the Irish rebels after they surrendered."[35]

Most Irish Americans, surprised by the events in Dublin, were confused and uncertain. Constitutional nationalists in Chicago affirmed their loyalty to the allies, while in New York a meeting of the United Irish League denounced the rising and expressed "its unqualified sorrow and amazement at the unpardonable wrong now being perpetrated against the whole people of Ireland by the present insane attempt at insurrection."[36] However, those Irish Americans who had abandoned Redmond over his support for Irish military service abroad were untroubled. New York's *Irish World,* which had been intensifying its attack on Redmond's leadership through the first four months of 1916, excitedly gave sketchy details, recalling in its pages the events of 1798 and 1803. It castigated Redmond and "his mercenary parliamentary colleagues" who, it argued, were "traitors to Ireland" and "morally responsible for the murder . . . of young Irishmen who have gone to their graves to take the king's shilling."[37]

The Irish Insurgents Acting on the Principle Which Won American Independence

Figure 9. "Irish Insurgents Acting on the Principle Which Won American Independence" (*Irish World and American Industrial Liberator,* 6 May 1916).

News of the executions changed everything, permanently. In Boston, the *Pilot* now enjoined the Irish in service on the battlefields of Europe and the martyrs of Dublin as patriots: "Ypres and Gallipoli are Irish names now, like Fontenoy. The eight who died the other day lifted up on eight crosses before the eyes of the world tried a different way, that was all."[38] All men and women of the Irish diaspora, it believed, would rally behind the martyrs: "Every son, grandson and great grandson of an Irishman whether he has continued to labor in peace in his own land; or from Canada, Australia, and even Ireland itself who took up arms for the allies had in his heart the stirring hope that directly or indirectly he was doing something for Ireland and would in the final analysis be behind the rebellion."[39] Though in the aftermath of the rising the *Pilot* still regarded the venture as an ill-conceived one, the matter had moved on, dealing a crushing blow to the IPP cause in the United States. By early August, there was no way back: "The fact is again demonstrated that England will never do justice to Ireland unless forced to do so by internal or external perils. . . . It would seem that the Dublin patriots saw things more clearly than the wiseacres," conceded the *Pilot*.[40] It was indeed the case, as one correspondent wrote grimly to John Redmond, that his life's work had been "destroyed" by the British retribution in the aftermath of the rising.[41]

Through the second half of 1916 and into 1917, Irish American hostility to Britain became more virulent. Hannah Sheehy-Skeffington visited the United States from December, venturing to Irish communities as distant as Butte to lecture on English repression in Ireland. Her tour presented tremendous opportunities to publicize the republican cause, and these were skillfully utilized. In January 1917 she presented President Woodrow Wilson with a petition and "had an interesting chat," pressing upon him Ireland's claim "as a small nation governed without consent."[42] A new organization, the Friends of Irish Freedom, backed by the Clan na Gael, garnered wide and influential support in Irish America and raised substantial sums to assist the families of those executed. Public meetings, lectures, and the circulation of numerous pamphlets across the United States further galvanized the immigrant community in support of Ireland's struggle and against Britain and its allies. The general feeling was summed up in February 1917 at a meeting of twelve hundred Irish in New York, which resolved that "fighting for the allies would be fighting for the combined subjection of Ireland, India and Egypt to British rule [and] would be a war against America and against Germany." By April the British ambassador, Sir Cecil Spring-Rice, spelled out the truth for London: "The fact that the Irish question is still unsettled is continually quoted against us, as a proof that it is not wholly true that the fight is one for the sanctity of engagements or the independence of small nations."[43]

But the fortunes of war soon overtook Irish America. In February 1917 Germany commenced unrestricted submarine warfare, and on 12 February an American ship, the *Lyman Law,* was torpedoed. In subsequent weeks, American citizens traveling on ships under different flags were also killed. As the death toll mounted, Irish America felt an increasing sense of foreboding. Isolationists and those who wished to preserve American neutrality tried desperately to wrest the initiative. However, events were moving beyond Irish America's reach. In mid-March, several more American steamers were sunk, and pressure mounted on President Wilson to act. Finally, on 2 April, he sought congressional approval for war against Germany, acknowledging the loyalty of most German Americans but warning all potential opponents: "If there is disloyalty, it will be dealt with a firm hand of stern repression."[44]

Though the war had loomed large on the American horizon, some Irish American nationalists appeared thunderstruck by the nation's declaration of war. On 7 April the *Irish World* commented aggressively, "We are now witnessing the culmination of a conspiracy that dates back to the closing decade of the nineteenth century. If we are today in a state of war it is largely due to that conspiracy." Also at fault, it believed, was international capitalism, a force pushing the world toward a "servile state." Yet this response, hopelessly unsustainable in America at war, soon gave way to a more measured reaction. Within a week of President Wilson's appearance before Congress, a meeting of prominent Irish American citizens at New York's Carnegie Hall celebrated the first anniversary of the declaration of the Irish republic. Those in attendance endorsed the text of a letter to be sent to the president that "unreservedly" pledged support for the nation's war effort but expressed the hope that "in pursuance of your noble declaration for justice to small nationalities you will raise your voice—powerful as the voice of America—in demand for justice to Ireland." This theme recurred in the *Irish World*'s next editorial page, too, where the war was now frankly acknowledged to be the result of German provocation and the commitment made that "to America and to America alone is our allegiance due."[45]

Though an uneasy calm settled, the situation of Irish Americans remained a difficult one. At its extremes the group faced intimidation and repression, while even the nonpolitical labored under a burden of suspicion. Such was the United States government's concern that the postmaster general, Albert Sydney Burlenson, prohibited the distribution of a speech by Thomas

Jefferson that called for the establishment of an Irish republic.[46] The issue of conscription added further to the weight of that burden. In April 1918 Prime Minister David Lloyd George introduced into the House of Commons a bill enabling conscription for war service in Ireland, a measure vigorously resisted in Ireland and opposed by many Irish in America. Yet many more Americans found the Irish antipathy to conscription incongruous now that the United States was at war and conscription in effect. Many questioned the loyalty and commitment of the Irish, and viewed Irish opposition to conscription in global terms. The *Christian Science Monitor,* for example, claimed that Cardinal Logue in Ireland, Cardinal Bégin in Canada, and Archbishop Mannix in Australia were partners in a worldwide stratagem to frustrate the allied war effort. Not surprisingly, the writer Charles McCarthy detected at this time a growing sense of antagonism reminiscent of times past: "I find there is a great anger in America against the Irish, and many old class prejudices being aroused."[47]

*

As in the United States, the events of 1916 injected poison into Australian domestic life, a situation worsened by bitter conflict over the issue of conscription. In January 1916 the prime minister, William Morris Hughes, traveled to London for wartime consultations. Hughes, born in London of Welsh parents, was feted in Britain and became convinced of the need for Australia to increase its contribution to the war effort.[48] Organizations for and against the conscription of Australian troops for overseas service were formed, dividing Australian from Australian. The proconscription Universal Service League, which in New South Wales included among its vice presidents the Anglican and Roman Catholic archbishops of Sydney, comprised academics, business leaders, and politicians. Most trade unions rallied against conscription. Amidst growing speculation, on 30 August 1916 Hughes announced that his government would seek the approval of the Australian people for the introduction of conscription. After a rancorous campaign the proposal was defeated at the ballot box by a narrow margin, following which the Labor government split. However, recruitments within Australia continued to fall through late 1916 and early 1917. In November 1917, following the United States entry into the war and the introduction of conscription in Canada and New Zealand, Hughes again determined to put a conscription proposal to the vote. At a plebiscite on 20 December the government's revised proposition was again defeated, this time by a wider margin.[49]

In the acrimonious arguments that surrounded both conscription plebiscites, the issue of Irish nationalism was an ever-present and emotive one. This was mainly due to the prominent anticonscription stance adopted by Daniel Mannix, coadjutor bishop in Melbourne at the time of the first vote and, following the death of Thomas Carr in May 1917, the new archbishop. Mannix was outspoken in his criticism of conscription: he believed that Australia had done "more than her full share" in the war; he categorized the struggle as "a sordid trade war"; and he described Prime Minister Hughes as "the little tsar."[50] Mannix's opponents saw his pronouncements as evidence of gross disloyalty to Australia and a sign of his preference of Ireland's republican ambitions over Australia's imperial interests. As a result, the cause of Irish nationalism was again cast as suspect, and the standing of many Irish Australians was tarnished. Sinn Féin was targeted in proconscription pamphlets as being an implacable enemy of Australia and the empire, along with the Industrial Workers of the World and, on occasion, the English suffragettes. The Reverend T. E. Ruth, a fierce opponent of Mannix's, published numerous pamphlets—including *Mannixisms, The priest in politics,* and *Dr. Mannix as political commander in chief of a sordid trade war*—all bitter, all inflaming a sense of anti-Irish feeling.[51]

However, despite the strenuous attacks of critics, neither Irish nationalism nor the dictates of Roman Catholic clergymen were primary factors in the defeat of the conscription plebiscites. By 1917 a strong nexus existed between the class, ethnic identity, and religion of many Irish in Australia, and such opposition to conscription as existed among the Irish-born and those of Irish descent was at least as heavily founded upon Australian-centered considerations as any determination to express overt support for the cause of Ireland.[52] Yet this is not to say that Ireland was unimportant in the conscription furor, because patently it was—as Patrick O'Farrell put it, "In Irish Australia Ireland had become a convenient allegory, the medium through which local points were made, the public language of inner feeling, a way of working home things out."[53] Even in the midst of the bitterness, though, a surprising ambivalence surrounded the whole Irish question in Australia. Though national and sectarian rancor was much inflamed, Irish Australians still lived side by side with their fellow Australians, and most seem to have conceded the injustice of Ireland's situation and the need for the matter to finally be resolved. In March 1917, the Australian Senate passed by twenty-nine votes to two a motion to present an address to the king expressing the hope that "a just measure of Home Rule may be granted (immediately) to the people of Ireland." It was indeed possible to separate the broader dilemmas of the Irish question from the tensions and overtones of the domestic conscription controversy.[54]

Yet Ireland was not finished as an issue of fear and division in wartime Australia. On 17 June 1918 seven members of Sydney's Irish National Association were detained under powers of the War Precautions Act and charged with various offences related to their association with Sinn Féin and advocacy of an independent Ireland. Speaking after the arrests, the acting prime minister, Mr. William Alexander Watt, said that although the objects of the INA were "quite consistent with loyalty and the employment of constitutional principles and methods, sinister attempts have been made by the republican extremists to pervert these objects." Government concerns about the activities of the Irish National Association in Australia were well founded—better founded, in fact, than was revealed at the time. Evidence subsequently confirmed that Albert Dryer, the secretary, and other members of the organization had connections with the Irish Republican Brotherhood in the United States and staged small-scale military training camps

Figure 10. The Irish internees in Darlinghurst Jail, Sydney, 1918–19. National Library of Australia.

west of Sydney in anticipation of fighting in Ireland itself. However, these military activities were not disclosed at a subsequent inquiry. That investigation found "no evidence that any of the interned men had any connection with any enemy persons in the Commonwealth [though] such of the internees as were members of the Irish Republican Brotherhood had by virtue of that membership hostile associations through German agencies in America. . . . In Australia they made use of the Irish National Association to further their aims, but it is not shown that the rank and file of the association had any knowledge of their connection with Germany." The signing of the armistice in November diminished the government's anxiety, though, and all the prisoners were released on 19 December 1918 except Dryer, who was detained until the following February.[55]

*

As the First World War drew to a close, Irish America prepared to reap the harvest of American intervention. Expectations weighed heavily that the postwar peace settlement would provide the forum in which independence would at last be secured, in line with President Wilson's commitments. Given the strength of these hopes, alternative proposals for the settlement of Ireland's future received short shrift. John Dillon's suggestion in the House of Commons in July 1918 that President Wilson himself be appointed arbitrator of the Irish question was summarily rejected by the *Irish World,* which believed "the honor and existence of a nation" were not negotiable. "She is prepared to present her claims before the coming peace congress [but] this is quite different from submitting to arbitration the vital question of Irish nationality."[56] The armistice saw expectations raised to an even higher plane. Prime Minister Lloyd George's declaration that Ireland must receive "the measure of self-government for which we are ostensibly fighting for other countries" appeared to confirm the legitimacy of those expectations.

The failure of the Versailles conference to fulfill Irish aspirations for self-determination has been well documented. After the armistice Irish Americans lobbied the Wilson administration vigorously to support Ireland's cause, its appeals strengthened by a congressional resolution in March 1919 in support of Irish self-determination. Momentum was maintained by convocation of the Third Irish Race Convention in Philadelphia in February, which brought together the Clan na Gael, republicans, and former Home Rule moderates to demand that the postwar peace conference address the Irish question and raise funds for the recently convened Dáil Éireann.

Representatives of the convention successfully secured an audience with the president and met with him in New York on 3 March. However, the interview proved disastrous: so dogmatic were the Irish spokesmen that Wilson later confided to a member of his staff that he had been inclined to tell them to "go to hell."[57]

The Irish Race Convention also appointed a group of three delegates, the American Commission on Irish Independence, to travel to Paris for the peace talks. Their objectives were to secure the presence of an Irish delegation at the talks and to reiterate demands for Irish self-determination. After initial meetings in Paris, including an audience with President Wilson, the delegation traveled to Ireland. Though evidence points to the British government's acquiescence on the understanding that the delegates' tour would be a low-key one, the mission to Ireland proved anything but sedate. The commissioners toured extensively, widely canvassed republican—though not unionist—opinion, and addressed the assembled Dáil Éireann. But reports of their strident message of support for the Irish republic caused outrage in Britain and provided the pretext, if not the ultimate grounds, for the British government to withdraw support for the mission. The controversy deeply embarrassed and alienated President Wilson, who told his long-serving secretary, the Irish American Joseph Tumulty, "I have tried to help in the Irish matter but the extraordinary indiscretion of the American delegation over here has almost completely blocked everything." However, this interpretation of the commissioners' activities was far from universally shared: the *Irish World* saw the delegation's mission as successful in having "stripped the Wilson administration of the cloak of hypocrisy in which it was enwrapped when it proclaimed its ardent solicitude for oppressed small nations."[58]

Though Irish America had high hopes for the Paris conference, events in Ireland had taken a course and momentum of their own. The general election of December 1918, which saw Sinn Féin win seventy-three seats in the House of Commons to the Irish Party's six, recast the Irish scene. While constitutional nationalists in Ireland and abroad struggled to come to terms with the momentous rebuff, the more militant strands of Irish American opinion delighted in the defeat of their foes. Their sense of euphoria was enhanced by the arrival in New York on 11 June 1919 of Eamon de Valera, president of the Dáil Éireann, who sought during his visit to America to gain recognition for the newly established republic and to secure Irish American funding to sustain the new revolutionary government. After his first public appearance in New York on 23 June, de Valera traveled widely to garner support, venturing as far as San Francisco, where on 18 July he addressed a crowd of twelve thousand. Despite the attacks of nativist critics, de Valera's visit to the United States in the latter half of 1919 initially did much to unite Irish American opinion and build support for his government.[59]

On 12 September the British government declared the Dáil Éireann illegal. Incited by newspaper banners proclaiming "England Makes War on the Irish Republic," Irish America rallied to defend the new parliament. A hastily convened mass meeting at the Lexington Avenue Opera House in New York City demanded the immediate recognition of the Irish Republic and a suspension of all United States loans to Britain pending its withdrawal from Ireland. For a time, outrage provided the mortar that held together the disparate segments of Irish America. However, by mid-1920, substantial cracks were appearing in that edifice. Bitter divisions, not only of personality but also over control, marked the latter months of de Valera's American tour. The revolutionary Harry Boland, in America with de Valera, wrote in May 1920, "I feel more and more convinced that Irishmen in Ireland must themselves win this fight, as the leaders in America have not and in the very nature of things cannot have the same viewpoint and spirit of the men at home."[60] De Valera returned to Ireland in December 1920 having attracted great publicity in the United States but without having won recognition for his republic. The Irish leader was only too well aware of the divisions left in his wake and is reported to have admitted, "If I were President of the United States myself, I could not, and would not recognize Ireland as a republic."[61]

Despite the divisions, Irish American anger at British policy remained caustic. Vitriolic denunciations of British activities in Ireland were published in pamphlets and books, and fund-raising occurred ever apace. In September 1920, at the behest of de Valera supporter William Maloney, a new strategy was invoked. A committee of 100 (later 150) was established to conduct investigations into conditions in Ireland. The group boasted an impressive lineup of federal and state politicians from both the Democratic and Republican parties as well as bishops of several denominations. Importantly, the committee's membership did not include any of the major Irish American activists, an omission that suited the intent of the organizers but offended leading figures in nationalist circles. The report, published in March 1921 and widely circulated in the United States and abroad, presented a stark though one-sided indictment of British policy. Defenders of Britain rose quickly in its defense: in Australia, the Loyalist League of Victoria dismissed the American report as "a farrago of falsehood and folly."[62]

*

In Australia, hopes in the aftermath of war had also been high. "It is not worth while to speculate whether the Irish Republic will come to pass this year or next," wrote the Sydney *Bulletin* optimistically, for the "outstanding fact is that events are shaping to make it inevitable." However, not all Irish in Australia thought so resolutely in terms of a republican solution. The same day, the *Catholic Press* reported the Archbishop of Sydney, Michael Kelly, urging that Ireland recognize what was within reach, "what was lawful and practicable."[63] "The world cannot do without England," Kelly told a Saint Patrick's Day audience, adding that "Catholic properties have had better protection from the Union Jack than either the Italian Flag or the Stars and Stripes." Here was Irish Australia sounding its voices, its multiple voices; but these were, with the exception of Archbishop Daniel Mannix, confused, distant, weak voices, without discernible influence on the wider world stage.

To rally enthusiasm, an Irish Race Convention was convened in Melbourne in November 1919, modeled on Philadelphia's gathering earlier that year. Orchestrated by Mannix, Irish Australia's most effective leader, the assembly affirmed the influence of the hierarchy on Australian Irish affairs and bestowed Mannix's favor upon de Valera's leadership.[64] The controversial archbishop maintained his high profile in subsequent months too. A spectacular Saint Patrick's Day parade was staged in Melbourne in 1920 at which fourteen winners of the Victoria Cross, the highest military honor available to Australian troops, escorted Mannix. Then in May, he left Australia for Europe on a tour that would further inflame hostility. On 8 August Mannix was seized by British authorities from the steamer *Baltic* and prevented from landing in Ireland; he was also prohibited from addressing audiences in Liverpool and Manchester. While Australian Catholics rallied to the defense of their bishop and took offence at the denial of his freedom of movement, others questioned his allegiance to Australia and demanded that an oath of allegiance be administered before he be permitted to set foot on Australian shores again.[65]

Mannix's overseas tour also provided an opportunity to sound out Irish American opinion. He visited the United States, met de Valera, and was left in no doubt as to the strength of America's commitment to the Irish Republic. "Short of going to war, America will do almost anything to help Ireland in her claim for self-determination," he told one interviewer upon his return to Australia—a puzzling analysis indeed given Irish Americans' disillusionment with the attitude of their government in postwar negotiations. "Outside a small section affected by British propaganda—and British propaganda is very active in the States—America is wholeheartedly behind Ireland," he continued, seemingly oblivious to the Wilson administration's lack of interest as well as the widening divisions within Irish America itself. And yet this was his judgment, one produced by a narrow, insular sampling of American attitudes and caressed to rally Australia's Irish and boost their confidence for the trials ahead.[66]

As the War of Independence escalated, the position of Australia's Irish became more and more difficult. The conflict posed a crisis of loyalty that overshadowed such pressing matters as the impending partition of Ireland. In an urgent debate on the death of the lord mayor of Cork in the federal House of Representatives in November 1920, the Labor member for Kalgoorlie, Hugh Mahon, stated that there were no policemen in Ireland, only "the agents provocateurs of a foreign government. . . . Is it not a shocking commentary on Britain's boasted love of freedom that the elect of the nation find their place, not in parliament but in the jails of the country," Mahon insisted. "I am confident that Australia will not stand for a policy so unrighteous that, if continued, it will lead to serious estrangement between the Dominions and the Imperial Government."[67] However, within weeks Mahon was expelled from parliament, his seat declared vacant following a public speech in which he allegedly declared the empire "bloody and accursed" and called for the establishment of an Australian republic. "We must divorce ourselves entirely from the Irish question, and anybody who counsels the disruption of the empire must be a traitor to this county," declared Prime Minister Hughes in a speech that emphatically confirmed the primacy of the imperial context within which Australia's Irish were still judged.[68]

*

On 9 July 1921 a truce was agreed upon between representatives of the Irish Republican Army and the British Army in Ireland to bring the hostilities to a close. For many Irish in America and Australia, and for the populations at large in both societies, the end of the bloodshed was welcome news. The commencement of Anglo-Irish talks in London in October promised much. But when news of the terms of the settlement, signed in London on 6 December, reached the United States, many Irish Americans greeted it with disbelief. The *Irish World,* seldom impressed with steps taken by the Irish themselves, declared the agreement a "treaty of surrender" and vowed to fight against it. However, more moderate opinion, tired after the emotional turmoil of the previous eight years, appeared ready and willing to acquiesce. Prominent Irish Americans including New York congressman William Bourke Cochran and Montana senator Thomas J. Walsh declared support for the agreement. Edward Doheny, president of the American Association for the Recognition of the Irish Republic, saw the measure as providing an opportunity for the normalization of Anglo-American relations.[69] In Australia, reaction was also generally supportive. The continued imperial connection posed no dilemmas for most Irish Australians, and most appear to have accepted it as a satisfactory outcome for the present. Echoing Michael Collins, the *Freeman's Journal* believed the treaty was "a stepping-stone to better things." Once it was ratified by the Dáil Éireann, most Australians regarded the matter as closed and believed that "Mr. de Valera must eventually bow to the inevitable, no matter how badly his dreams have been shaken."[70]

Ireland's descent into civil war in the wake of the agreement was repugnant to most Irish emigrants and those of Irish descent abroad. In the United States many sank into apathy, and others retreated into a permanent public silence. Though fringes within Irish America continued to repudiate the "freak state," even after the Irish electorate had expressed its view on the deal, it was only those who could not surrender their own vision of Ireland who refused to accede the point. Likewise, in Australia the war was viewed mainly with abhorrence. Reporting the shooting of Michael Collins, the *Freeman's Journal* remarked, "The sane and decent friends of Ireland stand behind true Irish aspirations, and Ireland has expressed what her aspirations are. Those who would murder those aspirations . . . can expect neither sympathy nor assistance from the Irish overseas."[71] Only a small number in Australia remained loyal to de Valera and an undivided republic, and they faced a lonely road ahead.

With a settlement reached and voted upon by the Irish themselves, it took a temerity found only amongst the most idealistic or the most foolish to continue the struggle. Moreover, with the numbers of immigrants arriving from Ireland in decline, and the assimilatory pressures in both societies so strong, most of the impetus of Irish nationalist movements in both societies was exhausted. The Union breached, the Irish and their descendants in the United States and Australia faced new struggles for their own and their children's advancement. These, rather than matters Irish, became the principal concern and predominant focus of attention for the future.

Conclusion

COMPARATIVE HISTORY RARELY
provides hard and fast answers—its principal power is to stimulate new
questions and bring to bear new perspectives on a subject. Through a
process of comparison, this book has demonstrated that explanations
grounded in Irish migrants' origins, prior historical experiences, or cultural
legacies, are in themselves inadequate explanations for their diverse adjust-
ments to life abroad. Instead, it proposes that the economic and political
contexts of Ireland's new worlds played a decisive role in shaping the distinctive experiences of immigrants in the United States and Australia.

Specifically, this study has highlighted the importance of the timing
of the onset of industrialization and urbanization *and* their relation to
large-scale Irish immigration as a critical determinant of the newcomers'
experiences. Important, too, were the political and ideological contexts
that enveloped these sweeping changes. These factors were not constant
across Ireland's new worlds but varied significantly, even within national
borders. America's earlier engagement with sweeping market reform, the
power of republican idealism, and the extent of the Irish flight during
the famine decade sharply delineated the experience of the American Irish
from that of their compatriots resident within Britain's empire in colonial Australia.

The complexity and diversity revealed in this comparison of Irish immigrants in the United States and Australia *should,* I hope, encourage historians
in both societies to challenge more deeply their assumptions about norms
of immigrant behavior and bring into sharper focus the specific and distinctive features of Irish settlement in their own nation. Should, but may not!
In a stocktaking of Irish America, Lawrence McCaffrey acknowledged the
"tempting possibilities" of comparative diaspora studies, but counseled
younger scholars to concentrate their efforts on the greater challenges of

"uncovering the many hidden facets of Irish America." McCaffrey believed "the best future in Irish studies for Americans is right here at home."[1] No doubt some Australian scholars would entertain similar beliefs as to the primacy of nationally framed inquiries.

McCaffrey is correct when he asserts that local and national studies are important. As historians, we ought to be sensitive to differences between neighboring New England towns, adjacent prairie states, or nearby Australian regions. But we also need the facility to adjust our focus and to recognize that from a global perspective the degrees of difference we take for granted may seem to others very slight indeed. More than half a century ago, Marc Bloch chided: "The authors of monographs must be once again reminded that it is their duty to read the literature on subjects analogous to theirs, and not only that bearing upon their own region . . . but also (something too often neglected) that dealing with more distant societies, separated by differences of political constitution or nationality from those they are studying."[2] Bloch's appeal for cross-cultural perspectives is as valid now as ever.

Perhaps more than anything else, the comparisons in this book emphasize the need to write in the host nation as a critical agent in immigrants' lives. By this I do not mean a homogeneous, nondescript nation but an organism grounded in historically specific processes of economic change and ideological formation. It is a simple enough demand—one advanced long ago by Frank Thistlethwaite in his memorable essay on nineteenth- and twentieth-century European migration—but a complicated task still too often unfulfilled.[3] Transnational comparisons and the uncovering of multilateral connections between different destinations across the Irish diaspora will help fulfill this objective and bring differences in immigrants' experiences into sharper relief.

At the same time, this book advocates the potential of comparison at a regional level to complement nationally oriented studies. Such exercises in comparison, whether of cities, country regions, or coasts, open new possibilities for the intensive study of immigrant communities and provide the opportunity to scrutinize that critical seam between regional life and nation-state where so many newcomers' lives are indelibly marked. They need to be conceived with verve and imagination, embrace a wide array of evidence, and draw on the best of the humanities and social sciences.

It would be a sad irony if, at a time when Ireland itself has moved increasingly to embrace the global dimensions of its historical experience, historians of those scattered Irish peoples were unable or unwilling to adequately acknowledge the transnational dimensions of those lives.[4] A strong onus exists on us all to reflect on the ways in which history can best be practiced to give acknowledgment and voice to the richness and diversity of immigrants' lives in Ireland's new worlds.

Abbreviations
Notes
Select Bibliography
Index

Abbreviations

ADB	*Australian Dictionary of Biography*
BP	*Pilot* (Boston)
CP	*Catholic Press* (Sydney)
FJ	*Freeman's Journal* (Sydney)
GH	*Goulburn Herald*
IA	*Irish-Australian* (Sydney)
IW	*Irish World and American Industrial Liberator* (New York)
HRA	*Historical Records of Australia*
MHS	Minnesota Historical Society (St. Paul)
ML	Mitchell Library, State Library of New South Wales, Sydney
NLI	National Library of Ireland
SMH	*Sydney Morning Herald*
UCB	Bancroft Library, University of California, Berkeley

Notes

Preface and Acknowledgments

1. Oscar Handlin, *Boston's Immigrants: A Study in Acculturation,* rev. ed. (1941; Cambridge, Mass.: Belknap Press, 1979), 86–87, 125–26. On the historiography of Irish America, see in particular, Donald Harman Akenson, "The Historiography of the Irish-Americans," in *Being Had: Historians, the Evidence and the Irish in North America* (Port Credit, Ont.: P. D. Meany, 1985), 37–75; Robert A. Burchell, "The Historiography of the American Irish," *Immigrants and Minorities* 1 (1982): 281–305.

2. William V. Shannon, *The American Irish: A Political and Social Portrait* (New York: Macmillan, 1963), 27.

3. Oliver MacDonagh, "The Irish Famine Emigration to the United States," *Perspectives in American History* 10 (1976): 435.

4. Lawrence J. McCaffrey, "A Profile of Irish America," in Owen D. Edwards and David N. Doyle, eds., *America and Ireland, 1776–1976: The American Identity and the Irish Connection* (Westport, Conn.: Greenwood Press, 1980), 81.

5. Kerby A. Miller, *Emigrants and Exiles: Ireland and the Irish Exodus to North America* (New York: Oxford University Press, 1985), 4–8.

6. Miller, *Emigrants and Exiles,* 4, 102–30.

7. The literature is very extensive. A selective list of recent studies on the Irish includes: (on South Africa) Donal McCracken, "Irish Identity and Settlement in South Africa before 1910," *Irish Historical Studies* 28 (1992): 134–49; Donal McCracken, ed., *The Irish in Southern Africa* (Durban: Ireland and Southern Africa Project, 1992); Donald Harman Akenson, *Occasional Papers on the Irish in South Africa* (Grahamstown: Institute of Social and Economic Research, Rhodes University, 1991); (on New Zealand) Brad Patterson, ed., *The Irish in New Zealand: Historical Contexts and Perspectives* (Wellington: Stout Centre, Victoria University of Wellington, 2002); Lyndon Fraser, ed., *A Distant Shore: Irish Migration and New Zealand Settlement* (Dunedin: Otago University Press, 2000); Lyndon Fraser, *To Tara Via Holyhead: Irish Catholic Migrants in Nineteenth-Century Christchurch* (Auckland: Auckland University Press, 1997); Donald Harman Akenson, *Half the World From Home: Perspectives on the Irish in New Zealand, 1860–1950* (Wellington: Victoria University Press, 1990); and Patrick O'Farrell, *Vanished Kingdoms: Irish in Australia and New Zealand* (Sydney: University of New South Wales Press, 1990); (on Australia) Patrick O'Farrell's *The Irish in Australia: 1788 to the Present* (Sydney: University of New South Wales Press, 2000) is the most important work and contains a substantial bibliography; David Fitzpatrick, *Oceans of Consolation: Personal Accounts of Irish Migration to Australia* (Ithaca, N.Y.: Cornell University Press, 1994); Malcolm Campbell, *Kingdom of the Ryans: The Irish in Southwest New South Wales*

1816–90 (Sydney: University of New South Wales Press, 1997); (on Canada) Donald Harman Akenson, *The Irish in Ontario: A Study in Rural History* (Kingston, Ont.: McGill-Queen's University Press, 1984); Bruce Elliott, *Irish Migrants in the Canadas: A New Approach* (Kingston, Ont.: McGill-Queen's University Press, 1987); Gordon Darroch and Lee Soltow, *Property and Inequality in Victorian Ontario: Structural Patterns and Cultural Communities in the 1871 Census* (Toronto: University of Toronto Press, 1994); Cecil J. Houston and William J. Smyth, *Irish Emigration and Canadian Settlement: Patterns, Links and Letters* (Toronto, 1990); Robert O'Driscoll and Lorna Reynolds, eds., *The Untold Story: The Irish in Canada,* 2 vols. (Toronto: Celtic Arts of Canada, 1988); and on the Irish worldwide, see Patrick O'Sullivan, ed., *The Irish World Wide: History, Heritage, Identity,* 6 vols. (Leicester: Leicester University Press, 1992–94).

8. Donald Harman Akenson, "Ontario: Whatever Happened to the Irish," *Canadian Papers in Rural History* 3 (1984): 230.

9. Akenson, *Half the World From Home;* see also his "Immigration and Ethnicity in New Zealand and the USA—The Irish Example," in Jock Phillips, ed., *New Worlds? The Comparative History of New Zealand and the United States* (Wellington: N.Z.-U.S. Education Foundation, 1991): 28–58.

10. David M. Emmons, *The Butte Irish: Class and Ethnicity in an American Mining Town, 1875–1925* (Urbana: University of Illinois Press, 1990); Timothy J. Meagher, *Inventing Irish America: Generation, Class, and Ethnic Identity in a New England City, 1880–1928* (Notre Dame, Ind.: University of Notre Dame Press, 2001); David T. Gleeson, *The Irish in the South, 1815–1877* (Chapel Hill: University of North Carolina Press, 2001); Kerby A. Miller et al., eds., *Irish Immigrants in the Land of Canaan: Letters and Memoirs from Colonial and Revolutionary America, 1675–1815* (New York: Oxford University Press, 2003).

11. For advocacy of transnational approaches to immigration history, see Jon Gjerde, "New Growth on Old Vines—the State of the Field: The Social History of Immigration To and Ethnicity In the United States," *Journal of American Ethnic History* 18, no. 4 (1999): 47.

12. James F. Hogan, *The Irish in Australia* (Melbourne: Australian Edition, 1888), 1.

13. Quoted in Sylvia L. Thrupp's editorial to the inaugural issue of *Comparative Studies in Society and History* 1 (1958): 1; Barrington Moore, *Social Origins of Dictatorship and Democracy: Lord and Peasant in the Making of the Modern World* (Boston: Beacon Press, 1967), xiii.

14. Thomas J. Archdeacon, "Problems and Possibilities in the Study of American Immigration and Ethnic History," *International Migration Review* 19 (1985): 112, 123.

15. Raymond Grew, "The Case for Comparing Histories," *American Historical Review* 85, no. 4 (October 1980): 763–78; George M. Fredrickson, "Comparative History," in Michael Kammen, ed., *The Past Before Us: Contemporary Historical Writing in the United States* (Ithaca, N.Y.: Cornell University Press, 1980), 457–73.

16. Theda Skocpol and Margaret Somers, "The Uses of Comparative History in Macrosocial Inquiry," *Comparative Studies in Society and History* 22 (1980): 175–81. See also Theda Skocpol, ed., *Vision and Method in Historical Sociology* (Cambridge: Cambridge University Press, 1984); Charles Tilly, *Big Structures, Large Processes, Huge Comparisons* (New York: Russell Sage Foundation, 1984); Victoria Bonnell, "The Uses of Theory, Concepts and Comparison in Historical Sociology," *Comparative Studies in Society and History* (1980): 156–73.

17. On the possibilities of "cross-national" history and the need to position such studies within transnational perspectives, see Kevin Kenny, "Diaspora and Comparison: The Irish as a Case Study," *Journal of American History* 90 (2003): 134–62.

1. Contrasting Fortunes

1. James S. Donnelly, Jr., *The Land and People of Nineteenth-Century Cork: The Rural Economy and the Land Question* (London: Routledge and Kegan Paul, 1975), 23.

2. Cormac Ó Gráda, "Poverty, Population and Agriculture, 1801–45," in W. E. Vaughan, ed., *Ireland under the Union, 1801–1870* (Oxford: Clarendon Press, 1989), 108; John B. O'Brien, "Population, Politics and Society in Cork, 1780–1900," in Patrick O'Flanagan and Cornelius Butler, eds., *Cork History and Society: Interdisciplinary Essays on the History of an Irish County* (Dublin: Geography Publications, 1993), 704–5.

3. Cormac Ó Gráda, *Ireland: A New Economic History* (Oxford: Clarendon Press, 1994), 273–313; Philip Ollerenshaw, "Industry 1820–1914," in Líam Kennedy and Philip Ollerenshaw, eds., *An Economic History of Ulster, 1820–1940* (Manchester: Manchester University Press, 1985), 62–108; Andy Bielenberg, *Cork's Industrial Revolution, 1780–1880: Development or Decline?* (Cork: Cork University Press, 1991), 3–5, 14–17, 31–36; O'Brien, "Population, Politics and Society," in O'Flanagan and Butler, *Cork History and Society,* 704–5.

4. Sean J. Connolly, "Union Government, 1812–23," in Vaughan, *Ireland under the Union, 1801–1870,* 57–60.

5. William Forbes Adams, *Ireland and Irish Emigration to the New World from 1815 to the Famine* (New Haven, Conn.: Yale University Press, 1932), 69–76, 423–27.

6. Miller, *Emigrants and Exiles,* 194; Cormac Ó Gráda, "Across the Briny Ocean: Some Thoughts on Irish Emigration to America, 1800–1850," in T. M. Devine and David Dickson, eds., *Ireland and Scotland, 1600–1850: Parallels and Contrasts in Economic and Social Development* (Edinburgh: John Donald Publishers, 1983), 118–30.

7. Adams, *Irish Emigration,* 126; David N. Doyle, "The Irish in North America, 1776–1845," in Vaughan, *Ireland under the Union, 1801–1870,* 685.

8. Frederick Maryat, *Diary in America: The Complete Account of His Trials, Wrangles and Tribulations in the United States and Canada, 1837–1838* (London: Nicholas Vane, 1960), 11, 56.

9. House of Commons, Select Committee on the Expediency of Encouraging Emigration from the United Kingdom, *Report,* 1826 (404), vol. 4, Minutes of Evidence, 49, 151, 168; House of Commons, Select Committee on Emigration from the United Kingdom, *Third Report,* 1827 (550), vol. 5, appendix 4, 574, estimated that in the period 1824–26, 54 percent of the United Kingdom population resident in New York State had arrived via Quebec, New Brunswick, and Nova Scotia; *Commission on Emigration and Other Population Problems* (Dublin: Stationery Office, 1954), statistical appendix, table 26, 314.

10. David Fitzpatrick, "Emigration, 1801–70," in Vaughan, *Ireland under the Union, 1801–1870,* 571, 608; David Fitzpatrick, *Irish Emigration, 1801–1921* (Dublin: Social History Society of Ireland, 1984), 9–12; Ó Gráda, "Across the Briny Ocean," 118, 120–21, 126.

11. Miller, *Emigrants and Exiles,* 223. C. J. Houston and W. J. Smyth identify 1834 as the year when Roman Catholics first outnumbered Protestants. "The Irish Diaspora: Emigration to the New World, 1720–1920," in B. J. Graham and L. J. Proudfoot, eds., *An Historical Geography of Ireland* (London: Academic Press, 1993), 346–47.

12. David N. Doyle, *Ireland, Irishmen and Revolutionary America, 1760–1820* (Dublin: Cultural Relations Committee of Ireland, 1981), 165–67.

13. Doyle, *Ireland,* 185–86.

14. Thomas Addis Emmet, *Memoir of Thomas Addis Emmet and Robert Emmet,* 2 vols. (New York: The Emmet Press, 1915), 1:391–400.

15. Augustus John Foster, *Jeffersonian America: Notes on the United States of America Collected in the Years 1805–6–7 and 1811–12 by Sir Augustus John Foster,* ed. Richard Beale Davis (San

Marino: The Huntington Library, 1954), 12; George Potter, *To the Golden Door: The Story of the Irish in Ireland and America* (Boston: Little, Brown, 1960), 180–84; Miller, *Emigrants and Exiles*, 264–66.

16. George Unthank, New York City, to John ———, Limerick, 16 February 1826. I am grateful to Kerby Miller of the University of Missouri–Columbia for a typescript of this letter.

17. Potter, *Golden Door*, 187–91, 198–99.

18. Vincent E. Powers, *"Invisible Immigrants": The Pre-Famine Irish Community in Worcester, Massachusetts, from 1826 to 1860* (New York: Garland Publishing, 1989), 300; Potter, *Golden Door*, 176–80.

19. Foster, *Jeffersonian America*, 155, 249–51, 260, 274; David A. Wilson, *United Irishmen, United States: Immigrant Radicals in the Early Republic* (Dublin: Four Courts Press, 1998), 58–95.

20. Max Berger, "The Irish Emigrant and American Nativism," *The Dublin Review* 219 (1946): 174–75.

21. Thomas F. Moriarty, "The Irish American Response to Catholic Emancipation," *Catholic Historical Review* 66 (1980): 353–73; David N. Doyle, "The Irish in North America, 1776–1845," in Vaughan, *Ireland under the Union, 1801–1870*, 696–99.

22. Thomas Addis Emmet to Archibald Rowan, 8 January 1827, Emmet, *Memoir*, 1:467.

23. Ged Martin, ed., *The Founding of Australia: The Argument About Australia's Origins* (Sydney: Hale and Iremonger, 1978); Alan Atkinson, *The Europeans in Australia* (Melbourne: Oxford University Press, 1997).

24. A. Roger Ekirch, *Bound for America: The Transportation of British Convicts to the Colonies, 1718–1775* (Oxford: Clarendon Press, 1987), 24–25; Bob Reece, *The Origins of Irish Convict Transportation to New South Wales* (Basingstoke, Hants.: Palgrave, 2001), 1–25.

25. O'Farrell, *Irish in Australia*, 22–23; Reece, *Origins*, 231–55; T. J. Kiernan, *Transportation from Ireland to Sydney: 1791–1816* (Canberra: privately printed, 1954), 30–37; A. G. L. Shaw, *Convicts and the Colonies: A Study of Penal Transportation from Great Britain and Ireland to Australia and Other Parts of the British Empire* (Melbourne: Melbourne University Press, 1977), 166–67.

26. Richard E. Reid, "Aspects of Irish Assisted Emigration to New South Wales, 1848–1870," 2 vols. (Ph.D. thesis, Australian National University, 1992), 1:v, 14, 101–3; Campbell, *Kingdom*.

27. Lloyd L. Robson, *The Convict Settlers of Australia: An Enquiry into the Origins and Character of the Convicts Transported to New South Wales and Van Diemen's Land, 1787–1852* (Melbourne: Melbourne University Press, 1965), 178–86; T. J. Kiernan, *Transportation*, 28–185; Trevor Parkhill, "Convicts, Orphans, Settlers: Patterns of Emigration from Ulster to Australia, 1790–1860," in John O'Brien and Pauric Travers, eds., *The Irish Emigrant Experience in Australia* (Dublin: Poolbeg, 1991), 7–12.

28. T. J. Kiernan, *Transportation*, 16.

29. Shaw, *Convicts and the Colonies*, 182–83; George Rudé, *Protest and Punishment: The Story of the Social and Political Protesters Transported to Australia, 1788–1868* (Oxford: Clarendon Press, 1978), 7–10.

30. Stephen Nicholas challenges the older scholarship of Shaw, Robson, and Manning Clark. Nicholas, ed., *Convict Workers: Reinterpreting Australia's Past* (Melbourne: Cambridge University Press, 1988). *Convict Workers* is persuasively critiqued by Raymond Evans and Bill Thorpe, "Power, Punishment and Penal Labour: Convict Workers and Moreton Bay," *Australian Historical Studies* 25 (April 1992): 90–111.

31. Data from the work of Kris Corcoran and Stephen Nicholas. Nicholas, *Convict Workers*, 202–12.

32. O'Farrell, *Irish in Australia,* 36.

33. House of Commons, Select Committee on Emigration, *Third Report,* 1827, 394–98.

34. House of Commons, Select Committee on Transportation, *Report,* 1838 (669), vol. 22, xx.

35. House of Commons, Select Committee on Transportation, *Report,* 1838, Minutes of Evidence, 7.

36. Charles A. Price, *The Great White Walls Are Built* (Canberra: Australian National University Press, 1974), 38–52.

37. Richard White, *Inventing Australia: Images and Identity, 1688–1980* (Sydney, Allen and Unwin, 1981), 29–46.

38. Caroline Chisholm, *Comfort for the Poor! Meat Three Times a Day!: Voluntary Information from the People of New South Wales Collected in that Colony by Mrs. Chisholm* (London, 1847), statement 25.

39. House of Commons, Select Committee on Transportation, *Report,* 1838, xxx–xxxi.

40. Edward Smith Hall, *The state of New South Wales in December, 1830: in a letter* (London: Joseph Cross, 1831), 19.

41. Fitzpatrick, "Emigration, 1801–70," 581.

42. R. B. Madgwick, *Immigration into Eastern Australia, 1788–1851* (1937; reprint, Sydney: Sydney University Press, 1969), 77–84, 88–111; A. J. Hammerton, "'Without Natural Protectors': Female Immigration to Australia, 1832–36," *Historical Studies* 16 (October 1975): 539–66.

43. Robin F. Haines, *Emigration and the Labouring Poor: Australian Recruitment in Britain and Ireland, 1831–60* (Basingstoke, Hants.: MacMillan, 1997), 21–23, 31–33; John McDonald and Eric Richards, "Workers for Australia: A Profile of British and Irish Migrants Assisted to New South Wales in 1841," *Journal of the Australian Population Association* 15, no. 1 (1998): 1–33; Robert J. Schultz, "The Assisted Immigrants, 1837–50: A Study of Some of the Aspects and Characteristics of the Immigrants Assisted to New South Wales and the Port Phillip District, 1837–1850," 2 vols. (Ph.D. thesis, Australian National University, 1971), 1:18, 43–49.

44. John Hunter to the Duke of Portland, 12 November 1796, *Historical Records of Australia* (hereafter *HRA*), series 1, ed. Frederick Watson (Sydney: Library Committee of the Commonwealth Parliament, 1914–25), 674; John Hunter to the Duke of Portland, 10 January 1798, *HRA* 2, 118; John Hunter to the Duke of Portland, 15 February 1798, *HRA* 2, 129; John Hunter to the Duke of Portland, 1 November 1798, *HRA* 2, 237.

45. Philip Gidley King to the Duke of Portland, 10 March 1801, *HRA* 3, 8–9.

46. Peter O'Shaughnessy, ed., *A Rum Story: The Adventures of Joseph Holt, Thirteen Years in New South Wales, 1800–12* (Sydney: Kangaroo Press, 1988), 79–87.

47. Philip Gidley King to Robert Hobart, 12 March 1804, *HRA* 4, 563–77; R. W. Connell, "The Convict Rebellion of 1804," *Melbourne Historical Journal* 5 (1965): 27–37.

48. Philip Gidley King to the Duke of Portland, 21 August 1801, *HRA* 3, 253; David Collins, *An Account of the English Colony in New South Wales With Remarks on the Dispositions, Customs, Manners &c. of the Native Inhabitants of the Country,* 2 vols. (London: T. Caddell Jun. and W. Davies, 1798 and 1802), 2:239.

49. John Hunter to the Duke of Portland, 10 January 1798, *HRA* 2, 118; John Hunter to the Duke of Portland, 15 February 1798, *HRA* 2, 129; Philip Gidley King to the Duke of Portland, 28 September 1800, *HRA* 2, 613, 637–51; Collins, *Account,* 1:160, 254–55, 304, 309, 325, 335, 446–47; 2:54–57, 77.

50. Potter, *Golden Door,* 180–83, 187–91.

51. Peter Cunningham, *Two Years in New South Wales; a series of letters comprising sketches of the*

actual state of society in that colony, 2 vols. (London: Henry Colburn, 1827), 2:245–46 (emphasis in the original).

52. Roger Therry, *Reminiscences of Thirty Years' Residence in New South Wales and Victoria* (London: Sampson Low, Son and Co., 1863), 413–14; Campbell, *Kingdom,* 28–29.

53. Kevin Kenny, *The American Irish: A History* (New York: Longman, 2000), 63–66; Peter Way, "Shovel and Shamrock: Irish Workers and Labor Violence in the Digging of the Chesapeake and Ohio Canal," *Labor History* 30 (1989): 489–517; Potter, *Golden Door,* 328–35.

54. Victor A. Walsh, "'A Fanatic Heart': The Cause of Irish-American Nationalism in Pittsburgh During the Gilded Age," *Journal of Social History* 15 (1981): 189–90.

55. Joyce Appleby, *Inheriting the Revolution: The First Generation of Americans* (Cambridge, Mass.: Belknap Press, 2000), 254.

56. Dale T. Knobel, *America for the Americans: The Nativist Movement in the United States* (New York: Twayne Publishers, 1996), 41–43; Bruce Laurie, *Artisans into Workers: Labor in Nineteenth-Century America* (New York: Hill and Wang, 1989), 25–27.

57. Knobel, *America,* 47; Miller, *Emigrants and Exiles,* 266.

58. Richard Jensen, "'No Irish Need Apply': A Myth of Victimization," *Journal of Social History* 36 (2002): 405–29.

59. Massachusetts Commission on Lunacy, *Report on Insanity and Idiocy in Massachusetts* (1855), quoted in Edith Abbott, *Historical Aspects of the Immigration Problem: Select Documents* (Chicago: University of Chicago Press, 1926), 614–15.

60. Sean Wilentz, *Chants Democratic: New York City and the Rise of the American Working Class, 1788–1850* (New York: Oxford University Press, 1984), 118.

61. Ó Gráda, "'Across the Briny Ocean,'" 120 and table 3, 125; Doyle, "Irish in North America, 1776–1845," 704.

62. Annual Report of the New York Association for Improving the Poor (1852), quoted in Abbott, *Historical Aspects,* 326.

63. Wilentz, *Chants Democratic,* 48; Charles Sellers, *The Market Revolution: Jacksonian America* (New York: Oxford University Press, 1991), 389; Dale T. Knobel, *Paddy and the Republic: Ethnicity and Nationality in Antebellum America* (Middletown, Conn.: Wesleyan University Press, 1986), 5–6; Kenny, *American Irish,* 61–62.

64. Richard J. Carwardine, *Evangelicals and Politics in Antebellum America* (New Haven, Conn.: Yale University Press, 1993), 1–2, 5–6.

65. Quote from Carwardine, *Evangelicals,* 80–81; Steven Mintz, *Moralists and Modernizers: America's Pre-Civil War Reformers* (Baltimore: Johns Hopkins University Press, 1995), 42–44.

66. Curtis D. Johnson, *Redeeming America: Evangelicals and the Road to the Civil War* (Chicago: Ivan R. Dee, 1993), 28–29.

67. Carwardine, *Evangelicals,* 81–88; Knobel, *America,* 56–61.

68. George Templeton Strong, *The Diary of George Templeton Strong: Young Man in New York, 1835–1849,* ed. Allen Nevins and Milton H. Thomas, 4 vols. (New York: MacMillan, 1952), 1:177.

69. Carwardine, *Evangelicals,* 46–49, 133–74; Knobel, *America,* 41–57.

70. Emmet, *Memoir,* 1:393.

71. Daniel O'Connell, *Speeches of Daniel O'Connell and Thomas Steele on the Subject of American Slavery* (Philadelphia: Anti-Slavery Office, 1843); *Daniel O'Connell upon American Slavery: With other Irish Testimonies,* Anti-Slavery Tracts, No. 5, New Series (New York: American Anti-Slavery Society, 1860; reprint, Westport, Conn.: Negro Universities Press, 1970).

72. Quoted in Gilbert Osofsky, "Abolitionists, Irish Immigrants and the Dilemmas of

Romantic Nationalism," *American Historical Review* 80 (1975): 891–92; Douglas C. Riach, "Daniel O'Connell and American Slavery," *Irish Historical Studies* 20 (1976): 3–5.

73. Maurice R. O'Connell, ed., *The Correspondence of Daniel O'Connell,* 8 vols. (Dublin: Irish Manuscripts Commission, 1972–80), 6:128–30.

74. Elizur Wright Junior to O'Connell, Maurice R. O'Connell, *Correspondence,* 6:193–94 (emphasis his).

75. Lawrence McCaffrey, *Daniel O'Connell and the Repeal Year* (Lexington: University of Kentucky Press, 1966).

76. Osofsky, "Abolitionists," 897–98; Colm Kerrigan, "Irish Temperance and US Anti-Slavery: Father Mathew and the Abolitionists," *History Workshop Journal* 31 (1991): 105–19.

77. Quoted in Osofsky, "Abolitionists," 902; James Cannings Fuller to O'Connell, 28 March 1842, Maurice R. O'Connell, *Correspondence,* 7:144–46; David R. Roediger, *The Wages of Whiteness: Race and the Making of the American Working Class* (London: Verso, 1991), 133–37.

78. Quoted in Noel Ignatiev, *How the Irish Became White* (New York: Routledge, 1995), 22.

79. Ian Tyrrell, *Sobering Up: From Temperance to Prohibition in Antebellum America, 1800–1860* (Westport, Conn.: Greenwood Press, 1977), 3–4, 16–32; Thomas F. Pegram, *Battling Demon Rum: The Struggle for a Dry America, 1800–1933* (Chicago: Ivan R. Dee, 1998), 4–8; Wilentz, *Chants Democratic,* 147–48, 272–86.

80. Tyrrell, *Sobering Up,* 125.

81. Strong, *Diary,* 1:150–51.

82. Strong, *Diary,* 1:150 (emphasis in the original).

83. Charles Dickens, *American Notes and Pictures from Italy* (London: Chapman and Hall, 1868), 78.

84. Dale Knobel, "'Celtic Exodus': The Famine Irish, Ethnic Stereotypes, and the Cultivation of American Racial Nationalism," in Margaret M. Mulrooney, ed., *Fleeing the Famine: North America and the Irish Refugees, 1845–1851* (Westport Conn.: Praeger, 2003), 84; Knobel, *Paddy,* 11–12; Tyrrell, *Sobering Up,* 297–305.

85. Laurie, *Artisans into Workers,* 49; Wilentz, *Chants Democratic,* 102–3; Knobel, *America,* 45–49.

86. Philip Hone, *The Diary of Philip Hone,* ed. Allan Nevins (New York: Dodd, Mead and Co., 1889; New York: Kraus Reprint, 1969), 1:190.

87. Stephen Roberts, *The Squatting Age in Australia, 1835–1847* (Melbourne: Melbourne University Press, 1964), 4.

88. R. W. Connell and T. H. Irving, *Class Structure in Australian History: Poverty and Progress,* 2nd ed. (Melbourne: Longman Cheshire, 1992), 35–47, 94–95.

89. *HRA* 1:187–94; John Ritchie, *Lachlan Macquarie: A Biography* (Melbourne: Melbourne University Press, 1986), 132–40.

90. W. A. Duncan, "Autobiography 1811–1854," Mitchell Library, State Library of New South Wales (hereafter ML), A2877 Reel CYPOS 161, p. 37; L. Thomas, *The Development of the Labour Movement in the Sydney District of N.S.W.* (Sydney: Australian Society for the Study of Labour History, 1962), 64–65; Patrick O'Farrell, "The Image of O'Connell in Australia," in Donal McCartney, ed., *The World of Daniel O'Connell* (Cork: Mercier Press, 1980), 114–15.

91. Samuel Marsden, "A Few General Observations on the Toleration of the Catholic Religion in New South Wales," ML MSS 18, ML.

92. O'Farrell, "Image of O'Connell," 112–14.

93. Hazel King, *Richard Bourke* (Melbourne: Oxford University Press, 1971), 226–29; Patrick

O'Farrell, *The Catholic Church and Community: An Australian History* (Sydney: University of New South Wales Press, 1985), 38–39.

94. Stuart Piggin, *Evangelical Christianity in Australia: Spirit, Word and World* (Melbourne: Oxford University Press, 1996), 10.

95. C. M. H. Clark, *A History of Australia*, vol. 3, *The Beginning of an Australian Civilization, 1824–1851* (Melbourne: Melbourne University Press, 1973), 408.

96. D. W. A. Baker, *Days of Wrath: A Life of John Dunmore Lang* (Melbourne: Melbourne University Press, 1985), 1–7, 161–67.

97. Baker, *Days of Wrath,* 191–92.

98. King, *Richard Bourke,* 228–32; O'Farrell, *Irish in Australia,* 42–43.

99. Andrew Markus, *Australian Race Relations, 1788–1993* (Sydney: Allen and Unwin, 1994), 56–58; Charles Price, *The Great White Walls Are Built: Restrictive Immigration to North America and Australasia, 1836–1888* (Canberra: Australian National University Press, 1974), 38–52.

100. *Sydney Morning Herald* (hereafter *SMH*), 20 April 1841; John Dunmore Lang, *The question of questions! or, Is this colony to be transformed into a province of the Popedom?: A letter to the Protestant land holders of New South Wales* (Sydney, 1841).

101. *SMH,* 31 August 1840.

102. *SMH,* 14 September 1841.

103. *Australasian Chronicle,* 17 March 1840.

104. *SMH,* 30 April 1841.

105. David Montgomery, "The Shuttle and the Cross: Weavers and Artisans in the Kensington Riots of 1844," *Journal of Social History* 5 (1972): 411–46; Michael Feldberg, *The Philadelphia Riots of 1844: A Study of Ethnic Conflict* (Westport, Conn.: Greenwood Press, 1975).

106. Knobel, *Paddy,* 25–26, 69–75, 84–87.

2. Crisis and Despair

1. Robert James Scally, *The End of Hidden Ireland: Rebellion, Famine, and Emigration* (New York: Oxford University Press, 1995), 191–204; Patrick O'Farrell, "Lost in Transit: Australian Reaction to the Irish and Scots Famines, 1845–1850," in Patrick O'Sullivan, ed., *The Meaning of the Famine,* vol. 6, *The Irish World Wide: History, Heritage, Identity* (London: Leicester University Press, 1997), 126–39.

2. Trevor McClaughlin, *Barefoot and Pregnant: Irish Famine Orphans in Australia* (Melbourne: Genealogical Society of Victoria, 1991); Reid, "Irish Assisted Emigration," 149–64.

3. Reid, "Irish Assisted Emigration," 164–76; Patrick J. Duffy, "Assisted Emigration from the Shirley Estate, 1843–54," *Clogher Record* 14, no. 2 (1992): 7–19, 28–31; Christopher O'Mahony and Valerie Thompson, *Poverty to Promise: The Monteagle Emigrants, 1838–58* (Sydney: Crossing Press, 1994), 1–15, 88–90.

4. Richard Davis, *The Young Ireland Movement* (Dublin: Gill and Macmillan, 1987), 102; D. George Boyce, *Nationalism in Ireland* (London: Routledge, 1995), 165–70.

5. Davis, *Young Ireland,* 148–49.

6. Davis, *Young Ireland,* 150–54; Boyce, *Ireland,* 174–76.

7. Davis, *Young Ireland,* 155–66; Robert Kee, *The Green Flag,* vol. 1, *The Most Distressful Country* (London: Penguin, 1989), 284–86.

8. *United Irishman,* 22 April 1848; Potter, *Golden Door,* 503–4; Michael Funchion, ed., *Irish American Voluntary Organizations* (Westport, Conn.: Greenwood Press, 1983), 101–5; Miller, *Emigrants and Exiles,* 308–12.

9. Quoted in Florence E. Gibson, *Attitudes of the New York Irish Toward State and National*

Affairs, 1848–1892 (London: Oxford University Press, 1951), 19 (emphasis in original); David Gleeson, "Parallel Struggles: Irish Republicanism in the American South, 1798–1876," *Éire-Ireland* 34, no. 2 (1999): 97–116; Potter, *Golden Door,* 503–4.

10. Quoted in Potter, *Golden Door,* 506; John Belchem, "Republican Spirit and Military Science: The 'Irish Brigade' and Irish-American Nationalism in 1848," *Irish Historical Studies* 29 (1994): 45; Belchem, "Nationalism, Republicanism and Exile: Irish Emigrants and the Revolutions of 1848," *Past and Present* 146 (1995): 103–35.

11. Quoted in Belchem, "Irish Brigade," 50; *United Irishman,* 22 April 1848.

12. *SMH,* 19 July 1848.

13. Richard Davis, *"To Solitude Consigned": The Tasmanian Journal of William Smith O'Brien, 1849–1853* (Sydney: Crossing Press, 1995), 39, 48–54; Blanche M. Touhill, *William Smith O'Brien and His Irish Revolutionary Companions in Penal Exile* (Columbia: University of Missouri Press, 1981), 17–75.

14. Touhill, *O'Brien,* 34–45; O'Farrell, *Irish in Australia,* 48–49.

15. Touhill, *O'Brien,* 40–41, 66–75, 116–210.

16. John Mitchel, *Jail Journal: Or Five Years in British Prisons* (Glasgow: Cameron, 1876), 235.

17. Mitchel, *Jail Journal,* 235–38.

18. John Martin to Mrs. Connell, 9 August 1851. Irish Political Prisoner Papers, ML 287/1, ML.

19. Mitchel, *Jail Journal,* 222, 251; John Martin to David Martin, n.d., Irish Political Prisoner Papers, ML 287/1, ML; Peter O'Shaughnessy, ed., *The Gardens of Hell: John Mitchel in Van Diemen's Land, 1850–1853* (Sydney: Kangaroo Press, 1988), 15–16.

20. O'Farrell, *Irish in Australia,* 206.

21. *SMH,* 26 July 1848; John Molony, *An Architect of Freedom: John Hubert Plunkett in New South Wales, 1832–1869* (Canberra: Australian National University Press, 1973), 72.

22. Geoffrey Serle, *The Golden Age: A History of the Colony of Victoria 1851–1861* (Melbourne: Melbourne University Press, 1977), 9–36, 382; Iain McCalman, Alexander Cook, and Andrew Reeves, eds., *Gold: Forgotten Histories and Lost Objects of Australia* (Melbourne: Cambridge University Press, 2001).

23. "Australian Life," *Dublin University Magazine* 58 (September 1861): 361.

24. Quoted in Serle, *Golden Age,* 162.

25. Serle, *Golden Age,* 155–69.

26. Strongest in support of the Irish as crucial instigators is C. H. Currey, *The Irish at Eureka* (Sydney: Angus and Robertson, 1954).

27. O'Farrell, *Irish in Australia,* 90–93.

28. David Headon and Elizabeth Perkins, eds., *Our First Republicans: John Dunmore Lang, Charles Harpur, Daniel Henry Deniehy, Selected Writings 1840–1860* (Sydney: Federation Press, 1998), 2–7, 58–59, 90–92.

29. Charles Gavan Duffy, *My Life in Two Hemispheres,* 2 vols. (London: T. Fisher Unwin, 1898), 2:130–34; Cyril Pearl, *The Three Lives of Gavan Duffy* (Kensington: New South Wales University Press, 1979), 143–71.

30. Charles Gavan Duffy, *Civil and Religious Liberty: Speech on the Presentation of a Property Qualification to Him August 20, 1856* (Melbourne: Michael T. Glason, 1856), 4, 7–8; Steven R. Knowlton, "The Enigma of Sir Charles Gavan Duffy: Looking for Clues in Australia," *Éire-Ireland* 31 (Fall/Winter 1996): 189–208.

31. William Westgarth, *Personal Recollections of Early Melbourne and Victoria* (Melbourne: George Robertson and Son, 1888), 80–82.

32. O'Farrell, *Irish in Australia,* 91–93; S. M. Ingham, "O'Shanassy, Sir John 1818–1883," in Douglas Pike, ed., *Australian Dictionary of Biography* (hereafter *ADB*), 16 vols. (Melbourne: Melbourne University Press, 1966–), 5:378–82; Ian Turner, "Lalor, Peter (1827–1889)," *ADB* 5:50–54.

33. United States Census Bureau [J. D. B. DeBow], *Statistical View of the United States: Compendium of the Seventh Census* (Washington, D.C.: U.S. Senate, 1854), 116–18.

34. David Grimsted, *American Mobbing, 1828–1861: Toward Civil War* (New York: Oxford University Press, 1998), 220–24; Knobel, *America,* 72–77.

35. Tyler Anbinder, *Nativism and Slavery: The Northern Know Nothings and the Politics of the 1850s* (New York: Oxford University Press, 1992), 53–74; Knobel, *America,* 88–95; Knobel, *Paddy,* 129–64.

36. Strong, *Diary,* 2:182–83.

37. Strong, *Diary,* 2:182, 241.

38. Evangeline Thomas, *Nativism in the Old Northwest, 1850–1860* (Washington, D.C.: Catholic University of America Press, 1936), 150–51; House of Lords, Select Committee on Colonization from Ireland, *Second Report,* 1848 (593), vol. 17, Minutes of Evidence, 339–41.

39. Thomas Darcy McGee, *A History of the Irish Settlers in North America from the earliest period to the census of 1850* (Boston: Patrick Donahue, 1852), 185–86.

40. John Francis Maguire, *The Irish in America* (London: Longman, Green and Co., 1868), 214–15; Potter, *Golden Door,* 542–43.

41. Quoted in Eilish Ellis, *Emigrants from Ireland, 1847–1852: State-Aided Emigration Schemes from Crown Estates in Ireland* (Baltimore: Genealogical Publishing Co., 1978), 60–68.

42. Strong, *Diary,* 7 July 1857, 2:348; see also, Max Berger, "The Irish Emigrant and American Nativism, As Seen by British Visitors 1836–1860," *The Dublin Review* 219 (October 1946): 177; Matthew Frye Jacobson, *Whiteness of a Different Color: European Immigrants and the Alchemy of Race* (Cambridge, Mass.: Harvard University Press, 1998), 68–73.

43. Joseph P. Ferrie, *Yankeys Now: Immigrants in the Antebellum United States, 1840–1860* (New York: Oxford University Press, 1999), 105; Steven Herscovici, "The Distribution of Wealth in Nineteenth-Century Boston: Inequality Among Natives and Immigrants, 1860," *Explorations in Economic History* 30 (1993): 323, 334; David W. Galenson, "Economic Opportunity on the Urban Frontier: Nativity, Work, and Wealth in Early Chicago," *Journal of Economic History* 51 (1991): 583–86; Timothy G. Conley and David W. Galenson, "Nativity and Wealth in Mid-Nineteenth-Century Cities," *Journal of Economic History* 58 (1998): 469–70.

44. Ferrie, *Yankeys Now,* 101–55.

45. Frederick Law Olmstead, *A Journey in the Seaboard Slave States With Remarks on their Economy* (New York: Dix and Edwards, 1856), 588–89.

46. E. R. R. Green, "The Irish in American Business and Professions," in David Noel Doyle and Owen Dudley Edwards, eds., *America and Ireland, 1776–1976: The American Identity and the Irish Connection* (Westport, Conn.: Greenwood Press, 1980), 193–204.

47. Dennis Clark, *The Irish in Philadelphia: Ten Generations of Urban Experience* (Philadelphia: Temple University Press, 1973), 47–48.

48. Joseph P. Ferrie, "Up and Out or Down and Out? Immigrant Mobility in the Antebellum United States," *Journal of Interdisciplinary History* 27 (Summer 1995): 33–55; Galenson, "Economic Opportunity," 581–603. See Kerby Miller's review of Ferrie's *Yankeys Now* in *Labor History* 41 (2000): 358–61 as to methodology.

49. Charles Shanabruch, *Chicago's Catholics: The Evolution of an American Identity* (Notre

Dame, Ind.: University of Notre Dame Press, 1981), 29–30; Brian C. Mitchell, *The Paddy Camps: The Irish of Lowell, 1821–1861* (Urbana: University of Illinois Press, 1988), 121–43.

50. Powers, *Invisible Immigrants,* 428.

51. Lawrence J. McCaffrey, *Textures of Irish America* (Syracuse, N.Y.: Syracuse University Press, 1992), 47.

52. Doyle, "The Irish in North America, 1776–1845," 713–14; Ellen Skerrett, "The Catholic Dimension," in Lawrence J. McCaffrey, ed., *The Irish in Chicago* (Urbana: University of Illinois Press, 1987), 23–41; Potter, *Golden Door,* 359–68.

53. Jay P. Dolan, *The American Catholic Experience: A History from Colonial Times to the Present* (New York: Doubleday and Co., 1985), 160–94; Charles R. Morris, *American Catholic: The Saints and Sinners Who Built America's Most Powerful Church* (New York: Vintage Books, 1997), 54–80; McCaffrey, *Textures,* 56, 64–65.

54. D. Gregory van Dussen, "American Methodism's *Christian Advocate* and Irish Catholic Immigration, 1830–1870," *Éire-Ireland* 26, no. 4 (1992): 91–94; Donna Merwick, *Boston's Priests, 1848–1910: A Study of Social and Intellectual Change* (Cambridge, Mass.: Harvard University Press, 1973), 32–43.

55. McCaffrey, *Textures,* 94; Roediger, *Wages of Whiteness,* 140–44.

56. Potter, *Golden Door,* 234–38, 377; Berger, "Irish Emigrant," 179; Thomas N. Brown, "The Political Irish: Politicians and Rebels," in Doyle and Edwards, *America and Ireland,* 38–40.

57. Thomas N. Brown, *Irish-American Nationalism, 1870–1890* (Philadelphia: J. B. Lippincott, 1966), 20, 23.

58. Brown, *Nationalism,* 24. See also McCaffrey, *Textures,* 137–38; Kenneth Moss, "St. Patrick's Day Celebrations and the Formation of Irish-American Identity, 1845–1875," *Journal of Social History* 29 (1995): 135–37.

59. Funchion, *Voluntary Organizations,* 223–26; van Dussen, "American Methodism's Christian Advocate," 76–99.

60. For full discussion see Malcolm Campbell, "The Other Immigrants: Comparing the Irish in Australia and the United States," *Journal of American Ethnic History* 14, no. 3 (1995): 3–22.

61. David Fitzpatrick, "The Irish in America: Exiles or Escapers?" *Reviews in American History* 15 (1987): 272–78.

62. David Fitzpatrick, *Oceans of Consolation: Personal Accounts of Irish Migration to Australia* (Ithaca, N.Y.: Cornell University Press, 1994), 616–17.

63. *Freeman's Journal* (Sydney) (hereafter *FJ*), 27 June 1850; *ADB,* 2:165–66.

64. See Mark Lyons, "Aspects of Sectarianism in New South Wales circa 1865 to 1880" (Ph.D. thesis, Australian National University, 1972), 1–13; *FJ,* 27 June 1850.

65. *Goulburn Herald* (hereafter *GH*), 2 March 1850; Pauline Hamilton, "'No Irish Need Apply': Prejudice as a Factor in the Development of Immigration Policy in New South Wales and Victoria, 1840–1870" (Ph.D. thesis, University of New South Wales, 1979), 356; McClaughlin, *Barefoot and Pregnant.*

66. *FJ,* 11 July 1850; *GH,* 9 March 1850, 30 March 1850, 20 April 1850.

67. *GH,* 9 March 1850, 30 March 1850, 20 April 1850; New South Wales Legislative Assembly, Select Committee on Irish Female Immigration, Votes & Proceedings, 1859, vol. 2, 18.

68. O'Farrell, *Catholic Church,* 127–29.

69. Campbell, *Kingdom,* 156–58.

70. Mary McClintock, *After the Battering Ram: The Trail of the Dispossessed from Derryveagh, 1861–1991* (n.p.: An Taisce, 1991), 6–7.

71. Henry Norbert Birt, *Benedictine Pioneers in Australia,* 2 vols. (London: Herbery and Daniel, 1911), 2:330–31.

72. Lyons, "Aspects of Sectarianism," 44, 45–57, 407–14; O'Farrell, *Irish in Australia,* 59–60.

73. Joseph M. Hernon, *Celts, Catholics and Copperheads: Ireland Views the American Civil War* (Columbus: Ohio State University Press, 1968), 5–6.

74. Hernon, *Celts,* 1–10, 53–57.

75. Hernon, *Celts,* 92–93; David T. Gleeson, *The Irish in the South, 1815–1877* (Chapel Hill: University of North Carolina Press, 2001), 140; Carl Wittke, *The Irish in America* (Baton Rouge: Louisiana State University Press, 1956), 148–49.

76. Robert G. Athearn, *Thomas Francis Meagher: An Irish Revolutionary in America* (New York: Arno Press, 1976), 110–67; Hernon, *Celts,* 92–96, 106–7.

77. Quoted in Ignatiev, *How the Irish Became White,* 88; Wittke, *Irish in America,* 135–38; Edward K. Spann, "Union Green: The Irish Community and the Civil War," in Ronald H. Bayor and Timothy J. Meagher, eds., *The New York Irish* (Baltimore: Johns Hopkins University Press, 1996), 193–209.

78. Strong, *Diary,* 4:132, 168; Kevin Kenny, *American Irish,* 122–24; Gibson, "Attitudes of the New York Irish," 141–51.

79. Gleeson, *Irish in the South,* 158–72; Hernon, *Celts,* 11–13; Wittke, *Irish in America,* 135–49.

80. Iver Bernstein, *The New York City Draft Riots: Their Significance for American Society and Politics in the Age of the Civil War* (New York: Oxford University Press, 1990); Edwin G. Burrows and Mike Wallace, *Gotham: A History of New York City to 1898* (New York: Oxford University Press, 1999), 887–99.

81. Strong, *Diary,* 4:342–43.

3. Irish Rural Life

1. Grace McDonald, *The History of the Irish in Wisconsin in the Nineteenth Century* (New York: Arno Press, 1976); James P. Shannon, *Catholic Colonization on the Western Frontier* (New York: Arno Press, 1976); Merle Curti, *The Making of an American Community. A Case Study of Democracy in a Frontier Community* (Palo Alto, Calif.: Stanford University Press, 1959).

2. Nancy L. Green, "The Comparative Method and Poststructural Structuralism: New Perspectives for Migration Studies," *Journal of American Ethnic History* 13, no. 4 (Summer 1994): 13; Marc Bloch, "A Contribution Towards a Comparative History of European Societies," in *Land and Work in Mediaeval Europe: Papers of Marc Bloch* (London: Routledge and Kegan Paul, 1967), 44–81.

3. Donald Akenson, "The Historiography of the Irish Americans," in *Being Had,* 37–75; David Doyle, "The Irish as Urban Pioneers in the United States, 1850–70," *Journal of American Ethnic History* 10 (Fall 1990–Winter 1991): 36–59; Campbell, "The Other Immigrants," 3–22.

4. United States Census Bureau [J. D. B. DeBow], *Statistical View of the United States: Compendium of the Seventh Census* (Washington, D.C.: U.S. Senate, 1854), 116–18; Campbell, *Kingdom,* 62–90.

5. Morton Winsberg, "Irish Settlement in the United States, 1850–90," *Éire-Ireland* 20, no. 1 (Spring 1985): 7–14.

6. Ann Regan, "The Irish," in June Drenning Holmquist (ed.), *They Chose Minnesota: A Survey of the State's Ethnic Groups* (St. Paul: Minnesota Historical Society Press, 1981), 132; Sarah P. Rubenstein, "The British, English, Scots, Welsh and British Canadians," in Holmquist, *They Chose Minnesota,* 118.

7. Fitzpatrick, *Irish Emigration,* 9–13.

8. Michael Callaghan, Saint Paul, Minnesota, to his brother, 28 September 1852. Callaghan Papers, A-C156, Minnesota Historical Society (hereafter MHS).

9. Mary Jane Hill Anderson, *Autobiography of Mary Jane Hill Anderson, Wife of Robert Anderson, 1827–1934* (Minneapolis: privately published, 1934), 3–17. On Galena, see Mary Josephine Read, "A Population Study of the Driftless Hill Land During the Pioneer Period, 1832–60" (Ph.D. dissertation, University of Wisconsin, 1941); McDonald, *Irish in Wisconsin,* chap. 2.

10. *Minnesota Democrat Weekly,* 19 May 1852. Extracted in Minnesota Federal Writers Project: Annals of Minnesota Subject Files, 1849–1942, M529 Reel 104, MHS.

11. Sister Mary Gilbert Kelly, *Catholic Immigrant Colonization Projects in the United States, 1815–60* (New York: U.S. Catholic Historical Society, 1939), 198–200; Henry A. Castle, "General James Shields," *Minnesota Historical Society Collections* 15 (1915): 711–30; "Address by John Ireland at the Unveiling of a Statue of Shields," *Minnesota Historical Society Collections* 15 (1915): 731–40.

12. Dennis Clark, *Hibernia America: The Irish and Regional Cultures* (Westport, Conn.: Greenwood Press, 1986), 120; Kelly, *Colonization Projects,* 200.

13. *Minnesota Democrat Weekly,* 17 March 1852; *Daily Minnesota Pioneer,* 21 November 1854; *Pioneer Democrat,* 18 March 1856; *Daily Minnesotan,* 18 July 1856, 7 May 1857. Annals of Minnesota Subject Files, 1849–1942, M529 Reel 104, MHS.

14. Regan, "Irish," 132. Staged migration was also a feature among Irish rural settlers in neighboring Wisconsin: see McDonald, *Irish in Wisconsin,* 11.

15. Michael J. Boyle, Diary, Entry for 17 March 1876. Boyle Papers, P1435, MHS.

16. William G. Gresham, *History of Nicollet and Le Sueur Counties Minnesota. Their Peoples, Industries and Institutions* (Indianapolis: B. F. Bowen, 1916), 407, 439, 528.

17. United States Census Office [Francis A. Walker], *A Compendium of the Ninth Census, 1870* (Washington, D.C.: Government Printing Office, 1872), 420.

18. John Ireland, "Fifty Years of Catholicity in the Northwest. Sermon Preached by Most Rev. John Ireland on the Fiftieth Anniversary of the Arrival of St. Paul's First Bishop, 2 July 1901," Irish-American Colonisation Company Papers, BB2 168, Box 3, F 4, MHS. See also Annie King Lacore Reminiscences, P1337, 9, MHS.

19. Lewis Doyle, Kilkenny township, Le Sueur County, Minnesota, to John Doyle, County Carlow, 23 January 1873. I am grateful to Professor Kerby Miller of the University of Missouri–Columbia for a transcript of the Hogan/Doyle family letters.

20. Philip H. Bagenal, *The American Irish and their Influence on Irish Politics* (Boston: Roberts Brothers, 1882), 79.

21. Ireland, "Fifty Years of Catholicity," Irish-American Colonisation Company Papers, BB2 168, Box 3, F 4, 3, MHS.

22. Campbell, *Kingdom,* 37–61; James Waldersee, *Catholic Society in New South Wales, 1788–1860* (Sydney: Sydney University Press, 1974).

23. William W. Burton, *The State of Religion and Education in New South Wales* (London: J. Cross, 1840), 278; Cunningham, *Two Years in New South Wales,* 2:109.

24. William Browne to Miss Margaret Lindsay, 4 November 1816; Browne to same, 24 August 1820, William Browne Papers, Ab 65/2, ML; Thomas Pope Besnard, *A Voice From the Bush in Australia* (Dublin: William Curry, 1839), 28–29.

25. Henry Lee, "Henry Osborne (1803–1859)," in Richard Reid and Keith Johnson, eds., *The Irish Australians: Selected Articles for Australian and Irish Family Historians* (Sydney: Society of Australian Genealogists, 1984), 24; P. McDonnell, "The Land That Osborne Left," *Familia: Ulster Genealogical Review* 2 (1987): 83–91.

26. John Dunmore Lang, *Notes of a Trip to the Westward and Southward in the Colony of New South Wales in the Months of March and April 1862* (Sydney: Hanson and Bennett, 1862), 42; Samuel Shumack, *An Autobiography or Tales and Legends of Canberra Pioneers* (Canberra: Australian National University Press, 1977), 108–9.

27. O'Farrell, *Irish in Australia*, 88–89, 154.

28. Fitzpatrick, *Oceans of Consolation*, 15–16; Campbell, *Kingdom*, 62–90; Reid, "Irish Assisted Emigration," especially chaps. 4–5.

29. Fitzpatrick, *Oceans of Consolation*, 16.

30. Colonial Secretary, Letters re Land, Entry for Edward Ryan, New South Wales State Archives.

31. Campbell, *Kingdom*, 80–82.

32. Lang, *Notes of a Trip*, 27.

33. *Express*, 2 July 1885; *Sydney Morning Herald*, 15 August 1859.

34. James Tobias Ryan, *Reminiscences of Australia* (Sydney: G. Robertson, 1895), 262; Waldersee, *Catholic Society*, 152–53.

35. Thomas and Anne Quilty to Ellen Quilty, Shanagolden, Limerick, 15 October 1850. Monteagle Papers, Menzies Library, University of New South Wales; O'Mahony and Thompson, *Poverty to Promise*, 73–74, 104–7; Gwendoline Wilson, *Murray of Yarralumla* (Melbourne: Oxford University Press, 1968).

36. Mary Durack, *Kings in Grass Castles* (London: Constable and Co., 1959), 45; Donald Carisbrooke, "Immigrants in the Bush," *Push from the Bush* 5 (December 1979): 48.

37. Campbell, *Kingdom*, 134–62.

38. On Irish persistence on the land, see Kieren D. Flanagan, "Emigration, Assimilation and Occupational Categories of Irish Americans in Minnesota" (M.A. thesis, University of Minnesota, 1969), table 18, 226–27.

39. Shumack, *Autobiography*, 45; and Fitzpatrick, *Oceans of Consolation*, 63, on land ownership.

40. McGee, *Irish Settlers*, 179–86; Bagenal, *American Irish*, 75–99; Kenny, *American Irish*, 143–44.

41. *Pilot* (Boston), 9 January 1869, 30 January 1869.

42. Lacore, Reminiscences, 3, MHS.

43. James P. Shannon, "Bishop Ireland's Connemara Experiment," *Minnesota History* 35 (March 1957): 208, quoting William Onahan; Marvin R. O'Connell, *John Ireland and the American Catholic Church* (St. Paul: Minnesota Historical Society Press, 1988), 135–61.

44. Gerard Moran, "'In Search of the Promised Land': The Connemara Colonization Scheme to Minnesota, 1880," *Éire–Ireland* 31, nos. 3–4 (Fall/Winter 1996): 130–49.

45. Prospectus of the Irish-American Colonisation Company Ltd., Irish-American Colonisation Company Papers, BB2 I68, Box 1, F 3, MHS.

46. John Sweetman, "The Sweetman Catholic Colony of Currie, Minnesota: A Memoir," *Acta et Dicta* 1, no. 3 (1911): 41–65; Sweetman, *Recent Experiences in the Emigration of Irish Families* (Dublin: M. H. Gill and Son, 1883); Alice E. Smith, "The Sweetman Irish Colony," *Minnesota History* 9 (1928): 331–46.

47. See Donald Harman Akenson, *Half the World from Home: Perspectives on the Irish in New Zealand, 1860–1950* (Wellington: Victoria University Press, 1990), 123–58; O'Farrell, *Irish in Australia*, 107; Gerard Moran, *Sending Out Ireland's Poor: Assisted Emigration to North America in the Nineteenth Century* (Dublin: Four Courts Press, 2004), 192–97.

48. Martin Mahony, *Sweetman Catholic Colony in Murray County, Minnesota: Letters from the Pastor and Others* (Currie, Minn.: Manager's Office, 1885), 5, 11.

49. Adna Weber, *The Growth of Cities in the Nineteenth Century: A Study in Statistics* (Ithaca, N.Y.: Cornell University Press, 1967), 1, 138–50.

50. Doyle, "Urban Pioneers."

51. James Middleton Papers, P1070, MHS. On farming activities, see his diary, especially volume 1, 1869.

4. The Pacific Irish

1. Handlin, *Boston's Immigrants;* on the historiography of the Irish in the United States, see Donald Akenson, "The Historiography of the Irish in the United States of America," in Patrick O'Sullivan, ed., *The Irish in the New Communities* (Leicester: Leicester University Press, 1993), 99–127.

2. Timothy J. Sarbaugh, "The Irish in the West: An Ethnic Tradition of Enterprise and Innovation, 1848–1991," *Journal of the West* 31, no. 2 (1992): 5–8; James P. Walsh, "The Irish in the New America: 'Way Out West,'" in Doyle and Edwards, *America and Ireland,* 165–76.

3. James Riordan to his sister, New Orleans, 20 September 1859, James Riordan Papers, Bancroft Library, University of California, Berkeley (hereafter UCB), C-B740.

4. Maguire, *Irish in America,* 262.

5. Hugh Quigley, *The Irish Race in California and on the Pacific Coast with an introductory historical dissertation on the principal races of mankind and a vocabulary of ancient and modern Irish family names* (San Francisco: A. Roman and Co., 1878).

6. Chisholm, *Comfort for the Poor;* O'Farrell, *Irish in Australia.*

7. Fitzpatrick, *Oceans of Consolation;* Patrick O'Farrell, *Letters from Irish Australia, 1825–1929* (Sydney: University of New South Wales Press, 1984); Angela McCarthy, *Irish Migrants in New Zealand, 1840–1937: The Desired Haven* (Woodbridge, Suffolk: The Boydell Press, 2005).

8. R. A. Burchell, *The San Francisco Irish, 1848–1880* (Berkeley: University of California Press, 1980), 184; Timothy J. Sarbaugh, "Exiles of Confidence: The Irish American Community of San Francisco, 1880–1920," in Timothy J. Meagher, ed., *From Paddy to Studs: Irish-American Communities in the Turn of the Century Era, 1880 to 1920* (Westport, Conn.: Greenwood Press, 1986), 161–79.

9. Oliver MacDonagh, "Emigration from Ireland to Australia: An Overview," in Colm Kiernan, ed., *Ireland and Australia, 1788–1988: Bicentenary Essays* (Dublin: Gill and Macmillan, 1986), 127; David Fitzpatrick, "Irish Emigration in the Later Nineteenth Century," *Irish Historical Studies* 22 (1980): 136–37; Donald Harman Akenson, *The Irish Diaspora: A Primer* (Toronto: P. D. Meany, 1993), 91–122. More negative assessments of the Irish experience in Australia may be found in two unpublished Ph.D. theses, Chris McConville, "Emigrant Irish and Suburban Catholic: Faith and Nation in Melbourne and Sydney, 1815–1933" (Ph.D. thesis, University of Melbourne, 1984), and Pauline Hamilton, "'No Irish Need Apply.'"

10. Patricia Nelson Limerick, "Will the Real California Please Stand Up?" *California History* 73 (1994): 268.

11. See James P. Walsh, "The Irish in Early San Francisco," in James P. Walsh, ed., *The San Francisco Irish, 1850–1976* (San Francisco: Irish Literary and Historical Society, 1978), 9–25; Roger Lotchin, *San Francisco, 1846–1856: From Hamlet to City* (New York: Oxford University Press, 1974), 102–3.

12. United States Census Bureau, 7th–14th censuses; Patrick J. Blessing, *The Irish in*

America: A Guide to the Literature and the Manuscript Collections (Washington, D.C.: Catholic University of America Press, 1992), 288–92.

13. See Malcolm Campbell, "Ireland's Furthest Shores: Irish Immigrant Settlement in Nineteenth-Century California and Eastern Australia," *Pacific Historical Review* 71 (2002): 59–90.

14. *Commission on Emigration and Other Population Problems, 1948–1954* (Dublin: Stationery Office, 1954), 314–15; James Jupp and Barry York, *Birthplaces of the Australian People: Colonial and Commonwealth Censuses* (Canberra: Center for Immigration and Multicultural Studies, 1995), 3–5, 17; O'Farrell, *Irish in Australia,* 63.

15. Hubert Howe Bancroft, *The History of California,* 7 vols. (Santa Barbara, Calif.: Wallace Herberd, 1970), 6:221.

16. Philip J. Ethington, *The Public City: The Political Construction of Urban Life in San Francisco, 1850–1900* (Cambridge: Cambridge University Press, 1994), 326–36; Catherine Ann Curry, "Three Irish Women and Social Action in San Francisco: Mother Teresa Comerford, Mother Baptist Russell, and Kate Kennedy," *Journal of the West* 31, no. 2 (1992): 66–72.

17. United States Census Office, *A Compendium of the Ninth Census,* 28–29, 400–401; Robert A. Burchell, "British Immigrants in Southern California, 1850–1870," *Southern California Quarterly* 53 (1971): 283–302.

18. See David Alan Johnson, *Founding the Far West: California, Oregon and Nevada, 1840–1890* (Berkeley: University of California Press, 1992), 238–42.

19. Burchell, *San Francisco Irish,* 58; Thomas R. Walker, "Economic Opportunity on the Urban Frontier: Wealth and Nativity in Early San Francisco," *Explorations in Economic History* 37 (2000): 258–77. Patrick J. Blessing focuses on Los Angeles and Sacramento and points to social mobility among Irish immigrants who persisted in these locations. "West Among Strangers: Irish Migration to California" (Ph.D. diss., University of California, Berkeley, 1977), 349–50.

20. MacDonagh, "Emigration from Ireland," 133.

21. Campbell, *Kingdom,* 145.

22. Tony Dingle, *The Victorians: Settling* (Sydney: Fairfax, Syme and Weldon, 1984), 26–27, 36–37.

23. Richard Broome, *The Victorians: Arriving* (Sydney: Fairfax, Syme and Weldon, 1984), 67–85; Dingle, *Settling,* 53–44.

24. Broome, *Arriving,* 82–85, 102–4; Chris McConville, *Croppies, Celts and Catholics: The Irish in Australia* (Melbourne: Edward Arnold, 1987), 47–61; Oliver MacDonagh, "Irish in Victoria in the Nineteenth Century," in James Jupp, ed., *The Australian People: An Encyclopedia of the Nation, Its People and Their Origins* (Sydney: Angus and Robertson, 1988), 578–82.

25. Barry Smith, "Stalwarts of the Garrison: Some Irish Academics in Australia," in O'Brien and Travers, *Irish Emigrant,* 120–47; Laurence Geary, "Australia *felix:* Irish Doctors in Nineteenth-Century Victoria," in O'Sullivan, ed., *Irish in the New Communities,* 162–79; Gordon Forth, "Anglo-Irish," in Jupp, *The Australian People,* 576–78.

26. T. A. Coghlan, *Results of a Census of New South Wales Taken on the Night of 31st March 1901* (Sydney: Government Printer, 1901), 770; United States Census Office [Francis A. Walker], *A Compendium of the Tenth Census, 1880* (Washington, D.C.: Government Printing Office, 1882), 1359–67.

27. N. G. Butlin, "Australian National Accounts," in Wray Vamplew, ed., *Australians, Historical Statistics* (Sydney: Fairfax, Syme and Weldon, 1987), 133.

28. Patrick O'Farrell and Deirdre O'Farrell, "The Status of Women: Some Opinions in Australian Catholic History c. 1860–1960," *Bulletin of Christian Affairs* 2 (1975): 3–42.

29. Roger Daniels, "On the Comparative Study of Immigrant and Ethnic Groups in the New World: A Note," *Comparative Studies in Society and History* 25 (1983): 401–4.

30. R. A. Burchell, "The Gathering of a Community: The British-Born of San Francisco in 1852 and 1872," *Journal of American Studies* 10 (1976): 279–312. This pattern was repeated in neighboring counties, such as Sonoma, where only 6 percent of the Irish-born gave their last place of residence as Ireland. See Dennis E. Harris, ed., *Redwood Empire Social History Project: California State Census, 1852, Sonoma County* (Sonoma: County of Sonoma, 1983), 37.

31. Burchell, *San Francisco Irish,* 34–35; Peter R. Decker, *Fortunes and Failures: White Collar Mobility in Nineteenth Century San Francisco* (Cambridge, Mass.: Harvard University Press, 1978), 13, 19–23; Bancroft, *History of California,* vi, 126–42.

32. Burchell, "Gathering of a Community," 282–83; Harris, *Redwood Empire,* 36–37.

33. Sherman L. Ricards and George. M. Blackburn, "The Sydney Ducks: A Demographic Analysis," *Pacific Historical Review* 42 (1973): 20; Burchell, "Gathering of a Community," 281–83.

34. Thomas Kerr, Diary of Things Worth Notice—During My Voyage to Calafornia [*sic*]— & Remarkable Events There (Yes and a good many things not worth notice too), MS 84/36C, UCB. Published as "An Irishman in the Gold Rush: The Journal of Thomas Kerr," *California Historical Society Quarterly* 7, no. 3 (1928): 205–27, and serialized in *California Historical Society Quarterly* 7 (1928): 395–404, and 8 (1929): 17–25, 167–82, 262–77.

35. James D. Phelan, "The Services of the Irish People in the Cause of Freedom," Address before the Knights of Saint Patrick, 27 November 1895, F858/P5/v6/X, UCB; Walsh, "James Phelan: Creating the Fortune, Creating the Family," *Journal of the West* 31, no. 2 (April 1992): 17–23; Ethington, *Public City,* 377–87.

36. John Riordan, "Garret McEnerney and the Irish Pursuit of Success," typescript 73/122/C/No. 96, UCB (edited version published in Walsh, *San Francisco Irish,* 72–84); Roger Lotchin, "John Francis Neylan, San Francisco Progressive" in Walsh, *San Francisco Irish,* 86–110; Frank Roney, *Irish Rebel and Labor Leader: An Autobiography,* ed. Ira Cross (Berkeley: University of California Press, 1931).

37. See, for example, Campbell, *Kingdom;* S. M. Ingham, *Enterprising Migrants: An Irish Family in Australia* (Melbourne: Hawthorn Press, 1975); Gordon Forth, *The Winters on the Wannon* (Geelong, Vic.: Deakin University Press, 1991).

38. Fitzpatrick, *Oceans of Consolation,* 15–16.

39. Haines, *Emigration and the Laboring;* Paula Hamilton "'Tipperarifying the Moral Atmosphere': Irish Catholic Immigration and the State, 1840–1860," in Sydney Labour History Group, eds., *What Rough Beast? The State and Social Order in Australian History* (Sydney: George Allen and Unwin, 1982), 13–30; Reid, "Irish Assisted Emigration."

40. Robin Haines, "Indigent Misfits or Shrewd Operators? Government-Assisted Emigrants from the United Kingdom to Australia 1831–1860," *Flinders University Working Papers in Economic History* 61 (May 1993): 12–13.

41. David N. Doyle, "Urban Pioneers," 36–59.

42. Bayard Taylor, *Eldorado or Adventures in the Path of Empire,* 18th ed. (New York: G. P. Putnam, 1861), 103; Bradford Luckingham, "Immigrant Life in Emergent San Francisco," *Journal of the West* 12 (1973): 600–617; Doris M. Wright, "The Making of Cosmopolitan California: An Analysis of Immigration, 1848–1870," *California Historical Society Quarterly* 19 (1940): 323–43.

43. Frank Soule, *The Annals of San Francisco* (New York: D. Appleton and Co., 1855), 411, 484; Mary P. Ryan, *Civic Wars: Democracy and Public Life in the American City during the Nineteenth Century* (Berkeley: University of California Press, 1997), 52–56.

44. Quoted in Albert L. Hurtado, *Intimate Frontiers: Sex, Gender and Culture in Old California*

(Albuquerque: University of New Mexico Press, 1999), 75, though for reaction to diversity see 75–76.

45. For example, Isabella Saxon, *Five Years Within the Golden Gate* (Philadelphia: J. B. Lippincott, 1868), 187, 193.

46. Quoted in Patrick J. Dowling, *California: The Irish Dream* (San Francisco: Golden Gate Publishers, 1988), 19. See also Roger Lotchin, *San Francisco, 1846–1856: From Hamlet to City* (New York: Oxford University Press, 1974) 114.

47. *Bishop's Directory of San Francisco* (San Francisco, 1875), 35–36; W. Gleeson, *History of the Catholic Church in California,* 2 vols. (San Francisco: A. L. Bancroft and Co., 1872), 2:281.

48. Quigley, *Irish Race in California,* 420; Sarbaugh, "Exiles of Confidence," 166; George T. Crowley, "The Irish in California," *Studies: An Irish Quarterly Review* 25 (1936): 451–62.

49. James P. Walsh, "Peter C. Yorke: San Francisco's Irishman Reconsidered," in Walsh, *San Francisco Irish,* 43–57; Ethington, *Public City,* 324–26; Joseph S. Brusher, "Peter C. Yorke and the A. P. A. in San Francisco," *Catholic Historical Review* 37 (1951): 129–50; Richard Gribble, *Catholicism and the San Francisco Labor Movement* (San Francisco: Mellon Research University Press, 1993).

50. F. R. Freehill, "Colonial 'Know-Nothingism': A Reply to Mr. B. R. Wise," *Centennial Magazine* 2–3 (August 1889–September 1890): 226–31; O'Farrell, *Irish in Australia,* 209–11; King, *Richard Bourke.*

51. Hilary M. Carey, *Believing in Australia: A Cultural History of Religions* (Sydney: Allen and Unwin, 1996), 94.

52. Osofsky, "Abolitionists," 889–912; Riach, "Daniel O'Connell," 3–25; Ignatiev, *How the Irish Became White.*

53. Mary Roberts Coolidge, *Chinese Immigration* (Taipei: Ch'Eng Wen Publishing, 1968), 270.

54. Roney, *Irish Rebel,* 266–69.

55. *Irish-Australian,* 6 October 1895.

56. *Irish-Australian,* 3, 17 November 1894; 30 March 1895.

57. Markus, *Australian Race Relations,* 59–84; Andrew Markus, *Fear and Hatred: Purifying California and Australia, 1850–1901* (Sydney: Hale and Iremonger, 1979).

5. New Worlds Converge

1. Mitchel, *Jail Journal,* 315.

2. Strong, *Diary,* 2:453.

3. William Leonard Joyce, *Editors and Ethnicity: A History of the Irish-American Press, 1848–1883* (New York: Arno Press, 1976), 79–80.

4. Brown, *Nationalism,* 26–27; Bryan McGovern, "John Mitchel: Ecumenical Nationalist in the Old South," *New Hibernia Review* 5, no. 2 (2001): 99–110; Louis J. Walsh, *John Mitchel* (Dublin: Talbot Press, 1934), 78–93.

5. Patrick O'Farrell, "Whose Reality? The Irish Famine in History and Literature," *Historical Studies* 29 (April 1982): 1–13; James S. Donnelly, Jr., "The Construction of the Memory of the Famine in Ireland and The Irish Diaspora, 1850–1900," *Éire-Ireland* 31, no. 2 (Summer 1996): 26–61.

6. Cited in Robert Kee, *The Green Flag, Volume Two: The Bold Fenian Men* (London: Penguin, 1989), 11.

7. John O'Leary, *Recollections of Fenians and Fenianism* (Shannon: Irish University Press, 1969), 152–70; R. V. Comerford, "Conspiring Brotherhoods and Contending Elites, 1857–63," in Vaughan, *Ireland under the Union, 1801–1870,* 415–30.

8. Brian Jenkins, *Fenians and Anglo-American Relations During Reconstruction* (Ithaca, N.Y.: Cornell University Press, 1969), 28–31; W. S. Neidhardt, *Fenianism in North America* (University Park: Pennsylvania State University Press, 1975), 9–15.

9. Neidhardt, *Fenianism,* 28–35; Jenkins, *Fenians,* 30–33; Kee, *Bold Fenian Men,* 28–30.

10. Neidhardt, *Fenianism,* 43–52; Kenny, *American Irish,* 128–29.

11. *Pilot* (Boston) (hereafter *BP*), 26 May 1866; Kee, *Bold Fenian Men,* 28–31.

12. Neidhardt, *Fenianism,* 59–75; Leon Ó Broin, *Fenian Fever: An Anglo-American Dilemma* (London: Chatto and Windus, 1971), 52–72.

13. Strong, *Diary,* 4:89.

14. *BP,* 16 June 1866.

15. *BP,* 30 June 1866.

16. R. V. Comerford, "Gladstone's First Irish Enterprise, 1864–70," in Vaughan, *Ireland under the Union, 1801–1870,* 438–41.

17. Mark Lyons, "Aspects of Sectarianism," 275.

18. James Rutledge, quoted in Alan Barcan, *Two Centuries of Education in New South Wales* (Sydney: University of New South Wales Press, 1988), 75.

19. O'Farrell, *Catholic Church,* 127–29, 151.

20. Michael Hogan, *The Sectarian Strand: Religion in Australian History* (Melbourne: Penguin, 1987), 100–127; Charles Gavan Duffy, *My Life,* 2:321–46.

21. Keith Amos, *The Fenians in Australia, 1865–1880* (Sydney: University of New South Wales Press, 1987), 78–99; O'Farrell, *Irish in Australia,* 208–10; G. C. Bolton, "The Fenians are Coming, the Fenians are Coming!" *Studies in Western Australian History* 4 (1981): 62–67.

22. Lyons, "Aspects of Sectarianism," 74–85; O'Farrell, *Irish in Australia,* 102–3.

23. *SMH,* 21, 22 January 1868.

24. *FJ,* 25 January 1868.

25. *SMH,* 13 March 1868; Lyons, "Aspects of Sectarianism," 89–100; Amos, *Fenians,* 52–53.

26. *FJ,* 14 March 1868 (country edition).

27. Amos, *Fenians,* 45–77; O'Farrell, *Irish in Australia,* 210–11.

28. Amos, *Fenians,* 45–77; Robert Travers, *The Phantom Fenians of New South Wales* (Sydney: Kangaroo Press, 1986), 63–79.

29. *SMH,* 14 March 1868.

30. *FJ,* 21 March 1850.

31. *Advocate,* 2 January 1869.

32. Lyons, "Aspects of Sectarianism," 85; 119–30; Amos, *Fenians,* 68–77.

33. *SMH,* 16 March 1868.

34. Richard Davis, *Irish Issues in New Zealand Politics, 1868–1922* (Dunedin: University of Otago Press, 1974), 11–24.

35. Henry Parkes, *Irish Immigration: Speech Delivered in the Legislative Assembly on the Second Reading of "A Bill to Authorise and Regulate Assisted Immigration"* (Sydney, 1869), 11; Pauline Hamilton, "'No Irish Need Apply,'" 423.

36. *Irishman* (Melbourne), 28 November 1872, 30 January 1873, 20 February 1873, 27 February 1873.

37. *Irish World* (hereafter *IW*), 12 November 1870; Michael A. Gordon, *Irish Political Violence in New York City, 1870 and 1871* (Ithaca, N.Y.: Cornell University Press, 1993).

38. Robert Ernst, *Immigrant Life in New York City, 1825–1863* (Port Washington, N.Y.: Ira J. Freedman, 1965), 193, 198–203.

39. See, for example, *IW,* 27 January 1872, 6 April 1872, 27 May 1873; Eric Foner, "Class,

Ethnicity and Radicalism in the Gilded Age: The Land League and Irish America," *Marxist Perspectives* 1, no. 2 (Summer 1978): 11–14; James Paul Rodechko, *Patrick Ford and His Search for America: A Case Study in Irish-American Journalism, 1870–1913* (New York: Arno Press, 1976), 58–90.

40. United States Census Office [Francis A. Walker], *Ninth Census Volume 1: The Statistics of the Population of the United States* (Washington, D.C.: Government Printer, 1872), 386, 389; Doyle, "Urban Pioneers," 43–48.

41. *Ninth Census,* 704–65.

42. *Ninth Census,* 704–65. On diversity in Pennsylvania, for example, see Stephanie A. Morris, "From Northwest Ireland to America, 1864–70: Tracing Migrants from Their Place of Origin to Their New Home in Philadelphia" (Ph.D. diss., Temple University, 1988), 170–201; on miners in Butte, see Emmons, *The Butte Irish.*

43. On the limits of the United States census data, see Akenson, *Being Had,* 38–75; and Donald Harman Akenson, "Data: What Is Known about the Irish in North America?" in O. MacDonagh and W. F. Mandle, eds., *Ireland and Irish-Australia: Studies in Cultural and Political History* (London: Croom Helm, 1986), 1–17.

44. *IW,* 2 March 1872, 6 April 1872, 14 December 1872.

45. *The Irish Cause on the Pacific. John Savage in California. Containing an Account of the Visit of the Chief Executive, F.B., to the Pacific Coast: The Great Demonstrations at Redwood City, and the Speeches on the Cause of Irish Independence* (New York: American News Company, 1870).

46. *IW,* 25 March 1871 (emphasis in the original).

47. Hasia Diner, *Erin's Daughters in America: Irish Immigrant Women in the Nineteenth Century* (Baltimore: Johns Hopkins University Press, 1983), 66.

48. Brown, *Nationalism,* 24; Lawrence J. McCaffrey, *Textures of Irish-America* (Syracuse, N.Y.: Syracuse University Press, 1992), 137–38; Donald Harman Akenson, *The United States and Ireland* (Cambridge, Mass.: Harvard University Press, 1973), 37.

49. William O'Brien and Desmond Ryan, eds., *Devoy's Post Bag, 1871–1928,* 2 vols. (Dublin: C. J. Fallon, 1948), 1:13; Anthony G. Evans, *Fanatic Heart: A Life of John Boyle O'Reilly, 1844–1890* (Nedlands, W.A.: University of Western Australia Press, 1997), 173–81; David Doyle, "John Boyle O'Reilly and Irish Adjustment in America," *Journal of the Old Drogheda Society* (1996): 7–25.

50. James Jeffrey Roche, *Life of John Boyle O'Reilly* (Philadelphia: John J. McVey, 1891), 115–21; Francis G. McManamin, *The American Years of John Boyle O'Reilly, 1870–1890* (New York: Arno Press, 1976), 116–23, 184–90; Thomas H. O'Connor, *The Boston Irish: A Political History* (Boston: Northeastern University Press, 1995), 134–36.

51. Kenny, *American Irish,* 155–57; Miller, *Emigrants and Exiles,* 524.

52. Foner, "Class, Ethnicity and Radicalism," 1–47; Malcolm Campbell, "Irish Nationalism and Immigrant Assimilation: Comparing the United States and Australia," *Australasian Journal of American Studies* 15, no. 2 (1996): 24–43.

53. John Boyle O'Reilly to John Devoy, 13 February 1871, in O'Brien and Ryan, *Devoy's Post Bag,* 1:30–32; Michael Funchion, ed., *Irish-American Voluntary Organizations* (Westport, Conn.: Greenwood Press, 1983), 165–68.

54. Miller, *Emigrants and Exiles,* 334–44.

55. Kevin Kenny, *Making Sense of the Molly Maguires* (New York: Oxford University Press, 1998), 13–44; Victor Walsh, "'A Fanatic Heart': The Cause of Irish-American Nationalism in Pittsburgh during the Gilded Age," *Journal of Social History* 15 (1981): 187–204.

56. Lyons, "Aspects of Sectarianism," 275–78; Hogan, *Sectarian Strand,* 97–100.

57. O'Farrell, *Irish in Australia,* 101–5.

58. O'Farrell, *Catholic Church,* 194–225; Hugh Jackson, *Churches and People in Australia and New Zealand* (Wellington: Allen and Unwin, 1987), 22–47.

59. Lyons, "Aspects of Sectarianism," 24, 45; Hogan, *Sectarian Strand,* 97–100.

60. Wray Vamplew, ed. *Australians: Historical Statistics* (Sydney: Fairfax, Syme and Weldon, 1987), 286–89, tables Manf. 1–12, 13–22; N. G. Butlin, *Investment in Australian Economic Development, 1861–1900* (Canberra: Department of Economic History, RSSS, Australian National University, 1972), 16–23.

61. Vamplew, *Historical Statistics,* 23, 40–41.

62. Jackson, *Churches,* 48–60.

63. Stuart Piggin, *Evangelical Christianity in Australia: Spirit, Word and World* (Melbourne: Oxford University Press, 1996), 57–58.

64. Hugh Laracy, "Patrick Hennebery in Australasia, 1877–1882," in Brad Patterson, ed., *The Irish in New Zealand: Historical Contexts and Perspectives* (Wellington: Stout Research Centre, Victoria University of Wellington, 2002), 103–16; Jackson, *Churches,* 65–76.

65. Richard Slotkin, *The Fatal Environment: The Myth of the Frontier in the Age of Industrialization, 1800–1890* (New York: Athenium, 1985), 33–47.

66. Charles Gavan Duffy, *The Opinion of the Country: Speech of the Hon. Sir Charles Gavan Duffy at Sale on Monday 9 April 1877* (Sale, Vic., 1877), 4; Campbell, *Kingdom,* 139–50.

67. D. W. A. Baker, "The Origins of Robertson's Land Acts," *Historical Studies: Selected Articles* (Melbourne: Melbourne University Press, 1967), 103–4; Bill Gammage, "Who Gained, and Who Was Meant to Gain, from Land Selection in New South Wales?" *Australian Historical Studies* 24 (April 1990): 104–22.

68. John McQuilton, *The Kelly Outbreak, 1878–1880: The Geographical Dimension of Social Banditry* (Melbourne: Melbourne University Press, 1979).

69. McQuilton, *Kelly Outbreak,* 170–90; O'Farrell, *Irish in Australia,* 138–42.

70. Alan O'Day, *Irish Home Rule, 1867–1921* (Manchester: Manchester University Press, 1998), 58–62.

71. A. M. Topp, "English Institutions and the Irish Race," *Melbourne Review* 6 (January 1881): 9–10.

72. Gregory Tobin, "The Sea-Divided Gael: A Study of the Irish Home Rule Movement in Victoria and New South Wales, 1880–1916" (M.A. thesis, Australian National University, 1969), 67; Louise Mazzaroli, "The Irish in New South Wales, 1884–1914: Some Aspects of the Irish Sub-Culture" (Ph.D. thesis, University of New South Wales, 1979), 40–41.

73. Laurence M. Geary, "The Australasian Response to the Irish Crisis, 1879–80," in Oliver MacDonagh and W. F. Mandle, eds., *Irish-Australian Studies: Papers Delivered at the Fifth Irish-Australian Conference* (Canberra: Australian National University, 1989), 99–126; Tobin, "Sea-Divided Gael," 74–76; O'Farrell, *Irish in Australia,* 221–22.

6. Call of the New

1. W. E. Vaughan and A. J. Fitzpatrick, *Irish Historical Statistics: Population, 1821–1971* (Dublin: Royal Irish Academy, 1978), 2; Timothy W. Guinnane, *The Vanishing Irish: Households, Migration, and the Rural Economy in Ireland, 1850–1914* (Princeton, N.J.: Princeton University Press, 1997), 88–90.

2. David Fitzpatrick, "The Disappearance of the Irish Agricultural Labourer, 1841–1912," *Irish Economic and Social History* 7 (1980): 66–85; Michael Turner, *After the Famine: Irish Agriculture, 1850–1914* (Cambridge: Cambridge University Press, 1996), 126–60; Cormac Ó Gráda, *Ireland: A New Economic History* (Oxford: Clarendon Press, 1994), 255–64.

3. Lyn Hollen Lees and John Modell, "The Irish Countryman Urbanised: A Comparative Perspective on Famine Migration," *Journal of Urban History* 3 (1977): 391–408.

4. Guinnane, *Vanishing Irish,* 104–7.

5. Donald Harman Akenson, *The Irish Diaspora: A Primer* (Toronto: P. D. Meany, 1993), 157–87; Kerby A. Miller with David N. Doyle and Patricia Kelleher, "'For Love and Liberty': Irish Women, Migration and Domesticity in Ireland and America, 1815–1920," in Patrick O'Sullivan, ed., *Irish Women and Irish Migration* (London: Leicester University Press, 1995), 41–65; Anne O'Connell, "'The Care of the Immigrant Girls': The Migration Process of Late-Nineteenth-Century Irish Women," *Éire-Ireland* 35 (Fall/Winter 2000–2001): 102–33.

6. Kevin H. O'Rourke and Jeffrey G. Williamson, *Globalization and History: The Evolution of a Nineteenth-Century Atlantic Economy* (Cambridge, Mass.: MIT Press, 1999), 15–23; George R. Boyer, Timothy J. Hatton and Kevin O'Rourke, "The Impact of Emigration on Real Wages in Ireland, 1850–1914," in Timothy J. Hatton and Jeffrey G. Williamson, eds., *Migration and the International Labor Market* (London: Routledge, 1994), 221–39; Ó Gráda, *New Economic History,* 226–42.

7. Haines, *Emigration and the Labouring Poor,* 33–35. This is not to agree with Haines's assertion (36) that preference for a nonagrarian lifestyle was a determining factor in the global pattern of Irish emigration.

8. Jonathan Hughes, *American Economic History* (London: Scott, Foreman, 1990), 267–78, 305–46.

9. Stephan Thernstrom, ed., *The Harvard Encyclopedia of American Ethnic Groups* (Cambridge, Mass.: Belknap Press, 1980), 476–86; Roger Daniels, *Coming to America: A History of Immigration and Ethnicity in American Life* (New York: Harper Perennial, 1990), 121–26.

10. Quoted in Abbott, *Historical Aspects,* 327–28; John Higham, *Strangers in the Land: Patterns of American Nativism, 1860–1925* (New York, Atheneum, 1975), 35–36; Jacobson, *Whiteness of a Different Color,* 39–90.

11. Jacob Riis, *How the Other Half Lives* (London: Sampson Low, 1891); Alan M. Kraut, *The Huddled Masses: The Immigrant in American Society, 1880–1921* (Arlington Heights, Ill.: Harlan Davidson, 1982).

12. McCaffrey, *Textures,* 89–102; Shannon, *American Irish,* 60–85.

13. David N. Doyle, *Irish Americans, Native Rights and National Empires: The Structure, Divisions and Attitudes of the Catholic Minority in the Decade of Expansion, 1890–1901* (New York: Arno Press, 1976), 38–90; Doyle, "Unestablished Irishmen: New Immigrants and Industrial America, 1870–1910," in Dirk Hoerder, ed., *American Labor and Immigration History: Recent European Research* (Urbana: University of Illinois Press, 1983), 193–219; Kenny, *American Irish,* 185–86.

14. Ann R. Miller, "The Industrial Affiliation of Workers: Differences by Nativity and Country of Origin," in Susan Cotts Watkins, ed., *After Ellis Island: Newcomers and Natives in the 1910 Census* (New York: Russell Sage Foundation, 1994), 257–311.

15. Michael J. White, Robert F. Dymowski, and Shilian Wang, "Ethnic Neighbors and Ethnic Myths: An Examination of Residential Segregation in 1910," in Watkins, *After Ellis Island,* 194–208.

16. James Gibbons, "Irish Immigration to the United States," *Irish Ecclesiastical Record* 1 (4th series, February 1897): 103.

17. Higham, *Strangers in the Land,* 26; Kerby A. Miller, in *Emigrants and Exiles* (500), describes "overall trends as encouraging."

18. Weber, *Growth of Cities,* 1, 138–50, 152.

19. Marchamp Longway, *London to Melbourne* (London: Remington and Co., 1889), 195; Tony Dingle, *The Victorians: Settling* (Sydney: Fairfax, Syme and Weldon, 1984), 152–56.

20. Longway, *London to Melbourne,* 274; John Freeman, *Lights and Shadows of Melbourne Life* (London: Sampson Low, 1888), 89–90.

21. Coghlan, *Census of New South Wales,* 272.

22. McConville, "Emigrant Irish," 133, 147–201; Archibald Michie, *Readings in Melbourne; With an Essay on the Resources and Prospects of Victoria for the Emigrant and Uneasy Classes* (London: Sampson Low, 1879), 194–95, 275–79.

23. David Montgomery, "The Irish and the American Labor Movement," in Doyle and Edwards, *America and Ireland,* 205–18; Kenny, *American Irish,* 185–92.

24. Markus, *Race Relations,* 110–24.

25. Higham, *Strangers in the Land,* 97–105.

26. Markus, *Fear and Hatred,* 121–79; Markus, *Race Relations,* 67–84, 110–24.

27. L. G. Redmond-Howard, *John Redmond, the Man and the Demand: A Biographical Study in Irish Politics* (London: Hurst and Blackett, 1910), 36–38. On the Redmond visit, see Malcolm Campbell, "John Redmond and the Irish National League in Australia and New Zealand, 1883," *History* 86 (2001): 348–62.

28. *SMH,* 16 February 1883.

29. *New South Wales Parliamentary Debates,* First Series, 1883, vol. 8, Legislative Assembly, 21 February 1883, adjournment debate; *FJ,* 24 February 1883.

30. *FJ,* 24 February 1883. Redmond's own account is given in R. Barry O'Brien, *The Life of Charles Stewart Parnell, 1846–1891,* 2 vols. (London: Smith, Elder, 1898), 1:370.

31. Hugh Mahon, *The Land League, with an introduction by J. E. Redmond MP* (Melbourne, 1883), vii–viii.

32. *Protestant Standard,* 24 February 1883.

33. *FJ,* 24 March 1883; Colm Kiernan, "Home Rule for Ireland and the Formation of the Australian Labor Party, 1883 to 1891," *Australian Journal of Politics and History* 38 (1992): 6–7.

34. *FJ,* 24 March 1883.

35. *FJ,* 9 June 1883.

36. Quoted in *FJ,* 9 June 1883; O'Farrell, *Irish in Australia,* 227.

37. John Redmond, *Historical and Political Addresses, 1883–1897* (Dublin: Sealy, Bryers and Walker), 179–201; John Redmond, *Ireland's Case Stated: Three Lectures by Mr. J. E. Redmond MP* (Melbourne: Advocate Office, 1883), 6.

38. Gregory Tobin, "Sea-Divided Gael", 109–10; Denis Gwynn, *The Life of John Redmond* (London: G. G. Harrap and Co., 1932), 52.

39. *IW,* 16 February 1884; *BP,* 9 February 1884; Funchion, *Chicago's Irish Nationalists,* 56–104.

40. *IW,* 8 March 1884.

41. Oliver MacDonagh, "Irish Culture and Nationalism Transplanted: St. Patrick's Day, 1888, in Australia," in Oliver MacDonagh, W. F. Mandle and Pauric Travers, eds., *Irish Culture and Nationalism* (New York; St. Martin's Press, 1983), 69–82.

42. Gregory Tobin, "Sea-Divided Gael," 143; Mazzaroli, "Irish in New South Wales," 43.

43. Quoted in Thomas Henry Grattan Esmonde, *Round the World with the Irish Delegates,* (Dublin: Sealy, Bryers and Walker, 1892), 85–86; F. S. L. Lyons, *John Dillon: A Biography* (London: Routledge and Kegan Paul, 1968), 102–6.

44. Bruce Mansfield, *Australian Democrat: The Career of William Edward O'Sullivan, 1846–1910* (Sydney: Sydney University Press, 1965), 283.

45. Lyons, *John Dillon,* 106; Patrick O'Farrell suggests £35,000 was raised. *Irish in Australia,* 232.

46. Lyons, *John Dillon,* 104.

47. Lyons, *John Dillon,* 153; O'Farrell, *Irish in Australia,* 241–42.

48. Anon., "Home Rule from a Federal Point of View," *Australian Magazine,* July 1886, 86–87.

49. *Irish-Australian* (hereafter *IA*), 6 October 1894, 12 January 1895; O'Farrell, *Irish in Australia,* 233–35.

50. *IA,* 13 July 1895.

51. O'Farrell, *Irish in Australia,* 236. The outcome of Davitt's observations was *Life and Progress in Australasia* (London: Methuen, 1898).

52. Mathew Frye Jacobson, *Special Sorrows: The Diasporic Imagination of Irish, Polish, and Jewish Immigrants in the United States* (Cambridge, Mass.: Harvard University Press, 1995), 206–14; Doyle, *Irish Americans,* 91–140.

53. Miller, *Emigrants and Exiles,* 540–41.

54. Meagher, *Inventing Irish America,* 9–12.

55. Funchion, *Voluntary Organizations,* 183–89; Jacobson, *Special Sorrows,* 30–31; Francis Carroll, *American Opinion and the Irish Question, 1910–23: A Study in Opinion and Policy* (Dublin: Gill and Macmillan, 1978), 7.

56. News cutting, Devoy Papers, MS 18,060, National Library of Ireland (hereafter NLI).

57. See especially the case studies in Meagher, *Paddy to Studs.*

58. John Dillon to Michael Davitt, 2 August 1899. Dillon Correspondence, MS 15,741, NLI.

59. John Redmond to W. Bourke Cochran, 31 March 1900, William Bourke Cochran Papers, Box 5 (Irish Correspondence, Gill-Redmond), New York Public Library; Alan J. Ward, *Ireland and Anglo-American Relations, 1899–1921* (London: Weidenfeld and Nicolson, 1969), 12–14.

60. John Redmond to William O'Brien, 16 August 1901, Redmond Papers, MS 10,496, Folder 5, NLI; Funchion, *Voluntary Organizations,* 272–74.

61. John Redmond, Scrapbook of 1902 Tour, Redmond Papers, MS 7,432, 7, 9–10, 22, NLI.

62. *SMH,* 19 March 1894.

63. *FJ,* 24 March 1894; Mazzaroli, "Irish in New South Wales," 56.

64. *FJ,* 16 February, 16 March 1895.

65. Quoted in O'Farrell, *Catholic Church,* 235.

66. *FJ,* 8 February 1896.

67. *SMH,* 18 March 1896; *Catholic Press,* 7, 21 March 1896; O'Farrell, *Catholic Church,* 231.

68. *Catholic Press,* 17 March 1900; O'Farrell, *Catholic Church,* 268. On Melbourne's Saint Patrick's Day celebrations, see T. P. Boland, *Thomas Carr: Archbishop of Melbourne* (St. Lucia, Qld.: University of Queensland Press, 1997), 282–83; on Adelaide, Clement Macintyre, "The Adelaide Irish and the Politics of Saint Patrick's Day, 1900–1918," in Rebecca Pelan, ed., *Irish-Australian Studies: Papers Delivered at the Seventh Irish-Australian Conference* (Sydney: Crossing Press, 1994), 182–96.

69. O'Farrell, *Irish in Australia,* 238–40; Ruán O'Donnell, "Michael Dwyer: Wicklow Chief and Irish-Australian Hero," in Pelan, *Irish-Australian Studies,* 206.

70. *The Scotch-Irish in America: Proceedings of the Scotch-Irish Congress at Columbia, Tennessee, May 8–11, 1889* (Cincinnati, Ohio: Scotch-Irish Society of America, 1889), 3–9; Michael Kammen, *Mystic Chords of Memory: The Transformation of Tradition in American Culture* (New York: Alfred A. Knopf, 1991), 219.

71. Preamble to the constitution of the American-Irish Historical Society, *Journal of the American-Irish Historical Society* 1 (1898): 7.

72. William D. Griffin, "American Irish Historical Society," in Funchion, *Voluntary Organizations*, 40–41; Ward, *Anglo-American Relations*, 40–41; Kammen, *Mystic Chords*, 218–19.

73. Jacobson, *Special Sorrows*, 208; Kammen, *Mystic Chords*, 228–53.

74. "Boston Globe Scrapbook: Matter Relating to the National Convention, August 30–31, 1904." American Irish Historical Society Archive, New York City.

75. Carroll, *American Opinion*, 8–9.

76. Albert Thomas Dryer, "The Independence of Ireland: Source Material for the History of the Movement in Australia," Dryer Papers, MS 6,610, Box 1, folder 11, National Library of Australia; O'Farrell, *Irish in Australia*, 241–50.

77. Commonwealth of Australia, *Parliamentary Debates*, House of Representatives, vol. 28 (Session 1905), 3807–18 (19 October 1905); Senate, vol. 28, 3761–81 (19 October 1905); Dryer, "Independence," Dryer Papers, National Library of Australia; William Redmond, *Through the New Commonwealth* (Dublin: Sealy, Bryers and Walker, 1906), 200–203.

78. H. K. Mack, *Why Ulster Fears* (Geelong, Vic., 1912), 5.

79. Carroll, *American Opinion*, 14–21; Ward, *Anglo-American Relations*, 30–69.

80. John Redmond to William Bourke Cochran, 12 April 1912; William Bourke Cochran to John Redmond, 13 April 1912, Cochran Papers, Box 5 (Irish Correspondence, Gill-Redmond), New York Public Library.

81. John Redmond to William Bourke Cochran, 7 April 1914, Cochran Papers, Box 5 (Irish Correspondence, Gill-Redmond), New York Public Library.

7. Casting Off Ties

1. *Commission on Emigration and Other Population Problems, 1948–1954* (Dublin: Stationery Office, 1954), 314–15; E. Dana Durand [Bureau of the Census], *Thirteenth Census of the United States Taken in the Year 1910: Abstract of the Census* (Washington, D.C.: Department of Commerce and Labor, 1913), 82, 188–89; Commonwealth of Australia, *Census of the Commonwealth of Australia 1911* (Melbourne: Commonwealth Statistician, 1914), vol. 3, pt. 14, 2072–73.

2. Eric Andrews, *The Anzac Illusion: Anglo-Australian Relations During World War I* (Melbourne: Cambridge University Press, 1993), 8–41.

3. Ernest Scott, *Australia During the War* (Sydney, 1936; facsimile ed., St. Lucia: University of Queensland Press, 1989), 22.

4. *SMH*, 6 August 1914; *Age*, 7 August 1914.

5. O'Farrell, *Catholic Church*, 304–5; Neil Byrne, *Robert Dunne, 1830–1917: Archbishop of Brisbane* (St. Lucia: University of Queensland Press, 1991), 232–33.

6. *Age*, 7 August 1914; Scott, *Australia During the War*, 24.

7. Quoted in Michael McKernan, *Australian Churches at War: Attitudes and Activities of the Major Churches, 1914–1918* (Sydney: Catholic Theological Faculty, 1980), 30; Boland, *Thomas Carr*, 404–5.

8. Bill Gammage, *The Broken Years: Australian Soldiers and the Great War* (Canberra: Australian National University Press, 1974), 7–11, 281; Andrews, *Anzac Illusion*, 42–46.

9. Emmons, *Butte Irish*, 347–48.

10. John Devoy to Bulmer Hobson, 3 July 1914, in O'Brien and Ryan, *Devoy's Post Bag*, 2:458; Terry Golway, *Irish Rebel: John Devoy and America's Fight for Ireland's Freedom* (New York: St. Martin's Press, 1998), 191–201.

11. *IW,* 3 October 1914; Denis Gwynn, *The Life of John Redmond* (London: George G. Harrap and Co., 1932), 391–92.

12. *IW,* 10 October 1914.

13. *IW,* 24 October 1914. See also 3, 10, 17, 31 October 1914.

14. *IW,* 24 October 1914; 31 October 1914.

15. *IW,* 17 October 1914.

16. Ward, *Anglo-American Relations,* 79–80; Carroll, *American Opinion,* 47–48.

17. *IW,* 10 October 1914, 7 November 1914.

18. Rosalie Moynahan, "Nemesis Holds Her Own," *IW,* 24 October 1914.

19. Carroll, *American Opinion,* 51–52.

20. Ward, *Anglo-American Relations,* 94; Carroll, *American Opinion,* 50–52.

21. Knobel, *America,* 244–46.

22. Quoted in Ward, *Anglo-American Relations,* 81.

23. Ward, *Anglo-American Relations,* 100.

24. Gerhard Fischer, *Enemy Aliens: Internment and the Homefront Experience in Australia, 1914–1920* (St. Lucia: University of Queensland Press, 1989).

25. Dryer, "Independence," Dryer Papers, National Library of Australia.

26. Dryer, "Independence," Dryer Papers, National Library of Australia; Garrath O'Keefe, "Australia's Irish Republican Brotherhood," *Journal of the Royal Australian Historical Society* 83 (December 1997): 136–52.

27. *Newcastle Herald,* 27 April 1916.

28. *Argus,* 1, 2 May 1916; Dryer, "Independence," Dryer Papers, National Library of Australia; Anon., *The Irish Rebellion and Australian Opinion* (Melbourne: Critchley Parker, 1916), 1–30.

29. *Catholic Press* (hereafter *CP*), 4, 11 May 1916; Colm Kiernan, *Daniel Mannix and Ireland* (Morwell, Vic.: Atella Books, 1984), 96.

30. Dryer, "Independence," Dryer Papers, National Library of Australia.

31. *Argus,* 2 May 1916.

32. *Bulletin,* 18 May 1916.

33. *Argus,* 16 May 1916; *FJ,* 11 May 1916; T. P. Boland, *James Duhig* (St. Lucia: University of Queensland Press, 1986), 128–39.

34. Carroll, *American Opinion,* 56–57.

35. Carroll, *American Opinion,* 57–63; Ward, *Anglo-American Relations,* 111–13.

36. Carroll, *American Opinion,* 63–65; William M. Leary, "Woodrow Wilson, Irish Americans and the Election of 1916," *Journal of American History* 54 (1967): 57–72.

37. *IW,* 6 May 1916; Carroll, *American Opinion,* 66–69.

38. *BP,* 13 May 1916.

39. *BP,* 3 June 1916.

40. *BP,* 5 August 1916.

41. Carroll, *American Opinion,* 64–65.

42. O'Brien and Ryan, *Devoy's Post Bag,* 2:519–20; Emmons, *Butte Irish,* 355–64.

43. Stephen Gwynn, ed., *The Letters and Friendships of Sir Cecil Spring-Rice: A Record* (London: Constable and Co., 1929), 2:392–93; Ward, *Anglo-American Relations,* 126–40.

44. Woodrow Wilson, *Address of the President of the United States Delivered at a Joint Session of the Two Houses of Congress, April 2, 1917* (Washington, D.C.: Edward J. Clode, 1917), 44; David M. Kennedy, *Over Here: The First World War and American Society* (New York: Oxford University Press, 1980).

45. *IW,* 7, 14 April 1917; Ward, *Anglo-American Relations,* 143–57.

46. Kennedy, *Over Here,* 77.

47. Quoted in Carroll, *American Opinion,* 108–20.

48. L. F. Fitzhardinge, *William Morris Hughes: A Political Biography* (Sydney: Angus and Robertson, 1964–79), 2:171–215, 279–306.

49. Scott, *Australia During the War,* 320–52, 397–428; see also Danny Cusack, *With an Olive Branch and a Shillelagh: The Life and Times of Senator Patrick Lynch* (Perth: Hesperian Press, 2004).

50. Scott, *Australia During the War,* 347, 420.

51. O'Farrell, *Irish in Australia,* 272.

52. Glenn Withers, "The 1916–1917 Conscription Referenda: A Cliometric Re-Appraisal," *Historical Studies* 20 (April 1982): 36–46.

53. O'Farrell, *Irish in Australia,* 272–73; Michael McKernan, "Catholics, Conscription and Archbishop Mannix," *Historical Studies* 17 (1977): 299–314.

54. Commonwealth of Australia, *Parliamentary Debates,* Senate, vol. 81 (Session 1914–17), 11050–61 (7 March 1917).

55. Patrick O'Farrell, "The Irish Republican Brotherhood in Australia: The 1918 Internments," in MacDonagh, Mandle, and Travers, *Irish Culture and Nationalism,* 182–93.

56. *IW,* 3 August 1918.

57. Carroll, *American Opinion,* 121–48; Ward, *Anglo-American Relations,* 166–88; Joseph P. O'Grady, "The Irish," in Joseph P. O'Grady, ed., *The Immigrants' Influence on Wilson's Peace Policies* (Louisville: University of Kentucky Press, 1967), 56–84.

58. *IW,* 7 June 1919; Francis M. Carroll, ed., *The American Commission on Irish Independence, 1919: The Diary, Correspondence and Report* (Dublin: Irish Manuscripts Commission, 1985), 18; Carroll, *American Opinion,* 131–39.

59. *IW,* 4 January 1919, 28 June 1919; Patrick McCartan, *With De Valera in America* (New York: Brentano, 1932); Timothy J. Sarbaugh, "Irish Republicanism vs. 'Pure Americanism': California's Reaction to Eamon de Valera's Visit," *California History* 60, part 2 (1981): 172–85.

60. Quoted in David Fitzpatrick, *Harry Boland's Irish Revolution* (Cork: Cork University Press, 2003), 166; Kenny, *American Irish,* 196–99.

61. Quoted in Ward, *Anglo-American Relations,* 233.

62. Ward, *Anglo-American Relations,* 238–41, Carroll, *American Opinion,* 162–70; Loyalist League of Victoria, *Slanders on Great Britain Refuted, or The Report of the Irish-American "Commission" with the Official Reply* (Melbourne: Loyalist League of Victoria, 1921).

63. *Bulletin,* 27 March 1919; *CP,* 27 March 1919; quoted in Dryer, "Independence," Dryer Papers, National Library of Australia.

64. Dryer, "Independence," Dryer Papers, National Library of Australia; O'Farrell, *Irish in Australia,* 279–81.

65. *FJ,* 4 August 1921; O'Farrell, *Irish in Australia,* 282–84; O'Farrell, *Catholic Church,* 340–44; Colm Kiernan, *Mannix,* 145–67.

66. *FJ,* 18 August 1921; Dermot Keogh, "Mannix, de Valera and Irish Nationalism," *Australasian Catholic Record* 65 (April 1988): 159–73.

67. Commonwealth of Australia, *Parliamentary Debates,* House of Representatives, vol. 94 (Session 1920–21), 6257–61 (11 November 1920).

68. Hugh Mahon, News clippings re expulsion from parliament, Hugh Mahon Papers, series 8, MS 937, National Library of Australia; W. M. Hughes to Hugh Mahon re expulsion, 10 November 1920, Mahon Papers, series 9, MSS 937/699, 937/700, National Library of Australia; Commonwealth of Australia, *Parliamentary Debates,* House of Representatives, vol. 94 (Session 1920–21), 6283–84, 6327–28, 6382–475 (9–11 November 1920).

69. *IW,* 7 January 1922; Carroll, *American Opinion,* 177–82.

70. *FJ,* 5, 12 January 1922; Dermot Keogh, "Mannix," 343.

71. *FJ,* 31 August 1922.

Conclusion

1. Lawrence J. McCaffrey, "Diaspora Comparisons and Irish-American Uniqueness," in Charles Fanning, ed., *New Perspectives on the Irish Diaspora* (Carbondale: Southern Illinois University Press, 2000), 25.

2. Marc Bloch, "A Contribution Towards a Comparative History of European Societies," in *Land and Work in Mediaeval Europe: Selected Papers of Marc Bloch* (London: Routledge and Kegan Paul, 1967), 72.

3. Frank Thistlethwaite, "Migration from Europe Overseas in the Nineteenth and Twentieth Centuries," *Rapports: Xie Congrès International des Sciences Historiques* 5 (1960): 34–35.

4. David Doyle, "Cohesion and Diversity in the Irish Diaspora," *Irish Historical Studies* 31 (1999): 411.

Select Bibliography

For reasons of manageability and space, background studies in the histories of Ireland, the United States, and Australia have been excluded. Local, family, and regional histories, especially those pertaining to chapters 4 and 5, have also been curtailed.

Primary Sources

Manuscript Material

American Irish Historical Society, New York
Boston Globe Scrapbooks.
Cohalan, Daniel. Papers.
Friends of Irish Freedom. Papers.

Bancroft Library, University of California, Berkeley
Biographical Sketch of the Murphy Family Prepared for Chronicles of the Builders of the Commonwealth. C-D 792–2.
Kerr, Thomas. Diary of Things Worth Notice—During My Voyage to Calafornia [*sic*]—& Remarkable Events There (Yes and a good many things not worth notice too), MS 84/36C.
Phelan, James D. "The Services of the Irish People in the Cause of Freedom: Address before the Knights of Saint Patrick, Nov. 27, 1895." F858/P5/v6/X.
Phelan, James. Papers. C-B 800, Carton 3.
Riordan, James. Papers. C-B 740.
Riordan, John. "Garret McEnerney and the Irish Pursuit of Success." Typescript 73/122/C/No. 96.
Scanlan Family. Papers. MS 70/32 C.
Sinclair, Samuel Fleming. "The Life and Travels of Samuel Fleming Sinclair." C-D 5111.

Menzies Library, University of New South Wales
Monteagle Papers.

Minnesota Historical Society, St. Paul, Minnesota
Boyle, Michael J. Papers, 1876–90. P1435.
Callahan Papers. A-C156.
Christie, James C., and family. Correspondence and Miscellaneous Papers. P1281.
Irish-American Colonization Company Papers. BB2.168
McBeath, James, and family. Papers. P794.
Middleton, James. Papers. P1070.

Minnesota Federal Writers Project. Annals of Minnesota Subject Files, 1849–1942. M529.
Lacore, Annie King. Reminiscences. P1337.
Rahilly, Patrick Henry. Papers. P942.

Mitchell Library, State Library of New South Wales, Sydney
Brady, William M. Papers, 1885–87. ML DOC 2156.
Browne, William. Papers. Ab 65/2.
Duncan, W. A. "Autobiography, 1811–1854." A2877 Reel CYPOS 161.
Hayes, Michael. Letters. A3586.
Irish Political Prisoner Papers. ML MSS 287/1.
Marsden, Samuel. "A Few General Observations on the Toleration of the Catholic Religion in New South Wales." ML MSS 18.
Martin, John. Letters. Am87.
Papers of the Irish Republican Association 1923. A3867.
Parkes, Henry. Correspondence. Vol.14, A884; Vol.46, A916.

National Library of Australia, Canberra
Atkinson, David. Letters. MS 670.
Dryer, Albert Thomas. "The Independence of Ireland: Source Material for the History of the Movement in Australia." Dryer Papers. MS 6610.
Foreign Office (UK). Correspondence Relating to the United States in Australia. Papers Concerning Australian involvement in the Fenian Brotherhood. mFm PR05779.
Mahon, Hugh. News clippings re expulsion from parliament. Hugh Mahon Papers. MS 937.

National Library of Ireland
Devoy Papers. MS 18,060.
Dillon Correspondence. MS 15,741.
Leslie, Shane. Papers. MSS 22,832, 22,835.
O'Brien, Mrs. William. Memoir. MS 8507.
Redmond, John. Papers. MSS 7432, 7435, 7443, 10,496, 15,277, 22,186.

New South Wales State Archives
Colonial Secretary. Letters re Land.

New York Public Library
William Bourke Cochran Papers, Boxes 4–5.

Newspapers
Advocate (Melbourne)
Age (Melbourne)
Argus (Melbourne)
Australasian Chronicle (Sydney)
Bulletin (Sydney)
Catholic Press (Sydney)
Express (Sydney)
Irish News (Melbourne)
Irish-Australian (Sydney)
Irishman (Melbourne)
Irish World and American Industrial Liberator (New York)
Monitor (San Francisco)
Newcastle Herald

Pilot (Boston)
Protestant Standard (Sydney)
Sydney Morning Herald
United Irishman

Parliamentary Papers and Reports

United Kingdom, Parliament
House of Commons, Select Committee on Emigration from the United Kingdom, *Third Report, 1827.*
House of Commons, Select Committee on the Expediency of Encouraging Emigration from the United Kingdom, *Report, 1826.*
House of Commons, Select Committee on the Laws which regulate the Linen Trade of Ireland, *Report, 1822.*
House of Commons, Select Committee on Transportation, *Report, 1838.*
House of Lords, Select Committee on Colonization from Ireland, *First Report, 1847–48.*
House of Lords, Select Committee on Colonization from Ireland, *Second Report, 1847–48.*
House of Lords, Select Committee on Colonization from Ireland, *Third Report, 1849.*

New South Wales, Parliament
New South Wales Legislative Assembly, Select Committee on Irish Female Immigration, *Report, 1859.*

United States, Congress
House of Representatives Committee on the Public Lands on Petitions of Irish Emigrant Associations in New York, Philadelphia, Baltimore and Pittsburgh, *Report, 1818.*

Printed Material
Anderson, Mary Jane Hill. *Autobiography of Mary Jane Hill Anderson, Wife of Robert Anderson, 1827–1934.* Minneapolis: privately published, 1934.
Anon. *The Irish Rebellion and Australian Opinion.* Melbourne: Critchley Parker, 1916.
Anon. "Australian Life." *Dublin University Magazine* 58 (September 1861): 361–66.
Bagenal, Philip H. *The American Irish and their Influence on Irish Politics.* Boston: Roberts Brothers, 1882.
Besnard, Thomas Pope. *A Voice From the Bush in Australia.* Dublin: William Curry, 1839.
Binns, John. *An Oration Commemorative of the Birth-Day of American Independence.* Philadelphia: C. and A. Conrad and Co., 1810.
Birt, Henry Norbert. *Benedictine Pioneers in Australia.* 2 vols. London: Herbery and Daniel, 1911.
Bishop's Directory of San Francisco. San Francisco, 1875.
Brace, Charles Loring. *The Dangerous Classes of New York and Twenty Years' Work Among Them.* New York: Wynkoop and Hallenbeck, 1872.
Burton, William W. *The State of Religion and Education in New South Wales.* London: J. Cross, 1840.
Chisholm, Caroline. *Comfort for the Poor! Meat Three Times a Day!: Voluntary Information from the People of New South Wales Collected in that Colony by Mrs. Chisholm.* London, 1847.
Cleary, P. S. *Australia's Debt to Irish Nation Builders.* Sydney: Angus and Robertson, 1933.
Coghlan, T. A. *Results of a Census of New South Wales Taken on the Night of 31st March 1901.* Sydney: Government Printer, 1901.
Collins, David. *An Account of the English Colony in New South Wales With Remarks on the Dispositions, Customs, Manners &c. of the Native Inhabitants of the Country.* 2 vols. London: T. Caddell Jun. and W. Davies, 1798 and 1802.

Coolidge, Mary Roberts. *Chinese Immigration.* Taipei: Ch'Eng Wen Publishing, 1968.

Cunningham, Peter. *Two Years in New South Wales; a series of letters comprising sketches of the actual state of society in that colony.* 2 vols. London: Henry Colburn, 1827.

Davitt, Michael. *Life and Progress in Australasia.* London: Methuen, 1898.

De Valera, Eamon. *Ireland's Request to the Government of the United States of America.* Melbourne: Tribune Publishing Co., 1921.

Dickens, Charles. *American Notes and Pictures from Italy.* London: Chapman and Hall, 1868.

Duffy, Charles Gavan. *My Life in Two Hemispheres.* 2 vols. London: T. Fisher Unwin, 1898.

————. "An Australian Example." *Contemporary Review* 52 (January 1888): 1–31.

————. *The Opinion of the Country: Speech of the Hon. Sir Charles Gavan Duffy at Sale on Monday 9 April 1877.* Sale, Vic., 1877.

————. *Civil and Religious Liberty: Speech on the Presentation of a Property Qualification to Him August 20, 1856.* Melbourne: Michael T. Glason, 1856.

Emmet, Thomas Addis. *Memoir of Thomas Addis Emmet and Robert Emmet.* 2 vols. New York: The Emmet Press, 1915.

Esmonde, Thomas Henry Grattan. *Round the World with the Irish Delegates.* Dublin: Sealy, Bryers and Walker, 1892.

Finn, Edmund (Garryowen). *The Chronicles of Early Melbourne, 1835–1852.* Melbourne: Ferguson and Mitchell, 1888.

Foster, Augustus John. *Jeffersonian America: Notes on the United States of America Collected in the Years 1805–6–7 and 1811–12 by Sir Augustus John Foster.* Edited by Richard Beale Davis. San Marino: The Huntington Library, 1954.

Freehill, F. R. "Colonial 'Know-Nothingism': A Reply to Mr. B. R. Wise." *Centennial Magazine* 2–3 (August 1889–September 1890): 226–31.

Freeman, John. *Lights and Shadows of Melbourne Life.* London: Sampson Low, 1888.

Gibbons, James. "Irish Immigration to the United States." *Irish Ecclesiastical Record,* 4th series, 1 (February 1897): 97–109.

Gleeson, W. *History of the Catholic Church in California.* 2 vols. San Francisco: A. L. Bancroft and Co., 1872.

Gresham, William G. *History of Nicollet and Le Sueur Counties Minnesota. Their Peoples, Industries and Institutions.* Indianapolis: B. F. Bowen, 1916.

Gwynn Stephen, ed. *The Letters and Friendships of Sir Cecil Spring-Rice: A Record.* 2 vols. London: Constable and Co., 1929.

Hall, Edward Smith. *The State of New South Wales in December, 1830: in a letter.* London: Joseph Cross, 1831.

Higgins, H. B. *Speech by the Hon. H. B. Higgins KC MP on Home Rule for Ireland.* Melbourne: Robert S. Brain, 1905.

Higgins, Patrick, and F. V. Connolly. *The Irish in America.* London: John Ouseley, 1909.

Hogan, James F. *The Irish in Australia.* Melbourne: Australian Edition, 1888.

Hone, Philip. *The Diary of Philip Hone.* Edited by Allan Nevins. 2 vols. New York: Dodd, Mead and Co., 1889. Reprint, New York: Kraus Reprint, 1969.

Howitt, William. *Land, Labour and Gold, or, Two Years in Victoria: with Visits to Sydney and Van Diemen's Land.* 2 vols. London: Longman, Brown, Green and Longmans, 1855.

Irish-Australian Almanac and Directory. Melbourne: Winter and Co. 1876, 1878.

The Irish Cause on the Pacific. John Savage in California. Containing an Account of the Visit of the Chief Executive, F.B., to the Pacific Coast: The Great Demonstrations at Redwood City, and the Speeches on the Cause of Irish Independence. New York: American News Company, 1870.

Kapp, Friedrich. *Immigration and the Commissioners of Emigration*. New York: The Nation Press, 1870.

Kelly, William. *Life in Victoria, or, Victoria in 1853 and Victoria in 1858*. 2 vols. London: Chapman Hall, 1859.

Lang, John Dunmore. *Notes of a Trip to the Westward and Southward in the Colony of New South Wales in the Months of March and April 1862*. Sydney: Hanson and Bennett, 1862.

———. *The Question of Questions! or, Is this colony to be transformed into a province of the Popedom?: A letter to the Protestant land holders of New South Wales*. Sydney, 1841.

Leslie, Shane. *The Irish Issue in its American Aspect*. London: T. Fisher Unwin, 1919.

Longway, Marchamp. *London to Melbourne*. London: Remington and Co., 1889.

Loyalist League of Victoria. *Slanders on Great Britain Refuted, or, The Report of the Irish-American "Commission" with the Official Reply*. Melbourne: Loyalist League of Victoria, 1921.

Mack, H. K. *Why Ulster Fears*. Geelong, Vic., 1912.

Maguire, John Francis. *The Irish in America*. London: Longman, Green and Co., 1868.

Mahon, Hugh. *The Land League, with an introduction by J. E. Redmond MP*. Melbourne, 1883.

Mahony, Martin. *Sweetman Catholic Colony in Murray County, Minnesota: Letters from the Pastor and Others*. Currie, Minn.: Manager's Office, 1885.

Maryat, Frederick. *Diary in America: The Complete Account of His Trials, Wrangles and Tribulations in the United States and Canada, 1837–1838*. London: Nicholas Vane, 1960.

McCartan, Patrick. *With De Valera in America*. New York: Brentano, 1932.

McGee, Thomas Darcy. *A History of the Irish Settlers in North America from the Earliest Period to the Census of 1850*. Boston: Patrick Donahue, 1852.

Michie, Archibald. *Readings in Melbourne; With an Essay on the Resources and Prospects of Victoria for the Emigrant and Uneasy Classes*. London: Sampson Low, 1879.

Mitchel, John. *Jail Journal; or, Five Years in British Prisons*. Glasgow: Cameron, 1876.

Morgan, F. (An Ulsterman). *The Rise and Progress of Orangeism*. Melbourne: privately printed, 1895.

O'Brien, Michael J. *A Hidden Phase of American History: Ireland's Part in America's Struggle for Liberty*. New York: Dodd, Mead and Co., 1919.

O'Brien, William, and Desmond Ryan, eds. *Devoy's Post Bag, 1871–1928*. 2 vols. Dublin: C. J. Fallon, 1948.

O'Connell, Daniel. *The Correspondence of Daniel O'Connell*. Edited by Maurice O'Connell. 8 vols. Dublin: Irish Manuscripts Commission, 1972–.

———. *Speeches of Daniel O'Connell and Thomas Steele on the Subject of American Slavery*. Philadelphia: Anti-Slavery Office, 1843.

———. *Daniel O'Connell upon American Slavery: With other Irish Testimonies*. Anti-Slavery Tracts, no. 5. New Series. New York: American Anti-Slavery Society, 1860. Reprint, Westport, Conn.: Negro Universities Press, 1970.

O'Donovan, Jeremiah. *Brief Account of the Author's Interview with his Countrymen, and of the Parts of the Emerald Isle whence they Emigrated*. Pittsburgh: privately printed, 1864.

O'Leary, John. *Recollections of Fenians and Fenianism*. Shannon: Irish University Press, 1969.

Olmstead, Frederick Law. *A Journey in the Seaboard Slave States With Remarks on their Economy*. New York: Dix and Edwards, 1856.

Parkes, Henry. *Irish Immigration: Speech Delivered in the Legislative Assembly on the Second Reading of "A Bill to Authorise and Regulate Assisted Immigration."* Sydney, 1869.

Quigley, Hugh. *The Irish Race in California and on the Pacific Coast with an introductory historical dissertation on the principal races of mankind and a vocabulary of ancient and modern Irish family names*. San Francisco: A. Roman and Co., 1878.

Redmond, John. *Historical and Political Addresses, 1883–1897*. Dublin: Sealy, Bryers and Walker, 1898.

———. *Ireland's Case Stated: Three Lectures by Mr. J. E. Redmond MP*. Melbourne: Advocate Office, 1883.

Redmond, William. *Through the New Commonwealth*. Dublin: Sealy, Bryers and Walker, 1906.

Redmond-Howard, L. G. *John Redmond, the Man and the Demand: A Biographical Study in Irish Politics*. London: Hurst and Blackett, 1910.

Riis, Jacob. *How the Other Half Lives*. London: Sampson Low, 1891.

Roche, James Jeffrey. *Life of John Boyle O'Reilly*. Philadelphia: John J. McVey, 1891.

Roney, Frank. *Irish Rebel and Labor Leader: An Autobiography*. Edited by Ira Cross. Berkeley: University of California Press, 1931.

Rossa, Diarmuid O'Donovan. *Rossa's Recollections, 1838–1898*. Shannon: Irish University Press, 1972.

Ryan, James Tobias. *Reminiscences of Australia*. Sydney: G. Robertson, 1895.

Saxon, Isabella. *Five Years Within the Golden Gate*. Philadelphia: J. B. Lippincott, 1868.

The Scotch-Irish in America: Proceedings of the Scotch-Irish Congress at Columbia, Tennessee May 8–11 1889. Cincinnati, Ohio: Scotch-Irish Society of America, 1889.

Shumack, Samuel. *An Autobiography, or, Tales and Legends of Canberra Pioneers*. Canberra: Australian National University Press, 1977.

Soule, Frank. *The Annals of San Francisco*. New York: D. Appleton and Co., 1855.

Strong, George Templeton. *The Diary of George Templeton Strong*. Edited by Allen Nevins and Milton H. Thomas. 4 vols. New York: MacMillan, 1952.

Sweetman, John. "The Sweetman Catholic Colony of Currie, Minnesota: A Memoir." *Acta et Dicta* 1, no. 3 (1911): 41–65.

———. *Recent Experiences in the Emigration of Irish Families*. Dublin: M. H. Gill and Son, 1883.

Taylor, Bayard. *Eldorado or Adventures in the Path of Empire*. 18th ed. New York: G. P. Putnam, 1861.

Therry, Roger. *Reminiscences of Thirty Years' Residence in New South Wales and Victoria*. London: Sampson Low, Son and Co., 1863.

Thomas, L. *The Development of the Labour Movement in the Sydney District of N.S.W.* Sydney: Australian Society for the Study of Labour History, 1962.

Topp, A. M. "English Institutions and the Irish Race." *Melbourne Review* 6 (January 1881): 9–27.

Turner, Henry Giles. *A History of the Colony of Victoria from its Discovery until its Absorption into the Commonwealth of Australia*. 2 vols. Melbourne: Longmans, Green and Co., 1904.

Watson, Frederick, ed. *Historical Records of Australia*. 33 vols. Sydney: Library Committee of the Commonwealth Parliament, 1914–25.

Westgarth, William. *Personal Recollections of Early Melbourne and Victoria*. Melbourne: George Robertson and Son, 1888.

Wilson, Woodrow. *Address of the President of the United States Delivered at a Joint Session of the Two Houses of Congress, April 2, 1917*. Washington, D.C.: Edward J. Clode, 1917.

Secondary Sources

Books and Articles

Abbott, Edith. *Historical Aspects of the Immigration Problem: Select Documents.* Chicago: University of Chicago Press, 1926.

———. *Immigration: Select Documents and Case Records.* Chicago: University of Chicago Press, 1924.

Adams, William Forbes. *Ireland and Irish Emigration to the New World from 1815 to the Famine.* New Haven, Conn.: Yale University Press, 1932.

Akenson, Donald Harman. *Being Had: Historians, the Evidence and the Irish in North America.* Port Credit, Ont.: P. D. Meany, 1985.

———. "The Historiography of the Irish in the United States." In *The Irish in the New Communities,* edited by Patrick O'Sullivan, 99–127. Leicester: Leicester University Press, 1992.

———. *The Irish Diaspora: A Primer.* Toronto: P. D. Meany, 1993.

———. *The Irish in Ontario: A Study in Rural History.* Kingston, Ont.: McGill-Queen's University Press, 1984.

———. *Small Differences: Irish Catholics and Irish Protestants, 1815–1922. An International Perspective.* Kingston, Ont.: McGill-Queen's University Press, 1988.

———. *The United States and Ireland.* Cambridge, Mass.: Harvard University Press, 1973.

Amos, Keith. *The Fenians in Australia: 1865–1880.* Sydney: University of New South Wales Press, 1988.

Anbinder, Tyler. *Nativism and Slavery: The Northern Know Nothings and the Politics of the 1850s.* New York: Oxford University Press, 1992.

Andrews, Eric. *The Anzac Illusion: Anglo-Australian Relations During World War I.* Melbourne: Cambridge University Press, 1993.

Athearn, Robert G. *Thomas Francis Meagher: An Irish Revolutionary in America.* New York: Arno Press, 1976.

Baker, D. W. A. *Days of Wrath: A Life of John Dunmore Lang.* Melbourne: Melbourne University Press, 1985.

Bancroft, Hubert Howe. *The History of California.* 7 vols. Santa Barbara, Calif.: Wallace Herberd, 1970.

Bayor, Ronald H. *Neighbors in Conflict: The Irish, Germans, Jews, and Italians of New York City, 1929–1941.* 2nd ed. Urbana: University of Illinois Press, 1988.

Bayor, Ronald H., and Timothy J. Meagher, eds. *The New York Irish.* Baltimore: Johns Hopkins University Press, 1996.

Belchem, John. "Nationalism, Republicanism and Exile: Irish Emigrants and the Revolutions of 1848." *Past and Present* 146 (1995): 103–35.

———. "Republican Spirit and Military Science: The 'Irish Brigade' and Irish-American Nationalism in 1848." *Irish Historical Studies* 29 (1994): 44–64.

Berger, Max. "The Irish Emigrant and American Nativism." *The Dublin Review* 219 (October 1946): 174–86.

Bernstein, Iver. *The New York City Draft Riots: Their Significance for American Society and Politics in the Age of the Civil War.* New York: Oxford University Press, 1990.

Bielenberg, Andy, ed. *The Irish Diaspora.* London: Longman, 2000.

Billington, Ray Allen. *The Origins of Nativism in the United States, 1800–1844.* New York: Arno Press, 1974.

Binder, Frederick M., and David M. Reimers. *All the Nations Under Heaven: An Ethnic and Racial History of New York City.* New York: Columbia University Press, 1995.

Blessing, Patrick J. "Irish Emigration to the United States, 1800–1920: An Overview." In *The Irish in America: Emigration, Assimilation and Impact,* edited by P. J. Drudy, 12–37. Cambridge: Cambridge University Press, 1985.

———. *The Irish in America: A Guide to the Literature and the Manuscript Collections.* Washington, D.C.: Catholic University of America Press, 1992.

Bodkin, Mathias. "Thomas Francis Meagher, 1822–1867." *Studies* 57 (Spring 1968): 49–53.

Bodnar, John. *The Transplanted: A History of Immigrants in Urban America.* Bloomington: Indiana University Press, 1985.

Boland, T. P. *James Duhig.* St. Lucia: University of Queensland Press, 1986.

———. *Thomas Carr: Archbishop of Melbourne.* St. Lucia: University of Queensland Press, 1997.

Bolton, Geoffrey C. "The Fenians Are Coming, The Fenians Are Coming!" *Studies in Western Australian History* 4 (1981): 62–67.

Boyce, D. George. *Nationalism in Ireland.* 3rd ed. London: Routledge, 1995.

Bratt, James D. "The Reorientation of American Protestantism, 1835–1845." *Church History* 67, no. 1 (1998): 52–82.

Broome, Richard. *The Victorians: Arriving.* Sydney: Fairfax, Syme and Weldon, 1984.

Brown, Thomas N. *Irish-American Nationalism, 1870–1890.* Philadelphia: J. B. Lippincott Company, 1966.

———. "The Origins and Character of Irish-American Nationalism." *Review of Politics* 18 (1956): 327–58.

Browne, Henry J. "Archbishop Hughes and Western Colonization." *Catholic Historical Review* 36 (1950): 257–85.

Brundage, David. "After the Land League: The Persistence of Irish-American Labor Radicalism in Denver, 1897–1905." *Journal of American Ethnic History* 11, no. 3 (1992): 3–26.

———. "Denver's New Departure: Irish Nationalism and the Labor Movement in the Gilded Age." *Southwest Economy and Society* 5, no. 3 (1981): 10–21.

Brusher, Joseph S. "Peter C. Yorke and the A.P.A. in San Francisco." *Catholic Historical Review* 38 (1951): 129–50.

Bull, Philip, Frances Devlin-Glass, and Helen Doyle, eds. *Ireland and Australia, 1798–1998: Studies in Culture, Identity and Migration.* Sydney: Crossing Press, 2000.

Bull, Philip, Chris McConville, and Noel McLachlan, eds. *Irish-Australian Studies: Papers Delivered at the Sixth Irish-Australian Conference, July 1990.* Sydney: Melbourne: La Trobe University, 1991.

Burchell, Robert A. "British Immigrants in Southern California, 1850–1870." *Southern California Quarterly* 53 (1971): 283–302.

———. "The Gathering of a Community: The British-Born of San Francisco in 1852 and 1872." *Journal of American Studies* 10 (1976): 279–312.

———. "The Historiography of the American Irish." *Immigrants and Minorities* 1 (1982): 281–305.

———. "Irish Property Holding in the West in 1870." *Journal of the West* 31, no. 2 (1992): 9–16.

———. *The San Francisco Irish, 1848–1880.* Berkeley: University of California Press, 1980.

Byrne, Neil. *Robert Dunne, 1830–1917: Archbishop of Brisbane.* St. Lucia: University of Queensland Press, 1991.

Byron, Reginald. *Irish America.* Oxford: Clarendon Press, 1999.

Calkin, Homer L. "The Irish in Iowa." *The Palimpsest* 45, no. 2 (1964): 33–96.

Campbell, Malcolm. "Emigrant Responses to War and Revolution, 1914–1921: Irish Opinion in the United States and Australia." *Irish Historical Studies* 32 (2000): 75–92.

———. "Immigrants on the Land: Irish Rural Settlement in Minnesota and New South Wales, 1830–1890." *New Hibernia Review* 2, no. 1 (1998): 43–61.

———. "Ireland's Furthest Shores: Irish Immigrant Settlement in Nineteenth-Century California and Eastern Australia." *Pacific Historical Review* 71 (2002): 59–90.

———. "Irish Nationalism and Immigrant Assimilation: Comparing the United States and Australia." *Australasian Journal of American Studies* 15, no. 2 (1996): 24–43.

———. "John Redmond and the Irish National League in Australia and New Zealand, 1883." *History* 86 (2001): 348–62.

———. *Kingdom of the Ryans: The Irish in Southwest New South Wales, 1816–90.* Sydney: University of New South Wales Press, 1997.

———. "The Other Immigrants: Comparing the Irish in Australia and the United States." *Journal of American Ethnic History* 14, no. 3 (1995): 3–22.

Carey, Hilary M. *Believing in Australia: A Cultural History of Religions.* Sydney: Allen and Unwin, 1996.

Carrier, N. H., and Jeffery, J. R. *External Migration: A Study of the Available Statistics, 1815–1950.* London: General Register Office, 1953.

Carroll, Francis M., ed. *The American Commission on Irish Independence, 1919: The Diary, Correspondence and Report.* Dublin: Irish Manuscripts Commission, 1985.

———. *American Opinion and the Irish Question, 1910–23: A Study in Opinion and Policy.* Dublin: Gill and MacMillan, 1978.

Carwardine, Richard J. *Evangelicals and Politics in Antebellum America.* New Haven, Conn.: Yale University Press, 1993.

Casper, Henry W. *History of the Catholic Church in Nebraska: The Church on the Northern Plains, 1838–1874.* Milwaukee: Bruce Press, 1960.

Cassirer, Reinhard. "United Irishmen in Democratic America." *Ireland Today* 3, no. 2 (1938): 131–37.

Clark, Dennis. *Hibernia America: The Irish and Regional Cultures.* Westport, Conn.: Greenwood Press, 1986.

———. *The Irish in Philadelphia: Ten Generations of Urban Experience.* Philadelphia: Temple University Press, 1973.

Clifford, James. "Diasporas." *Cultural Anthropology* 9 (1994): 302–38.

Conzen, Kathleen Neils. *Immigrant Milwaukee, 1836–60: Accommodation and Community in a Frontier City.* Cambridge, Mass.: Harvard University Press, 1976.

Conzen, Kathleen Neils, David A. Gerber, Ewa Morawska, George Pozzetta, and Rudolph J. Vecoli. "The Invention of Ethnicity: A Perspective from the U.S.A." *Journal of American Ethnic History* 12, no. 1 (1992): 3–41.

Costello, Con. *Botany Bay: The Story of the Convicts Transported from Ireland to Australia, 1791–1853.* Cork: The Mercier Press, 1987.

Coughlan, Neil. "The Coming of the Irish to Victoria." *Historical Studies* 12 (1965): 68–86.

Cousins, S. H. "The Regional Patterns of Emigration During the Great Irish Famine, 1846–51." *Transactions and Papers of the Institute of British Geographers* 28 (1960): 119–34.

———. "The Regional Variation in Emigration from Ireland between 1821 and 1841." *Transactions of the Institute of British Geographers* 37 (1965): 15–30.

Currey, C. H. *The Irish at Eureka.* Sydney: Angus and Robertson, 1954.

Curry, Catherine Ann. "Three Irish Women and Social Action in San Francisco: Mother Teresa Comerford, Mother Baptist Russell, and Kate Kennedy." *Journal of the West* 31, no. 2 (1992): 66–72.

Curti, Merle. *The Making of an American Community: A Case Study of Democracy in a Frontier Community.* Palo Alto, Calif.: Stanford University Press, 1959.

Daniels, Roger. *Coming to America: A History of Immigration and Ethnicity in American Life.* New York: Harper Perennial, 1990.

———. "On the Comparative Study of Immigrant and Ethnic Groups in the New World: A Note." *Comparative Studies in Society and History* 25 (1983): 401–4.

Darroch, Gordon. "Half Empty or Half Full: Images and Interpretations in the Historical Analysis of the Catholic Irish in Nineteenth-Century Canada." *Canadian Ethnic Studies* 25, no. 1 (1993): 1–8.

Darroch, A. Gordon, and Michael Ornstein. "Ethnicity and Occupational Structure in Canada in 1871: The Vertical Mosaic in Historical Perspective." *Canadian Historical Review* 61 (1980): 305–33.

Darroch, Gordon, and Lee Soltow. *Property and Inequality in Victorian Ontario: Structural Patterns and Cultural Communities in the 1871 Census.* Toronto: University of Toronto Press, 1994.

Davis, Richard. *Irish Issues in New Zealand Politics, 1868–1922.* Dunedin: University of Otago Press, 1974.

———. *"To Solitude Consigned": The Tasmanian Journal of William Smith O'Brien, 1849–1853.* Sydney: Crossing Press, 1995.

———. *The Young Ireland Movement.* Dublin: Gill and Macmillan, 1987.

Davis, Richard, Jennifer Livett, Anne-Maree Whitaker, and Peter Moore, eds. *Irish-Australian Studies: Papers Delivered at the Eighth Irish-Australian Conference, Hobart, July 1995.* Sydney: Crossing Press, 1996.

Dayton, Tim. "Thoreau and the Irish-Americans: Ethnicity, Class, and Culture in the Nineteenth-Century United States." *Cea Critic* 55 (1992): 26–38.

Decker, Peter R. *Fortunes and Failures: White Collar Mobility in Nineteenth-century San Francisco.* Cambridge, Mass.: Harvard University Press, 1978.

Dingle, Tony. *The Victorians: Settling.* Sydney: Fairfax, Syme and Weldon, 1984.

Diner, Hasia R. *Erin's Daughters in America: Irish Immigrant Women in the Nineteenth Century.* Baltimore: Johns Hopkins University Press, 1983.

Dolan, Jay P. *The American Catholic Experience: A History from Colonial Times to the Present.* New York: Doubleday and Co., 1985.

———. *The Immigrant Church: New York's Irish and German Catholics, 1815–1865.* Baltimore: Johns Hopkins University Press, 1975.

Donnelly, James S. *The Great Irish Potato Famine.* Stroud, Glos.: Sutton Publishing, 2001.

Dowling, Patrick J. *California: The Irish Dream.* San Francisco: Golden Gate Publishers, 1988.

Doyle, David N. "Cohesion and Diversity in the Irish Diaspora." *Irish Historical Studies* 31 (1999): 411–34.

———. *Ireland, Irishmen and Revolutionary America, 1760–1820.* Dublin: Cultural Relations Committee of Ireland, 1981.

———. *Irish Americans, Native Rights and National Empires: The Structure, Divisions and Attitudes of the Catholic Minority in the Decade of Expansion, 1890–1901.* New York: Arno Press, 1976.

———. "The Irish and American Labour, 1880–1920." *Saothar* 1, no. 1 (1975): 42–53.

———. "The Irish as Urban Pioneers in the United States, 1850–70." *Journal of American Ethnic History* 10, nos. 1–2 (1990–91): 37–59.

———. "The Irish in Australia and the United States: Some Comparisons." *Irish Economic and Social History* 16 (1989): 73–94.

———. "The Irish in Chicago." *Irish Historical Studies* 26 (1989): 293–303.

———. "The Irish in North America, 1776–1845." In *Ireland under the Union, 1801–1870*, edited by W. E. Vaughan, 682–725. Oxford: Clarendon, 1989.

———. "John Boyle O'Reilly and Irish Adjustment in America." *Journal of the Old Drogheda Society* (1996): 6–25.

———. "The Regional Bibliography of Irish America, 1800–1930: A Review and Addendum." *Irish Historical Studies* 23 (1983): 254–83.

———. "The Remaking of Irish-America." In *Ireland under the Union, 1870–1921*, edited by W. E. Vaughan, 725–63. Oxford: Clarendon Press, 1996.

Doyle, David Noel, and Owen Dudley Edwards, eds. *America and Ireland, 1776–1976: The American Identity and the Irish Connection*. Westport, Conn.: Greenwood Press, 1980.

Duffy, Patrick J. "Assisted Emigration from the Shirley estate, 1843–54." *Clogher Record* 14, no. 2 (1992): 7–62.

Dunne, Finley Peter. *Mr Dooley in Peace and War*. Urbana: University of Illinois Press, 1988.

Durack, Mary. *Kings in Grass Castles*. London: Constable and Co., 1959.

Durey, Michael. *Transatlantic Radicals and the Early American Republic*. Lawrence: University of Kansas Press, 1997.

Eichacker, Joanne Mooney. *Irish Republican Women in America: Lecture Tours, 1916–1925*. Dublin: Irish Academic Press, 2003.

Ekirch, A. Roger. *Bound for America: The Transportation of British Convicts to the Colonies, 1718–1775*. Oxford: Clarendon Press, 1987.

Elliott, Bruce. *Irish Migrants in the Canadas: A New Approach*. Kingston, Ont.: McGill-Queen's University Press, 1987.

Ellis, Peter Beresford, and Joseph A. King. "Fenian casualties and prisoners: Fenian invasion of British North America, June 1866." *Irish Sword* 18, no. 73 (1992): 271–84.

Emmick, Nancy J. "Bibliographical Essay on Irish-Americans in the West." *Journal of the West* 31, no. 2 (1992): 87–94.

Emmons, David M. *The Butte Irish: Class and Ethnicity in an American Mining Town, 1875–1925*. Urbana: University of Illinois Press, 1990.

Erie, Steven P. *Rainbow's End: Irish-Americans and the Dilemmas of Urban Machine Politics, 1840–1985*. Berkeley: University of California Press, 1988.

Ernst, Robert. *Immigrant Life in New York City, 1825–1863*. Port Washington, N.Y.: Ira J. Friedman, 1965.

Ethington, Philip J. *The Public City: The Political Construction of Urban Life in San Francisco, 1850–1900*. Cambridge: Cambridge University Press, 1994.

Evans, Anthony G. *Fanatic Heart: A Life of John Boyle O'Reilly, 1844–1890*. Nedlands, W.A.: University of Western Australia Press, 1997.

Fanning, Charles, ed. *New Perspectives on the Irish Diaspora*. Carbondale: Southern Illinois University Press, 2000.

Feldberg, Michael. *The Turbulent Era: Riot and Disorder in Jacksonian America*. New York: Oxford University Press, 1980.

Ferrie, Joseph P. "Up and Out or Down and Out? Immigrant Mobility in the Antebellum United States." *Journal of Interdisciplinary History* 27 (1995): 33–55.

———. "The Wealth Accumulation of Antebellum European Immigrants to the U.S., 1840–60." *Journal of Economic History* 54 (1994): 1–33.

———. *Yankeys Now: Immigrants in the Antebellum United States, 1840–1860.* (New York: Oxford University Press, 1999.

Fischer, Gerhard. *Enemy Aliens: Internment and Homefront Experience in Australia, 1914–1920.* St. Lucia: University of Queensland Press, 1989.

Fitzpatrick, David. "The Disappearance of the Irish Agricultural Labourer, 1841–1912." *Irish Economic and Social History* 7 (1980): 66–85.

———. "Emigration, 1801–70." In *Ireland under the Union, 1801–1870,* edited by W. E. Vaughan, 562–622. Oxford: Clarendon Press, 1989.

———. "Emigration, 1871–1921." In *Ireland under the Union, 1870–1921,* edited by W. E. Vaughan, 606–45. Oxford: Clarendon Press, 1996.

———. *Harry Boland's Irish Revolution.* Cork: Cork University Press, 2003.

———. *Irish Emigration, 1801–1921.* Dublin: Social History Society of Ireland, 1984.

———. "Irish Emigration in the Later Nineteenth Century." *Irish Historical Studies* 22 (1980): 126–43.

———. *Oceans of Consolation: Personal Accounts of Irish Migration to Australia.* Ithaca, N.Y.: Cornell University Press, 1994.

Foley, Tadhg, and Fiona Bateman, eds. *Irish-Australian Studies: Papers Delivered at the Ninth Irish-Australian Conference, Galway, April 1997.* Sydney: Crossing Press, 2000.

Foner, Eric. "Class, Ethnicity and Radicalism in the Gilded Age: The Land League and Irish America." *Marxist Perspectives* 1, no. 2 (1978): 6–55.

Forth, Gordon. *The Winters on the Wannon.* Geelong, Vic.: Deakin University Press, 1991.

Fortner, Robert S. "The Culture of Hope and the Culture of Despair: The Print Media and 19th Century Irish Emigration." *Éire–Ireland* 13, no. 3 (1978): 32–48.

Funchion, Michael. *Chicago's Irish Nationalists, 1881–1890.* New York: Arno Press, 1976.

Funchion, Michael, ed. *Irish-American Voluntary Organizations.* Westport, Conn.: Greenwood Press, 1983.

Gabaccia, Donna. *From the Other Side: Women, Gender, and Immigrant Life in the U.S., 1820–1990.* Bloomington: Indiana University Press, 1994.

Galbally, Ann. *Redmond Barry: An Anglo-Irish Australian.* Melbourne: Melbourne University Press, 1995.

Galenson, David W. "Economic Opportunity on the Urban Frontier: Nativity, Work, and Wealth in Early Chicago." *Journal of Economic History* 51 (1991): 581–603.

Gallman, J. Matthew. *Receiving Erin's Children: Philadelphia, Liverpool, and the Irish Famine Migration, 1845–1855.* Chapel Hill: University of North Carolina Press, 2000.

Gerber, David A. *The Making of an American Pluralism: Buffalo, New York, 1825–60.* Champaign: University of Illinois Press, 1989.

Gibson, Florence E. *Attitudes of the New York Irish toward State and National Affairs, 1848–1892.* London: Oxford University Press, 1951.

Gjerde, Jon. "New Growth on Old Vines—the State of the Field: The Social History of Immigration To and Ethnicity In the United States." *Journal of American Ethnic History* 18, no. 4 (1999): 40–65.

Glazer, Nathan, and Daniel Patrick Moynihan. *Beyond the Melting Pot: The Negroes, Puerto Ricans, Jews, Italians and Irish of New York City.* Cambridge: Massachusetts Institute of Technology, 1963.

Gleeson, David T. *The Irish in the South, 1815–1877.* Chapel Hill: University of North Carolina Press, 2001.

———. "Parallel Struggles: Irish Republicanism in the American South, 1798–1876." *Éire-Ireland* 34, no. 2 (1999): 97–116.

Golway, Terry. *Irish Rebel: John Devoy and America's Fight for Ireland's Freedom.* New York: St. Martin's Press, 1998.

Gordon, Michael A. *Irish Political Violence in New York City, 1870 and 1871.* Ithaca, N.Y.: Cornell University Press, 1993.

Graham, B. J., and L. J. Proudfoot. *An Historical Geography of Ireland.* London: Academic Press, 1993.

Green, Nancy L. "The Comparative Method and Poststructural Structuralism: New Perspectives for Migration Studies." *Journal of American Ethnic History* 13, no. 4 (1994): 3–22.

Greenberg, Amy S. "Irish in the City: Recent Developments in American Urban History." *The Historical Journal* 42 (1999): 571–81.

Gribben, Arthur, ed. *The Great Famine and the Irish Diaspora in America.* Amherst: University of Massachusetts Press, 1999.

Gribble, Richard. *Catholicism and the San Francisco Labor Movement, 1896–1921.* San Francisco: Mellon Research University Press, 1993.

Griffen, Patrick. *The People with No Name: Ireland's Ulster Scots, America's Scots Irish, and the Creation of a British Atlantic World, 1689–1764.* Princeton, N.J.: Princeton University Press, 2001.

Grimes, Seamus, and Gearóid Ó Tuathaigh, eds. *The Irish-Australian Connection.* Galway: University College, 1988.

Grimstead, David. *American Mobbing, 1828–1861: Toward Civil War.* New York: Oxford University Press, 1998.

Guinnane, Timothy. *The Vanishing Irish: Households, Migration, and the Rural Economy in Ireland, 1850–1914.* Princeton, N.J.: Princeton University Press, 1997.

Gwynn, Denis. *The Life of John Redmond.* London: George G. Harrap and Co., 1932.

Haines, Robin F. *Emigration and the Labouring Poor: Australian Recruitment in Britain and Ireland, 1831–60.* Basingstoke, Hants.: MacMillan, 1997.

Haines, Robin, and Ralph Shlomowitz. "Emigrations from Europe to Colonial Destinations: Some Nineteenth-Century Australian and South African Perspectives." *Itineria* 20, no. 1 (1996): 133–51.

Hamilton, Paula. "'Tipperarifying the Moral Atmosphere': Irish Catholic Immigration and the State, 1840–1860." In *What Rough Beast? The State and Social Order in Australian History,* edited by Sydney Labour History Group, 13–30. Sydney: George Allen and Unwin, 1982.

Hammerton, A. J. "'Without Natural Protectors': Female Immigration to Australia, 1832–36." *Historical Studies* 16 (October 1975): 539–66.

Handlin, Oscar. *Boston's Immigrants: A Study in Acculturation.* Revised ed. Cambridge, Mass.: Belknap Press, 1979.

———. *The Uprooted.* 2nd ed. Boston: Little, Brown, 1973.

Hansen, Marcus Lee. *The Atlantic Migration, 1607–1860: A History of the Continuing Settlement of the United States.* New York: Harper Torchbooks, 1961.

Harris, Dennis E., ed. *Redwood Empire Social History Project: California State Census, 1852, Sonoma County.* Sonoma, Calif.: County of Sonoma, 1983.

Hartford, William F. *Working People of Holyoke: Class and Ethnicity in a Massachusetts Mill Town, 1850–1960.* New Brunswick: Rutgers University Press, 1992.

Hatton, Timothy J., and Jeffrey G. Williamson. "After the Famine: Emigration from Ireland, 1850–1913." *Journal of Economic History* 53 (1993): 575–600.

Hatton, Timothy J., and Jeffrey G. Williamson, eds. *Migration and the International Labour Market.* London: Routledge, 1994.

Hernon, Joseph M. *Celts, Catholics and Copperheads: Ireland Views the American Civil War.* Columbus: Ohio State University Press, 1968.

Higham, John. *Strangers in the Land: Patterns of American Nativism, 1860–1925.* New York: Atheneum, 1975.

Hoerder, Dirk, ed. *American Labor and Immigration History: Recent European Research.* Urbana: University of Illinois Press, 1983.

———. *"Struggle a Hard Battle": Essays on Working-Class Immigrants.* DeKalb: Northern Illinois University Press, 1986.

Hogan, Michael. *The Sectarian Strand: Religion in Australian History.* Melbourne: Penguin, 1987.

Hollett, David. *Passage to the New World: Packet Ships and Irish Famine Emigrants, 1845–1851.* Gwent, U.K.: P. M. Heaton Publishing, 1995.

Holmquist, June Drenning, ed. *They Chose Minnesota: A Survey of the State's Ethnic Groups.* St. Paul: Minnesota Historical Society Press, 1981.

Hueston, Robert Francis. *The Catholic Press and Nativism, 1840–1860.* New York: Arno Press, 1976.

Ignatiev, Noel. *How the Irish Became White.* New York: Routledge, 1995.

Jackson, Hugh. *Churches and People in Australia and New Zealand.* Wellington: Allen and Unwin, 1987.

Jacobson, Matthew Frye. *Special Sorrows: The Diasporic Imagination of Irish, Polish, and Jewish Immigrants in the United States.* Cambridge, Mass.: Harvard University Press, 1995.

———. *Whiteness of a Different Color: European Immigrants and the Alchemy of Race.* Cambridge, Mass.: Harvard University Press, 1998.

Jenkins, Brian. *Fenians and Anglo-American Relations during Reconstruction.* Ithaca, N.Y.: Cornell University Press, 1969.

Johnson, Curtis D. *Redeeming America: Evangelicals and the Road to the Civil War.* Chicago: Ivan R. Dee, 1993.

Johnson, James H. "The Distribution of Irish Emigration in the Decade before the Great Famine." *Irish Geography* 21 (1988): 78–87.

Jones, Maldwyn Allen. *American Immigration.* Chicago: University of Chicago Press, 1960.

Joyce, William Leonard. *Editors and Ethnicity: A History of the Irish-American Press, 1848–1883.* New York: Arno Press, 1976.

Jupp, James, ed. *The Australian People: An Encyclopedia of the Nation, Its People and Their Origins.* Sydney: Angus and Robertson, 1988.

Kammen, Michael. *Mystic Chords of Memory: The Transformation of Tradition in American Culture.* New York: Alfred A. Knopf, 1991.

Kazal, Russell A. "Revisiting Assimilation: The Rise, Fall and Reappraisal of a Concept in American Ethnic History." *American Historical Review* 100 (1995): 437–71.

Kee, Robert. *The Green Flag.* 3 vols. London: Penguin, 1989.

Kelly, Mary Gilbert. *Catholic Immigrant Colonization Projects in the United States, 1815–60.* New York: U.S. Catholic Historical Society, 1939.

Kennedy, David M. *Over Here: The First World War and American Society.* New York: Oxford University Press, 1980.

Kenny, Kevin. *The American Irish: A History.* New York: Longman, 2000.

———. *Making Sense of the Molly Maguires.* New York: Oxford University Press, 1998.

Kenny, Kevin, ed. *New Directions in Irish-American History.* Madison: University of Wisconsin Press, 2003.

Keogh, Dermot. "Mannix, de Valera and Irish Nationalism." *Australasian Catholic Record* 65 (April 1988): 159–73.

———. "Mannix, de Valera and Irish Nationalism, Part 2." *Australasian Catholic Record* 65 (July 1988): 343–57.

Kerrigan, Colm. "Irish Temperance and U.S. Anti-Slavery: Father Mathew and the Abolitionists." *History Workshop Journal* 31 (1991): 105–19.

Kiernan, Colm. *Daniel Mannix and Ireland.* Morwell, Vic.: Atella Books, 1984.

———. "Home Rule for Ireland and the Formation of the Australian Labor Party, 1883–1901." *Australian Journal of Politics and History* 38 (1992): 1–11.

Kiernan, Colm, ed. *Australia and Ireland, 1788–1988: Bicentenary Essays.* Dublin: Gill and Macmillan, 1986.

———. *Ireland and Australia.* Sydney: Angus and Robertson, 1984.

Kiernan, T. J. *Transportation from Ireland to Sydney: 1791–1816.* Canberra: privately printed, 1954.

King, Hazel. *Richard Bourke.* Melbourne: Oxford University Press, 1971.

Knobel, Dale T. *America for the Americans: The Nativist Movement in the United States.* New York: Twayne Publishers, 1996.

———. *Paddy and the Republic: Ethnicity and Nationality in Antebellum America.* Middletown, Conn.: Wesleyan University Press, 1986.

Laurie, Bruce. *Artisans into Workers: Labor in Nineteenth-Century America.* New York: Hill and Wang, 1989.

Leary, William M. "Woodrow Wilson, Irish Americans and the Election of 1916." *Journal of American History* 54 (1967): 57–72.

Leyburn, James G. *The Scotch-Irish: A Social History.* Chapel Hill: University of North Carolina Press, 1962.

Luebke, Frederick C., ed. *Ethnicity on the Great Plains.* Lincoln: University of Nebraska Press, 1980.

Lyons, F. S. L. *John Dillon: A Biography.* London: Routledge and Kegan Paul, 1968.

MacDonagh, Oliver. *The Emancipist: Daniel O'Connell, 1830–47.* London: Weidenfeld and Nicolson, 1989.

———. "Emigration from Ireland to Australia: An Overview." In *Ireland and Australia, 1788–1988: Bicentenary Essays,* edited by Colm Kiernan, 121–37. Dublin: Gill and Macmillan, 1986).

———. "The Irish Famine Emigration to the United States." *Perspectives in American History* 10 (1976): 357–446.

———. *A Pattern of Government Growth: The Passenger Acts and Their Enforcement, 1800–60.* London: MacGibbon and Kee, 1961.

———. *The Sharing of the Green: A Modern Irish History for Australians.* Sydney: Allen and Unwin, 1996.

MacDonagh, Oliver, and W. F. Mandle, eds. *Ireland and Irish-Australia: Studies in Cultural and Political History.* London: Croom Helm, 1986.

———. *Irish-Australian Studies: Papers Delivered at the Fifth Irish-Australian Conference.* Canberra: Australian National University, 1989.

MacDonagh, Oliver, W. F. Mandle, and Pauric Travers, eds. *Irish Culture and Nationalism, 1750–1950.* London: Macmillan, 1983.

MacGinley, M. E. R. "The Irish in Queensland: An Overview." In *The Irish Emigrant Experience in Australia,* edited by John O'Brien and Pauric Travers, 103–19. Dublin: Poolbeg, 1991.

———. "Irish Migration to Queensland, 1885–1912." *Queensland Heritage* 3, no. 1 (November 1974): 12–17.

Madgwick, R. B. *Immigration into Eastern Australia, 1788–1851.* New York, 1937. Reprint, Sydney: Sydney University Press, 1969.

Mageean, Deirdre M. "Emigration from Irish Ports." *Journal of American Ethnic History* 13, no. 1 (Fall 1993): 6–30.

Mansfield, Bruce. *Australian Democrat: The Career of William Edward O'Sullivan, 1846–1910.* Sydney: Sydney University Press, 1965.

Markus, Andrew. *Australian Race Relations, 1788–1993.* Sydney: Allen and Unwin, 1994.

———. *Fear and Hatred: Purifying California and Australia, 1850–1901.* Sydney: Hale and Iremonger, 1979.

McCaffrey, Lawrence J., "Daniel O'Connell and the Irish-American Nationalist and Political Profiles." In *The World of Daniel O'Connell,* edited by Donal McCartney, 100–111. Cork: Mercier Press, 1980.

———. "Diaspora Comparisons and Irish-American Uniqueness." In *New Perspectives on the Irish Diaspora,* edited by Charles Fanning, 15–27. Carbondale: Southern Illinois University Press, 2000.

———. *The Irish Diaspora in America.* Washington, D.C.: Catholic University of America Press, 1984.

———. "A Profile of Irish America." In *America and Ireland, 1776–1976: The American Identity and the Irish Connection,* edited by David N. Doyle and Owen D. Edwards, 81–91. New York: Greenwood Press, 1980.

———. *Textures of Irish America.* Syracuse, N.Y.: Syracuse University Press, 1992.

McCaffrey, Lawrence J., ed. *The Irish in Chicago.* Urbana: University of Illinois Press, 1987.

McCartan, Patrick. *With De Valera in America.* New York: Brentano, 1932.

McClaughlin, Trevor. *Barefoot and Pregnant: Irish Famine Orphans in Australia.* Melbourne: Genealogical Society of Victoria, 1991.

———, ed. *Irish Women in Colonial Australia.* Sydney: Allen and Unwin, 1998.

McConville, Chris. *Croppies, Celts and Catholics: The Irish in Australia.* Melbourne: Edward Arnold, 1987.

McDonald, Grace. *History of the Irish in Wisconsin in the Nineteenth Century.* Washington, D.C.: Catholic University of America Press, 1954. Reprint, New York: Arno Press, 1976.

McGovern, Bryan. "John Mitchel: Ecumenical Nationalist in the Old South." *New Hibernia Review* 5, no. 2 (2001): 99–110.

McKernan, Michael. *Australian Churches at War: Attitudes and Activities of the Major Churches, 1914–1918.* Sydney: Catholic Theological Faculty, 1980.

———. "Catholics, Conscription and Archbishop Mannix." *Historical Studies* 17 (1977): 299–314.

McManamin, Francis G. *The American Years of John Boyle O'Reilly, 1870–1890.* New York: Arno Press, 1976.

McQuilton, John. *The Kelly Outbreak, 1878–1880: The Geographical Dimension of Social Banditry.* Melbourne: Melbourne University Press, 1979.

Meagher, Timothy J. *Inventing Irish America: Generation, Class, and Ethnic Identity in a New England City, 1880–1928*. Notre Dame, Ind.: University of Notre Dame Press, 2001.

———. "'Irish All the Time': Ethnic Consciousness among the Irish in Worcester, Massachusetts, 1880–1905." *Journal of Social History* 19 (1985): 273–303.

———. "'Why Should We Care for a Little Trouble or a Walk through the Mud': St. Patrick's and Columbus Day Parades in Worcester, Massachusetts, 1845–1915." *New England Quarterly* 58 (1985): 5–26.

Meagher, Timothy J., ed. *From Paddy to Studs: Irish-American Communities in the Turn of the Century Era, 1880 to 1920*. Westport, Conn.: Greenwood Press, 1986.

Merwick, Donna. *Boston's Priests, 1848–1910: A Study of Social and Intellectual Change*. Cambridge, Mass.: Harvard University Press, 1973.

Miller, Kerby A. *Emigrants and Exiles: Ireland and the Irish Exodus to North America*. New York: Oxford University Press, 1985.

Miller, Kerby A., Arnold Shrier, Bruce D. Boling, and David N. Doyle, eds. *Irish Immigrants in the Land of Canaan: Letters and Memoirs from Colonial and Revolutionary America, 1675–1815*. New York: Oxford University Press, 2003.

Miller, Kerby A., with David Doyle and Bruce Boling. "Emigrants and Exiles: Irish Cultures and Irish Emigration to North America, 1790–1922." *Irish Historical Studies* 22 (1980): 97–125.

Mitchell, Brian C. *The Paddy Camps: The Irish of Lowell, 1821–61*. Urbana: University of Illinois Press, 1988.

Modell, John, and Lees, Lyn H. "The Irish Countryman Urbanized: A Comparative Perspective on Famine Migration." *Journal of Urban History* 3, no. 4 (1977): 391–408.

Molony, John N. *An Architect of Freedom: John Hubert Plunkett in New South Wales, 1832–1869*. Canberra: Australian National University Press, 1973.

Montgomery, David. "The Shuttle and the Cross: Weavers and Artisans in the Kensington Riots of 1844." *Journal of Social History* 5 (1972): 411–46.

Moody, T. W. "Irish-American Nationalism." *Irish Historical Studies* 15 (1967): 438–45.

Moran, Gerard. "Aspects of Irish Labour in North America." *Saothar* 17 (1992): 118–21.

———. "'In Search of the Promised Land': The Connemara Colonization Scheme to Minnesota, 1880." *Éire-Ireland* 31, nos. 3 and 4 (1996): 130–49.

———. *Sending Out Ireland's Poor: Assisted Emigration to North America in the Nineteenth Century*. Dublin: Four Courts Press, 2004.

Moriarty, Thomas, F. "The Irish American Response to Catholic Emancipation." *Catholic Historical Review* 66 (1980): 353–73.

Morris, Charles R. *American Catholic: The Saints and Sinners Who Built America's Most Powerful Church*. New York: Vintage Books, 1997.

Morton, Grenfell. "Ulster Emigrants to Australia, 1850–1890." *Ulster Folklife* 18 (1972): 111–20.

Moss, Kenneth. "St. Patrick's Day Celebrations and the Formation of Irish-American Identity, 1845–1875." *Journal of Social History* 29 (1995): 125–48.

Murphy, Mary. *Mining Cultures: Men, Woman and Leisure in Butte, 1914–41*. Urbana: University of Illinois Press, 1997.

Myers, Phillip E. "The Fenians in Iowa." *The Palimpsest* (1981): 56–64.

Neidhardt, W. S. *Fenianism in North America*. University Park: Pennsylvania State University Press, 1975.

Neville, Grace. "Westward Bound: Emigration to North America in the Irish Folklore Commission Archives." *Etudes Irlandaises* 17, no. 1 (1992): 195–207.

Nicholas, Stephen, ed. *Convict Workers: Reinterpreting Australia's Past.* Melbourne: Cambridge University Press, 1988.

Niehaus, Earl F. *The Irish in New Orleans, 1800–1860.* Baton Rouge: Louisiana University Press, 1965.

Nolan, Janet. *Ourselves Alone: Women's Emigration from Ireland, 1885–1920.* Lexington: University Press of Kentucky, 1989.

Ó Gráda, Cormac. "Across the Briny Ocean: Some Thoughts on Irish Emigration to America, 1800–1850." In *Ireland and Scotland 1600–1850: Parallels and Contrasts in Economic and Social Development,* edited by T. M. Devine and David Dixon, 118–30. Edinburgh: John Donald Publishers, 1983.

———. *Black '47 and Beyond: The Great Irish Famine in History, Economy and Memory.* Princeton, N.J.: Princeton University Press, 1999.

———. *Ireland: A New Economic History.* Oxford: Clarendon Press, 1994.

———. "Some Aspects of Nineteenth-Century Irish Emigration." In *Comparative Aspects of Scottish and Irish Economic and Social History, 1600–1900,* edited by L. M. Cullen and T. C. Smout, 65–73. Edinburgh: John Donald, 1977.

O'Brien, John B. "Population, Politics and Society in Cork, 1780–1900." In *Cork History and Society: Interdisciplinary Essays on the History of an Irish County,* edited by Patrick O'Flanagan and Cornelius Butler, 699–720. Dublin: Geography Publications, 1993.

O'Brien, John, and Pauric Travers, eds. *The Irish Emigrant Experience in Australia.* Dublin: Poolbeg, 1991.

O'Connell, Anne. "'The Care of the Immigrant Girls': The Migration Process of Late-Nineteenth-Century Irish Women. *Éire-Ireland* 35, nos. 3 and 4 (2000–2001): 102–33.

O'Connell, Marvin R. *John Ireland and the American Catholic Church.* St. Paul: Minnesota Historical Society Press, 1988.

O'Connor, Thomas H. *The Boston Irish: A Political History.* Boston: Northeastern University Press, 1995.

O'Day, Alan. "Revising the Diaspora." In *The Making of Modern Irish History: Revisionism and the Revisionist Controversy,* edited by D. George Boyce and Alan O'Day, 188–215. London: Routledge, 1996.

O'Fahey, Charles J. "Reflections on the St. Patrick's Day Orations of John Ireland." *Ethnicity* 2 (1975): 244–57.

O'Farrell, Patrick. *The Catholic Church and Community: An Australian History.* Sydney: University of New South Wales Press, 1985.

———. "Emigrant Attitudes and Behaviour as a Source for Irish History." In *Historical Studies* 10, edited by G. A. Hayes-McCoy, 109–31. Dublin: Irish Committee for Historical Sciences, 1976.

———. "The Image of O'Connell in Australia." In *The World of Daniel O'Connell,* edited by Donal McCartney, 112–24. Cork: Mercier Press, 1980.

———. *The Irish in Australia: 1788 to the Present.* 3rd ed. Sydney: University of New South Wales Press, 2000.

———. "The Irish in Australia and New Zealand, 1791–1870." In *Ireland under the Union, 1801–1870,* edited by W. E. Vaughan, 661–81. Oxford: Clarendon Press, 1989.

———. "The Irish in Australia and New Zealand, 1870–1990." In *Ireland under the Union, 1870–1921,* edited by W. E. Vaughan, 703–24. Oxford: Clarendon Press, 1996.

———. *Letters from Irish Australia, 1825–1929.* Sydney: University of New South Wales Press, 1984.

————. *Vanished Kingdoms: Irish in Australia and New Zealand*. Sydney: University of New South Wales Press, 1990.

O'Farrell, Patrick, and Dierdre O'Farrell. "The Status of Women: Some Opinions in Australian Catholic History c. 1860–1960." *Bulletin of Christian Affairs* 2 (November 1975): 2–42.

O'Farrell, Patrick, and Dierdre O'Farrell, eds. *Documents in Australian Catholic History: 1788–1884*. 2 vols. London: Geoffrey Chapman, 1969.

O'Grady, Joseph P. "The Irish." In *The Immigrants' Influence on Wilson's Peace Policies*, edited by Joseph P. O'Grady, 56–84. Louisville: University of Kentucky Press, 1967.

O'Mahony, Christopher, and Valerie Thompson. *Poverty to Promise: The Monteagle Emigrants, 1838–58*. Sydney: Crossing Press, 1994.

O'Rourke, Kevin H., and Jeffrey G. Williamson. *Globalization and History: The Evolution of a Nineteenth-Century Atlantic Economy*. Cambridge, Mass.: MIT Press, 1999.

O'Shaughnessy, Peter, ed. *The Gardens of Hell: John Mitchel in Van Diemen's Land, 1850–1853*. Sydney: Kangaroo Press, 1988.

————. *A Rum Story: The Adventures of Joseph Holt, Thirteen Years in Australia, 1800–1812*. Sydney: Kangaroo Press, 1988.

Osofsky, Gilbert. "Abolitionists, Irish Immigrants and the Dilemmas of Romantic Nationalism." *American Historical Review* 80 (1975): 889–912.

O'Sullivan, Patrick, ed. *The Irish World Wide: History, Heritage, Identity*. 6 vols. Leicester: Leicester University Press, 1992–97.

Patrick, Ross, and Heather Patrick. *Exiles Undaunted: The Irish Rebels Kevin and Eva O'Doherty*. St. Lucia: University of Queensland Press, 1989.

Pawsey, Margaret. *The Popish Plot: Culture Clashes in Victoria, 1860–1863*. Sydney: Studies in the Christian Movement, 1983.

Pelan, Rebecca, ed., assisted by Noel Quirke and Mark Finnane. *Irish-Australian Studies: Papers Delivered at the Seventh Irish-Australian Conference*. Sydney: Crossing Press, 1994.

Potter, George. *To the Golden Door: The Story of the Irish in Ireland and America*. Boston: Little, Brown, 1960.

Powers, Vincent E. *Invisible Immigrants: The Pre-Famine Irish Community in Worcester, Massachusetts, from 1826 to 1860*. New York: Garland Publishing, 1989.

Read, Gordon. "Liverpool—the Floodgate of the Old World: A Study in Ethnic Attitudes." *Journal of American Ethnic History* 13, no. 1 (Fall 1993): 31–47.

Reece, Bob. *The Origins of Irish Convict Transportation to New South Wales*. Basingstoke, Hants.: Palgrave, 2001.

Reece, Bob, ed. *Exiles from Erin: Convict Lives in Ireland and Australia*. London: MacMillan, 1991.

————. *Irish Convict Lives*. Sydney: Crossing Press, 1993.

————. *The Irish in Western Australia*. Perth: Centre for Western Australian History, 2000.

Regan, Ann. "The Irish." In *They Chose Minnesota: A Survey of the State's Ethnic Groups*, edited by June Drenning Holmquist, 130–52. St. Paul: Minnesota Historical Society Press, 1981.

Riach, Douglas C. "Daniel O'Connell and American Anti-slavery." *Irish Historical Studies* 20 (1976): 3–25.

Ricards, Sherman L., and George M. Blackburn. "The Sydney Ducks: A Demographic Analysis." *Pacific Historical Review* 42 (1973): 20–31.

Richards, Eric. "How Did Poor People Emigrate from the British Isles to Australia in the Nineteenth Century?" *Journal of British Studies* 33 (1993): 250–79.

———. "The Importance of Being Irish in Colonial South Australia." In *The Irish Emigrant Experience in Australia,* edited by John O'Brien and Pauric Travers, 62–102. Dublin: Poolbeg, 1991.

———. "Irish Life and Progress in Colonial South Australia." *Irish Historical Studies* 27 (1991): 216–36.

Richards, Eric, ed. *Poor Australian Immigrants in the Nineteenth Century: Visible Immigrants Two.* Canberra: Australian National University, 1991.

Richards, Eric, Richard Reid, and David Fitzpatrick, eds. *Visible Immigrants: Neglected Sources for the History of Australian Immigration.* Canberra: Australian National University, 1989.

Robins, Joseph A. "Irish Orphan Emigration to Australia, 1848–50." *Studies: An Irish Quarterly Review* 57 (Winter 1968): 372–87.

Robson, Lloyd L. *The Convict Settlers of Australia: An Enquiry into the Origins and Character of the Convicts Transported to New South Wales and Van Diemen's Land, 1787–1852.* Melbourne: Melbourne University Press, 1965.

Rodechko, James Paul. *Patrick Ford and His Search for America: A Case Study in Irish-American Journalism, 1870–1913.* New York: Arno Press, 1976.

Roediger, David R. *The Wages of Whiteness: Race and the Making of the American Working Class.* London: Verso, 1991.

Ronanyne, Jarlath, and Robert Pascoe, eds. *The Irish Imprint in Australia.* Melbourne: Victoria University of Technology, 1994.

Roney, Frank. *Irish Rebel and Labor Leader: An Autobiography.* Edited by Ira Cross. Berkeley: University of California Press, 1931.

Rudé, George. *Protest and Punishment: The Story of the Social and Political Protesters Transported to Australia, 1788–1868.* Oxford: Clarendon Press, 1978.

———. "Early Irish Rebels in Australia." *Historical Studies* 16 (1974): 17–35.

Ryan, Dennis P. *Beyond the Ballot Box: A Social History of the Boston Irish, 1845–1917.* Rutherford: Farleigh-Dickinson University Press, 1983.

Ryan, Mary P. *Civic Wars: Democracy and Public Life in the American City during the Nineteenth Century.* Berkeley: University of California Press, 1997.

Sarbaugh, Timothy. "Exiles of Confidence: The Irish American Community of San Francisco, 1880–1920." In *From Paddy to Studs: Irish-American Communities in the Turn of the Century Era, 1880 to 1920,* edited by Timothy J. Meagher, 161–79. Westport, Conn.: Greenwood Press, 1986.

———. "The Irish in the West: An Ethnic Tradition of Enterprise and Innovation, 1848–1991." *Journal of the West* 31, no. 2 (1992): 5–8.

———. "Irish Republicanism vs. 'Pure Americanism': California's Reaction to Eamon de Valera's Visits." *California History* 60, part 2 (1981): 172–85.

Scally, Robert James. *The End of Hidden Ireland: Rebellion, Famine and Emigration.* New York: Oxford University Press, 1995.

Schrier, Arnold. *Ireland and the American Emigration, 1850–1900.* Minneapolis: University of Minnesota Press, 1958.

Scott, Ernest. *Australia During the War.* Vol. 11 of *The Official History of Australia in the War of 1914–1918.* Sydney, 1936. Facsimile ed., St. Lucia: University of Queensland Press, 1989.

Serle, Geoffrey. *The Golden Age: A History of the Colony of Victoria, 1851–1861.* Melbourne: Melbourne University Press, 1977.

Shannon, James P. *Catholic Colonization on the Western Frontier.* New York: Arno Press, 1976. Originally published as *The Irish Americans* (New Haven, Conn.: Yale University Press, 1957).

Shannon, William V. *The American Irish: A Political and Social Portrait.* New York: Macmillan, 1963.

Shaw, A. G. L. *Convicts and the Colonies: A Study of Penal Transportation from Great Britain and Ireland to Australia and Other Parts of the British Empire.* Melbourne: Melbourne University Press, 1977.

Shaw, Douglas V. *The Making of an Immigrant City: Ethnic and Cultural Conflict in Jersey City, New Jersey, 1850–77.* New York: Arno Press, 1976.

Sheedy, Kieran. *Upon the Mercy of the Government: The Story of the Surrender, Transportation, and Imprisonment of Michael Dwyer and His Wicklow Comrades, and Their Subsequent Lives in New South Wales.* Dublin: Radio Telefís Éireann, 1988.

Stansell, Christine. *City of Women: Sex and Class in New York, 1789–1860.* New York: Alfred A. Knopf, 1986.

Takaka, Ronald. *A Different Mirror: A History of Multicultural America.* Boston: Little, Brown and Co., 1993.

Tansill, Charles Callan. *America and the Fight for Irish Freedom, 1866–1922.* New York: Devin-Adair Co., 1957.

Thernstrom, Stephan. *The Other Bostonians: Poverty and Progress in the American Metropolis, 1880–1970.* Cambridge, Mass.: Harvard University Press, 1973.

———. *Poverty and Progress: Social Mobility in a Nineteenth-Century City.* Cambridge, Mass.: Harvard University Press, 1964.

Thistlethwaite, Frank. "Migration from Europe Overseas in the Nineteenth and Twentieth Centuries." *Rapports: Xie Congrès International des Sciences Historiques* 5 (1960): 32–60.

Thomas, M. Evangeline. *Nativism in the Old Northwest, 1850–1860.* Washington, D.C.: Catholic University of America Press, 1936.

Touhill, Blanche M. *William Smith O'Brien and His Irish Revolutionary Companions in Penal Exile.* Columbia: University of Missouri Press, 1981.

Travers, Robert. *The Phantom Fenians of New South Wales.* Sydney: Kangaroo Press, 1986.

Truxes, Thomas M. *Irish-American Trade, 1660–1783.* Cambridge: Cambridge University Press, 1988.

Turbin, Carole. *Working Women of Collar City: Gender, Class and Community in Troy, New York, 1864–86.* Urbana: University of Illinois Press, 1992.

Tyrrell, Ian R. *Sobering Up: From Temperance to Prohibition in Antebellum America, 1800–1860.* Westport, Conn.: Greenwood Press, 1977.

Vamplew, Wray, ed. *Australians: Historical Statistics.* Sydney: Fairfax, Syme and Weldon, 1987.

Van Dussen, D. Gregory. "American Methodism's *Christian Advocate* and Irish Catholic Immigration, 1830–1870." *Éire-Ireland* 26, no. 4 (1992): 76–99.

Vaughan, W. E., ed. *Ireland under the Union, 1801–1870.* Vol. 5 of A New History of Ireland. Oxford: Clarendon Press, 1989.

Vaughan, W. E., ed. *Ireland under the Union, 1870–1921.* Vol. 6 of A New History of Ireland. Oxford: Clarendon Press, 1996.

Vecoli, Rudolph J. "An Inter-Ethnic Perspective on American Immigration History." *Mid-America* 75, no. 2 (1993): 223–35.

Vinyard, JoEllen. *The Irish on the Urban Frontier: Nineteenth-Century Detroit, 1850–1880.* New York: Arno Press, 1976.

Wade, Richard C. *The Urban Frontier: The Rise of Western Cities, 1790–1830.* Urbana: University of Illinois Press, 1996.

Waldersee, James. *Catholic Society in New South Wales, 1788–1860.* Sydney: Sydney University Press, 1974.

Walkowitz, Daniel. *Worker City, Company Town: Iron and Cotton-Worker Protest in Troy and Cohhoes, New York, 1854–84.* Urbana: University of Illinois Press, 1978.

Walsh, James P. "American-Irish: West and East." *Éire-Ireland* 6, no. 2 (1971): 25–32.

———. "James Phelan: Creating the Fortune, Creating the Family." *Journal of the West* 31, no. 2 (April 1992): 17–23.

Walsh, James P., ed. *The San Francisco Irish, 1850–1976.* San Francisco: Irish Literary and Historical Society, 1978.

Walsh, Victor A. "Across 'the Big Wather': The Irish-Catholic Community of Mid-Nineteenth-Century Pittsburgh." *The Western Pennsylvania Historical Magazine* 66 (1983): 1–23.

———. "'Drowning the Shamrock': Drink, Teetotalism, and the Irish Catholics of Gilded-Age Pittsburgh." *Journal of American Ethnic History* 10, nos. 1–2 (Fall/Winter 1991): 60–79.

———. "'A Fanatic Heart': The Cause of Irish-American Nationalism in Pittsburgh during the Gilded Age." *Journal of Social History* 15 (1981): 187–204.

Ward, Alan J. *Ireland and Anglo-American Relations, 1899–1921.* London: Weidenfield and Nicolson, 1969.

Ward, Margaret. *Unmanageable Revolutionaries.* London: Pluto Press, 1983.

Watkins, Susan Cotts, ed. *After Ellis Island: Newcomers and Natives in the 1910 Census.* New York: Russell Sage Foundation, 1994.

Way, Peter. *Common Labour: Workers and the Digging of North American Canals, 1780–1860.* Cambridge: Cambridge University Press, 1993.

———. "Shovel and Shamrock: Irish Workers and Labor Violence in the Digging of the Chesapeake and Ohio Canal." *Labor History* 30 (1989): 489–517.

Weber, Adna F. *The Growth of Cities in the Nineteenth Century: A Study in Statistics.* Ithaca, N.Y.: Cornell University Press, 1967.

Wells, Ronald A. *Ulster Migration to America: Letters from Three Irish Families.* New York: Peter Lang, 1991.

Whitaker, Anne-Marie. *Unfinished Revolution: United Irishmen in New South Wales, 1800–1810.* Sydney: Crossing Press, 1994.

Wilentz, Sean. *Chants Democratic: New York City and the Rise of the American Working Class, 1788–1850.* New York: Oxford University Press, 1984.

———. "Industrializing America and the Irish: Towards the New Departure." *Labor History* 20 (1979): 579–95.

Williams, John. *Ordered to the Island: Irish Convicts and Van Diemen's Land.* Sydney: Crossing Press, 1994.

Wilson, David A. *United Irishmen, United States: Immigrant Radicals in the Early Republic.* Dublin: Four Courts Press, 1998.

Wilson, Gwendoline. *Murray of Yarralumla.* Melbourne: Oxford University Press, 1968.

Winsberg, Morton D. "Irish Settlement in the United States, 1850–1890." *Éire-Ireland* 20, no. 1 (1985): 7–14.

Wittke, Carl. *The Irish in America.* Baton Rouge: Louisiana University Press, 1956.

Yans-McLaughlin, Virginia, ed. *Immigration Reconsidered: History, Sociology, and Politics.* New York: Oxford University Press, 1991.

Wyman, Mark. *Immigrants in the Valley: Irish, Germans and Americans in the Upper Mississippi Country, 1830–1860.* Chicago: Nelson Hall, 1984.

Unpublished Theses and Dissertations

Beadles, John A. "The Syracuse Irish, 1812–1928: Immigration, Catholicism, Socio-Economic States, Politics and Irish Nationalism." Ph.D. diss., Syracuse University, 1974.

Blessing, Patrick J. "West Among Strangers: Irish Migration to California." Ph.D. diss., University of California, Berkeley, 1977.

Fallon, Patricia. "The Irish in Country Places: A Regional Study." M.A. diss., Griffith University, 1994.

Flanagan, Kieren D. "Emigration, Assimilation and Occupational Categories of Irish Americans in Minnesota." M.A. thesis, University of Minnesota, 1969.

Gibson, Florence E. "Attitudes of the New York Irish Toward State and National Affairs, 1848–1892." Ph.D. diss., Columbia University, 1951.

Gleeson, David Thomas. "The Irish in the South, 1815–1877." Ph.D. diss., Mississippi State University, 1997.

Gothard, Janice. "Government Assisted Migration of Single Women from Britain to Australia, 1860–1900." Ph.D. thesis, Murdoch University, 1991.

Hamilton, Pauline. "'No Irish Need Apply': Prejudice as a Factor in the Development of Immigration Policy in New South Wales and Victoria, 1840–1870." Ph.D. thesis, University of New South Wales, 1979.

Lyons, Mark. "Aspects of Sectarianism in New South Wales circa 1865 to 1880." Ph.D. thesis, Australian National University, 1972.

Mazzaroli, Louise. "The Irish in New South Wales, 1884–1914: Some Aspects of the Irish Sub-Culture." Ph.D. thesis, University of New South Wales, 1979.

McConville, Chris. "Emigrant Irish and Suburban Catholic: Faith and Nation in Melbourne and Sydney, 1815–1933." Ph.D. thesis, University of Melbourne, 1984.

Millett, William M. "The Irish and Mobility Patterns in Northampton, Massachusetts, 1846–1883." Ph.D. diss., University of Iowa, 1980.

Morris, Stephanie A. "From Northwest Ireland to America, 1864–70: Tracing Migrants from Their Place of Origin to Their New Home in Philadelphia." Ph.D. diss., Temple University, 1988.

O'Donnell, Ruán. "Marked for Botany Bay: The Wicklow United Irishmen and the Development of Political Transportation from Ireland." Ph.D. thesis, Australian National University, 1996.

Read, Mary Josephine. "A Population Study of the Driftless Hill Land During the Pioneer Period, 1832–60." Ph.D. diss., University of Wisconsin, 1941.

Reid, Richard E. "Aspects of Irish Assisted Emigration to New South Wales, 1848–1870." Ph.D. thesis, Australian National University, 1992.

Schultz, Robert J. "The Assisted Immigrants, 1837–50: A Study of Some of the Aspects and Characteristics of the Immigrants Assisted to New South Wales and the Port Phillip District, 1837–1850." Ph.D. thesis, Australian National University, 1971.

Tobin, Catherine. "The Lowly Muscular Digger: Irish Canal Workers in Nineteenth-Century America." Ph.D. diss., University of Notre Dame, 1987.

Tobin, Gregory. "The Sea-Divided Gael: A Study of the Irish Home Rule Movement in Victoria and New South Wales, 1880–1916." M.A. thesis, Australian National University, 1969.

Walsh, Victor A. "Across the Big Wather: Irish Community Life in Pittsburgh and Allegheny City, 1850–1885." Ph.D. diss., University of Pittsburgh, 1983.

Woodburn, Susan. "The Irish in New South Wales, Victoria and South Australia, 1788–1880." M.A. thesis, University of Adelaide, 1979.

Index

HISTORY of IRELAND
and the IRISH DIASPORA

Remembering the Year of the French:
Irish Folk History and Social Memory
Guy Beiner

Ireland's New Worlds: Immigrants, Politics, and Society
in the United States and Australia, 1815–1922
Malcolm Campbell

The Slow Failure: Population Decline
and Independent Ireland, 1920–1973
Mary E. Daly

The Eternal Paddy:
Irish Identity and the British Press, 1798–1882
Michael de Nie

Old World Colony: Cork and South Munster, 1630–1830
David Dickson

Sinn Féin: A Hundred Turbulent Years
Brian Feeney

Stakeknife: Britain's Secret Agents in Ireland
Martin Ingram and Greg Harkin

New Directions in Irish-American History
Edited by Kevin Kenny

The Same Age as the State
Máire Cruise O'Brien

The Bible War in Ireland: The "Second Reformation"
and the Polarization of Protestant-Catholic Relations, 1800–1840
Irene Whelan

Tourism, Landscape, and the Irish Character:
British Travel Writers in Pre-Famine Ireland
William H. A. Williams